DIARIES AND SELECTED LETTERS

Mikhail Bulgakov

Translated by Roger Cockrell

ALMA CLASSICS

ALMA CLASSICS
an imprint of

ALMA BOOKS LTD
London House
243–253 Lower Mortlake Road
Richmond
Surrey TW9 2LL
United Kingdom
www.almaclassics.com

This translation first published by Alma Classics in 2013
© the Estate of Mikhail and Elena Bulgakov 2001
Translation and Introduction © Roger Cockrell, 2013
Notes, Index and Extra Material © Alma Classics, 2013
Pictures © the Estate of Mikhail Bulgakov

Supported using public funding by
ARTS COUNCIL
ENGLAND
LOTTERY FUNDED

Printed and bound by CPI Group (UK) Ltd, Croydon, CR0 4YY

ISBN: 978-1-84749-303-3

Contents

Introduction

"Am I thinkable in the USSR?"
*Mikhail Bulgakov, letter to the Soviet
government, 28th March 1930*

This volume of Mikhail Bulgakov's diaries and letters covers a period of twenty years, from the time of Bulgakov's arrival in Moscow in the autumn of 1921 to his death in the same city in March 1940. In the early years, Bulgakov was overwhelmingly preoccupied with domestic concerns and day-to-day survival in an environment that was often less than welcoming. But his thoughts were also directed outwards and, as a journalist and avid reader of newspapers, he became a keen observer of the social and political scene. Many comments in the diary relate to the volatile international situation outside Soviet Russia, particularly the potentially explosive events in Germany and the growing hostility and conflict between Soviet-style socialism and fascism. As regards Great Britain, he was less than impressed by its imperialist ambitions and its population of "slow-witted Brits" (see diary entry of 20th–21st December 1924).

By this time, however, Bulgakov's desire to become a writer and his growing awareness of his special talent had already taken shape within him. He knew that the future would be difficult: "I bitterly regret," he wrote on 26th October 1923, "that I gave up medicine, thereby condemning myself to an uncertain existence. But God will see I only did this because of my love of writing." Once the decision had been made, however, he entered the literary scene in the early to mid-1920s with an astonishing burst of creative energy, producing a major novel, *The White Guard*, several stories and a number of plays. Initially he met with some success: one story, *The Fatal Eggs*, was published, together with part of *The White Guard*, and a dramatic adaptation of the same novel, *The Days of the Turbins*, was staged in Moscow to great acclaim. But there it was to end, and a pattern was soon set that lasted for the rest of his life, in which he was attacked by a universally hostile and often virulent press, harassed by the secret police and subjected to crippling censorship.

After appealing to the government, he was given work as an assistant director at the Moscow Arts Theatre, but his urge to write remained undiminished. He found himself trapped, increasingly depressed, frustrated and overwhelmed by exhaustion and a sense of hopelessness. "I am unable to write anything," he wrote to Maxim Gorky on 6th September 1929. "Everything has been banned, I am ruined, persecuted and totally alone." He was to all intents and purposes imprisoned in the city that he had come to love. "I have been injected with the psychology of a prisoner," he wrote on 30th May 1932. He felt sufficiently safe to reveal his innermost thoughts and fears to only a very few correspondents – among them, his wife Yelena Sergeyevna, in a whole series of letters while she was away from Moscow in the summer of 1938, his brother Nikolai in Paris, the composer Boris Asafyev, the writer Yevgeny Zamyatin and his first biographer, Pavel Popov, with whom he was on especially friendly terms. With the renowned director and co-founder of the Moscow Arts Theatre, Konstantin Stanislavsky, the relationship was altogether more ambivalent, ranging from "delighted admiration" at Stanislavsky's skill as a director during rehearsals (31st December 1931) to "radical disagreement" with the Arts Theatre's impossible demands concerning the staging of his play *Molière* (22nd April 1935). As for the Moscow Arts Theatre's other co-founder, Vladimir Nemirovich-Danchenko, Bulgakov seems to have had little but contempt for him. "Oh, yes," he writes with heavy sarcasm to his wife on 3rd June 1938, "I am simply dying with impatience to show my novel to such a philistine." At times Bulgakov could be brutally abrupt. In his diary entry of the 23rd to 24th December 1924 he referred to the novelist Alexei Tolstoy as a "dirty, dishonest clown", and elsewhere he accused the theatre director Vsevolod Meyerhold of being "so lacking in principles" that it was as if he walked about "just in his underpants" (letter of 14th June 1936).

We will never know how much Bulgakov's anger and sense of despair would have been mitigated had he been allowed to go abroad, but we are left in no doubt how vitally important such permission was for him. Although at one stage he asked to be deported (letter to Stalin of July 1929), he emphasized in many other letters that he wanted only to be able to travel abroad for a couple of months. For personal and medical reasons he wanted his wife to accompany him, but they were both prepared to leave Yelena's young son behind as a pledge of their return. At one stage, permission appeared to have been granted, only for hopes to be cruelly dashed. It was simply not to be, it seemed, and he was left with his yearning and his dreams. "I dreamt about Rome," he wrote in a letter of 11th July 1934, "a balcony, just as described in Gogol, pine trees, roses... a manuscript." The Rome of Gogol, the Paris of Molière (which occupied a place in his heart that was second only to his beloved native city of Kiev), sunshine and the Mediterranean – all lured and beckoned, all so close and yet so unattainable, except through his imagination. And by the mid-1930s imagination seemed to be all that remained to him. He continued to work on his "novel", but he had given up all hope of it ever seeing the light of day. The most that he could hope for, as he wrote to Yelena on 15th June 1938, was that the novel would be of sufficient worth for it to be put away "into a dark drawer".

Bulgakov lived a tragically short life, not even seeing his fiftieth birthday, but it is something of a miracle that he was allowed to continue as long as he did, at a time when other similarly inclined fellow writers were disappearing into the maw of the gulag. Unlike many of his contemporaries, Bulgakov had not shared in any initial rush of enthusiasm for the 1917 revolution. Boris Pasternak, for example, speaking through his hero Yury Zhivago, saw the revolution as "magnificent surgery", whereas for Bulgakov it was the harbinger of a tragedy that would lead Russia to the abyss. Furthermore, Bulgakov remained openly unrepentant about his political sympathies. In his letter to the secret police (OGPU) of 22nd September 1926 he stated that during the civil war he had been "entirely on the side of the Whites, whose retreat filled me with horror and incomprehension". How then did he escape imprisonment, or even worse? Was it perhaps through the intercession of Stalin? Certainly, Stalin particularly admired *The Days of the Turbins*, and there has been speculation of a "special relationship" between them. We also know, however, that Stalin was adamantly opposed to the staging of other plays such as *Escape* and *The Crimson Island* – and, in any case, if such a relationship had existed, why did he never give permission for Bulgakov to travel abroad?

There is no certain answer to such questions. Arbitrariness is one of the defining features of a totalitarian society; Bulgakov's rhetorical question whether he was "thinkable" in such a society may therefore well have seemed justifiable. Yet whatever the perception of him by the government and the Communist Party (as well as, sadly, by so many of his colleagues in the literary and theatrical world), he was so much more than merely "thinkable". For in a society pervaded by fear and terror, in which lying and deception had become the official medium of state policy and in which the dominant tone was conformism and the prevailing attitude one of sycophancy and self-seeking ambition, a figure such as Bulgakov was in fact indispensable. For there could have been no more powerful counter-statement to Stalin's Russia than his stories, novels and plays, whether or not they were published or performed during his lifetime (Woland's assertion in *The Master and Margarita* that "manuscripts don't burn" comes to mind).

"My ship is sinking," he wrote on 16th January 1930, "and the water's already up to the bridge. I must drown courageously." In her farewell to Bulgakov, expressed in a short poem written shortly after his death, Anna Akhmatova spoke in characteristically understated but all the more powerful terms of the writer's significance for her personally and for Russia. These diary entries and letters represent not merely a unique record of one of the darkest periods in recent Russian history, but a testament to an exceptionally talented writer whose strength of spirit and rich and fertile imagination were to prove a source of inspiration to future generations.

– Roger Cockrell, 2013

Diaries and
Selected Letters

Note on the Text

The text for this selection of Bulgakov's diaries and letters is based on *Mikhail i Yelena Bulgakovy: Dnevnik Mastera i Margarity*, compiled and edited by V.I. Losev (Moscow: Vagrius, 2004). The more complete edition of the diaries and letters (*Dnevnik, pis'ma 1914–1940*) published in Moscow by Sovremenny Pisatel' in 1997 has also been consulted. Lacunae in the text have been indicated by <...>, while [...] denotes an editorial cut. First names, patronymics and dates have been provided in the notes whenever these could be traced.

1921

To Varvara Mikhailovna Voskresenskaya*

Dear Mama,
How are you? Are you well? [...]

I'm really sorry that, in a short letter, I can't tell you in detail exactly what Moscow's like nowadays. Suffice it to say that people are undergoing a mad struggle for existence and having to adjust to the new conditions. Since my arrival I think I've managed to achieve everything it's possible to achieve in the six weeks I've been here. I have a job – not the most important thing, I know, but you have to be able to earn a living. And that's something I've succeeded in doing, believe it or not. In only a miserly way so far, it's true, but Taska* and I have been managing to eat and to stock up with potatoes. She's mended her shoes and we've begun to buy wood for the fire, etc.

The work has been frenzied, not easy at all. Morning to night, day after day, without a break.

Soviet institutions have been completely reorganized, with people being fired. This includes my own firm, which clearly won't last very long. So I'll shortly be out of a job. But that's not important: I've taken steps, before it's too late, to switch to private work. You'll no doubt already be aware that that's the only way to exist in Moscow – either that or setting oneself up in business. [...]

I'm trying to get myself a position in the linen industry. And, what's more, yesterday I was offered a job as a journalist for an industrial newspaper that has just started up. I don't yet know on what terms. It's a genuine commercial enterprise, and they're taking me on for a trial period. Yesterday I had to take an examination, as it were. Tomorrow they should be offering me an advance of half a million. This will mean that they think highly of me, and it's possible I'll be put in charge of the news section. And so that's what lies in store for me: linen, an industrial newspaper and (casual) private work. The search for work of this sort is precisely what I had in mind when I was in Kiev. Any other kind of work would be impossible. It would mean, at best, that we'd starve.

[...] I know masses of people here – journalists, theatre people or simply business people. That means a lot in today's Moscow, which is changing to a new way of life, something that it hasn't experienced for ages – mad competition, everyone racing around showing initiative and so on. You have to live like this, otherwise you'll die. And I have no desire to die.

[...] Poor Taska is flailing away trying to grind rye with an axe head and prepare food from all kinds of rubbish. But she's marvellous! In a word, we're both thrashing around, beating our heads against the ice like fish. Just so long as we have a roof over our heads. Andrei's room is a life-saver.* When Nadya comes,* this question will become fearsomely more difficult of course. But I'm putting this out of my mind for now and trying not to think about it, since I have quite enough to worry about each day as it is.

In Moscow only hundreds of thousands and millions are worth anything. A pound of black bread costs 4,600 roubles, a pound of white 14,000. And the cost is increasing all the time! The shops are full of goods, but you can't afford anything! The theatres are full, but as I was walking past the Bolshoi on business yesterday (going anywhere not on business is out of the question nowadays!) the girls were selling tickets for 75, 100, 150 thousand roubles each! Moscow has everything: shoes, cloth, meat, sturgeon, conserves, delicacies – everything! Cafés are opening, spreading like mushrooms. And, everywhere, hundreds of thousands of roubles! Hundreds of thousands! A roaring wave of speculation.

I have just one dream: to get through the winter, to survive December, which will be the most difficult month, I should imagine. I cannot express just how helpful Taska is to me. With the enormous distances that I have to cover each day running (literally) around

Moscow, she saves me a massive amount of energy and strength, feeding me and leaving me to do only those things she can't do for herself: chopping wood in the evenings and carting potatoes about in the mornings.

We both go around Moscow in our miserable little coats. I walk along with one side of the coat in front of the other (the left side lets in much more cold air for some reason). I dream of getting Tatyana something warm for her feet. She's only got her thin little shoes. But maybe it will be all right! Just so long as we have a room and good health!

[…] I'm writing all this just to show you the circumstances in which I have to realize my *idée fixe*: to re-establish within the space of three years the norm of an apartment, clothes, food and books. Whether or not I'll be successful, we'll have to see.

I won't tell you, because you won't believe me, just how frugally Taska and I are living. We're careful with every little piece of firewood.

Such is life's harsh school.

In the evenings I work in fits and starts on my *Country Doctor's Notebook*.* Could turn out to be quite a big piece. I'm also working on *The Ailment*.* But I don't have time, I don't have time! *That's what's really painful!* […]

PS: Can you guess what my most pleasant memory has been recently? Lying on your sofa and drinking tea with French rolls. I would give so much to be able to do that again, if only for a couple of days, drinking tea and not thinking about anything. I'm just so tired. […]

1st December

To Nadezhda Zemskaya

[...] I'm head of the current news section at the *Business and Industrial Herald*, and if I go out of my mind you'll know why. Can you imagine what it means to produce an independent newspaper?! There should be an article by Boris* in the second number, on the aviation industry, on cubic capacity and stockpiles and that sort of thing. I'm being driven completely mad. What about the supply of newsprint? What if we don't get any advertising? Then there's the news! And the censorship! I'm at boiling point all day long.

I've written a piece on *Eugene Onegin** for the theatrical journal *The Screen*. It hasn't been accepted. The reason: suitable for a literary journal, but not for a theatrical one. I've written a literary article dedicated to Nekrasov,* 'The Muse of Revenge'. Accepted by the arts-publications bureau of the Main Political Education Committee [of the Commissariat of Enlightenment]. They paid me 100. It was forwarded to the *Artistic Herald*, which is due to be published under the aegis of the MPEC. I know already either that the journal won't appear, or that at the last minute someone or other will take a dislike to 'The Muse'... and so on. Such a mess.

Please don't be surprised by such an outrageously incoherent letter – it's not deliberate, just that I'm literally worn out. I've given up on everything. Writing is out of the question. The only time I'm happy is when Taska pours me some hot tea. The two of us are now eating immeasurably better than at first. I wanted to write a long letter to you describing Moscow, but this is what you've got instead. [...]

1922

13th January

To Nadezhda Zemskaya

[...] I'm enclosing with this letter the correspondence from *Business Renaissance*. I hope you'll feel able (I will try to repay you by doing something for you in Moscow) to send it to one of the Kiev newspapers of your choice (preferably one of the large dailies) as a matter of urgency and offer it to them.

The results could be as follows:

(1) They won't accept it; (2) they will accept it; (3) they will accept it and find it interesting. If (1), then there's nothing more to say. If (2), then collect the fee agreed by the journal and send it on to me, deducting for yourself any amount which you calculate you've spent on postage and any other expenses arising from your correspondence with me (entirely up to you how much).

If (3), then please put me forward as their Moscow correspondent on any topic of their choice or for some "basement" satirical article on Moscow.* They can then send me an invitation and advance. Tell them that I'm head of the news section, a professional journalist at the *Herald*. If they print the *Renaissance* piece, send me two copies by registered post. Please forgive me for troubling you [...]. You'll understand what I must be feeling today, as I disappear up the chimney with the *Herald*.

In a word, overwhelmed. [...]

Bulgakov's Diary

25th January
(Tatyana's name day)

Given up writing the diary for a bit. A pity – there's been a lot of interesting things going on all this time.

I'm still without a job. Taska and I not eating well. So I don't feel like writing.

Black bread now 20 thousand a pound; white <...> thousand. [...]

26th January

Joined a troupe of roving actors. We'll be playing in the suburbs. 125 roubles a performance. Miserly amount. It will mean I'll have no time for writing of course – vicious circle.

Taska and I now half-starving.

Didn't mention that Korolenko's death* has been marked in the newspapers by masses of complimentary comments.

Vodka at N.G.'s.*

9th February

My life's never been so black as it is now. Taska and I are starving. Had to ask uncle for a little flour, vegetable oil and some potatoes. Boris has a million. Been all over Moscow at a run, but no job. [...]

<...> They may be turning No. 3 into a home for starving children.

Professor Ch. has gone overboard, striking the following off the lists of those who receive special rations: all actors, infant prodigies (Meyerhold's son* was one of those on the list!) and "academics", such as those from Sverdlovsk University. <...>

14th February

This evening, at the former women's college on Virgin Fields, *A Doctor's Notebook** was discussed. By half-past six all doorways were crammed with dark masses of students. There were several thousand of them. In the lecture hall <...>

Veresayev is not at all attractive, looks like an elderly Jew, but he's kept himself very well. He has very narrow eyes, large, bushy eyebrows and a bald patch. Low-pitched voice. I found him very likeable. A completely different impression from the one he used to give when lecturing. A contrast perhaps with the professors. Whereas they ask difficult, boring questions, Veresayev is always close to his students – they look for challenging questions and truthful resolutions. He doesn't speak very much, but when he does, it always sounds somehow clever and intelligent.

There were two women with him, evidently his wife and daughter. Very nice wife. <...>

15th February

The weather's got much worse. There's a frost today. Walking around on totally worn-out soles. My felt boots are useless. We're half starving. Up to my ears in debt [...]

24th March

To Nadezhda Zemskaya

[...] I shan't even begin to describe what life in Moscow's like. It's so extraordinary I'd need eight pages to describe it properly; you wouldn't be able to understand it otherwise. [...] But I'll mention a few random points anyway.

Most obviously I've noticed the following: (1) badly dressed people have disappeared; (2) the number of trams has increased and, if you are to believe the rumours, shops are going bust, theatres (apart from those putting on grotesque shows) are going bust, together with private publishing houses. It's impossible to talk about prices, since the currency is falling so rapidly that sometimes the price of things changes within a single day. [...]

The rest, I repeat, is indescribable. Apartment prices are unbelievable. Luckily for me, this nightmare of an apartment on the fifth floor in which I've been struggling to live for six months is inexpensive (700 thousand for March). [...]

I'm completely overwhelmed by work. I don't have any time for writing or for learning French as I should. I'm building a library (prices at second-hand booksellers – the ignorant, insolent swine – are higher than in the shops). [...]

It's now two in the morning. I'm so tired that I can't even actually remember what I've written! Some rubbish or other, but the main thing is it seems I've forgotten what it was...

24th March

*To Vera Bulgakova**

[...] I'm working very hard for the large newspaper *The Worker* and the Head of the Scientific and Technical Department. With Boris Mikhailovich Zemsky. Started only recently. The worst issue in Moscow is the question of housing. I'm living in a room left to me by Andrei Zemsky. Bolshaya Sadovaya 10, Apartment 50. A really nasty room, the neighbours also. I don't feel I've settled in, had so much trouble getting everything organized. I won't begin writing about the cost of living in Moscow. My salary is about 45 million a month (that's the rate for March). It's not enough. I need to do all I can to earn some more. I have many acquaintances in Moscow (journalists and artists), but I rarely see any of them, because I'm working so hard, racing around Moscow exclusively on newspaper business. [...]

1923

To Vera Bulgakova

Dear Vera,

Thank you all for your telegram. I was very pleased to hear that you're in Kiev. Unfortunately, I couldn't deduce from the telegram whether you had returned for good or just for the time being. My dream is that all of us should at last be able to settle down safely in Moscow and Kiev.

I think that you and Lyolya* might be able to get together amicably and arrange to live in the same place where Mama lived. Maybe I'm mistaken, but I feel this would be better for Ivan Pavlovich too* – perhaps one of the family who is so closely linked to him and who owes him so much could live nearby. I can't stop thinking about Kolya and Vanya* and how sad it is that we can't make things easier for them in any way. I'm also very sad when I think about Mama's death and the fact that it means that there's now nobody in Kiev living close to Ivan Pavlovich. My one wish is that your arrival in Kiev doesn't lead to any disagreements within the family but, on the contrary, brings you all closer together. That's why I was so glad to read your reference to the "friendly family". That's the main thing, for all of us. It's true: just a little goodwill and life would be so wonderful for you all. I'm speaking for myself: after so many tough years I value peace and quiet above all else! I would so love to be among family. But it can't be helped. Living here in Moscow, in circumstances that are immeasurably more difficult than yours, I am nonetheless thinking the whole time how to place my life onto a normal footing [...]

I'd like to ask a special favour of you: please live together in friendship and do it in memory of Mama.

I'm working so hard and am dreadfully tired. Maybe I'll be able to come to Kiev for a bit in the spring to see you and Ivan Pavlovich. If you manage to settle down in Kiev, have a word with Ivan Pavlovich and Varvara* to see if you can do something to preserve Mama's plot of land in Bucha.* I would be so sorry if this were to disappear. […]

    Your brother Mikhail

Bulgakov's Diary

24th May

Haven't taken up my diary for ages. On 21st April travelled from Moscow to Kiev, where I stayed until 12th May. In Kiev operated on myself (cancerous lump behind my left ear). I didn't get to the Caucasus as I had planned and returned to Moscow on 12th May. That's when things really started to happen. The Soviet representative Vatslav Vatslavovich Vorovsky was murdered in Lausanne by Conradi.* On the 12th there was a grandly staged demonstration in Moscow. Vorovsky's murder coincided with Curzon's ultimatum to Russia* to take back Weinstein's* impudent diplomatic messages that had been sent via the British trade representative in Moscow, to pay compensation for the English fishing vessels detained in the White Sea, to desist from propagandizing in the Far East and so on and so on.

The air was full of talk of a diplomatic bust-up, even of war. But the general opinion, it's true, was that it wouldn't come to war. And quite right too: how could we go to war with Britain? But there may well be a blockade. The news that both Poland and Romania are getting agitated (Marshall Foch has visited Poland*) is also very bad. In general we're poised on the brink of events. In today's newspapers there are reports that British warships are being sent to the White and Black Seas, and news that Curzon rejects any idea of compromise and demands that Krasin* (who set off by airplane for London immediately after the ultimatum) precisely fulfils the terms of the ultimatum.

Moscow is such a rowdy city, especially when compared to Kiev. Most striking of all is the huge amount of beer-drinking that goes on here. Even I'm drinking quite a bit. And, in general, I've let myself go recently. Count Alexei Tolstoy has arrived from Berlin.* Dissolute, insolent behaviour. Drinks a lot.

Have gone off the rails – written nothing for six weeks.

Wednesday 11th July

The biggest gap in my diary so far. In the meantime there have been events of extraordinary importance.

The sensational row with Britain has ended quietly, peacefully and shamefully. The government has made extremely humiliating concessions, even including the payment of compensation for the execution of two British subjects, persistently accused by the Soviet newspapers of being spies.

And then recently there was an even more remarkable event: Patriarch Tikhon* suddenly made a written statement renouncing his error in his attitude towards the Soviet authorities, saying he was no longer their enemy and so on.

He was released from confinement. Moscow full of countless rumours, and there is an absolute storm in the White émigré newspapers abroad. Disbelief, different interpretations and so on.

The day before yesterday the Patriarch's statement appeared on walls and fences, beginning with the words: "We, by the grace of God, the Patriarch of Moscow and all Russia…"

Essentially he's saying that he's the friend of the Soviet government and, while condemning the Whites, he's also condemning the Living Church. No church reforms other than the adoption of the new orthography and calendar.

There's an unbelievable row within the Church now. The Living Church is beside itself with rage. They wanted to get rid of Patriarch Tikhon entirely, but now he's speaking publicly and still in his post, etc.

We're having a revoltingly cold and wet summer.

White bread is 14 million a pound. The value of the chervonets* is climbing all the time and is now worth 832 million.

25th July

The 1923 Moscow summer has been extraordinary. Not a day goes by without it raining at least once, sometimes several times. In June we had two exceptional downpours, with roads being flooded and Neglinny Alley collapsing. Something similar today – another downpour with large hailstones.

Life here as chaotic as ever, rushed, nightmarish. Am spending a lot on drink, sadly. Colleagues at the *Hooter** drinking a lot. Played billiards on Neglinny. Two days ago *The Hooter* moved into the Palace of Labour on the Solyanka, and now during the day I am some distance away from *On the Eve.**

My writing is progressing sluggishly. The Berlin book* has still not been published, I'm pushing ahead with my satirical sketches in the *On the Eve*. *The Hooter* takes up the best part of my day, meaning that my novel is hardly moving at all.

Moscow is extraordinarily lively. Traffic increasing all the time.

The chervonets today is worth 975 million, the gold rouble 100. State Bank exchange rates.

That's just wonderful, isn't it?

22nd August

Haven't taken up my diary for months, omitting to record important events.

27th August
Evening

Just got back from a lecture by the Change of Landmarks group:* Professor Klyuchnikov, A. Tolstoy, Bobrishchev-Pushkin and Vasilyevsky-Ne-Bukva.*

The Zimin Theatre was packed. There were masses of people on the stage, journalists, acquaintances, etc. Sat next to Katayev.* In his talk on literature Tolstoy mentioned me and Katayev, among other contemporary writers.

Still no sign of my 'Notes on a Cuff'.
The Hooter's tormenting me, preventing me from writing.

Sunday, 2nd September

Chervonets banknotes today, by the grace of God, worth 2,050 million roubles (two billion fifty million roubles). Up to my eyes in debt. With little money, the future looks bleak.

Sofochka arrived yesterday, with her mother, husband and child.* On their way to Saratov. They're due to leave tomorrow by fast train, going back to a place where they once had a wonderful family life. But now they'll be leading a difficult and poverty-stricken nomadic existence.

Went with Katayev today to see Alexei Tolstoy at his Ivankovo dacha. He was very pleasant. The only thing wrong was his and his wife's incorrigible Bohemian attitude towards young writers.

All that, however, is redeemed by his genuinely large talent.

When Katayev and I left he accompanied us as far as the dam. Half-moon in the star-studded sky, silence. Tolstoy talked about the need to begin a school of neo-realism. He even waxed a little lyrical. "Looking at the moon, let us vow to…"

He's fearless, but he looks to me and to Katayev for support. His ideas on literature are always correct and apposite, at times magnificent.

In amongst my bouts of depression and nostalgia for the past, living in these absurd, temporarily cramped conditions, in a totally disgusting room in a totally disgusting house, I sometimes, as now, experience a brief upsurge of confidence and strength. I can sense my thoughts soaring upwards, and I believe I'm immeasurably stronger than any other writer I know. But in my present circumstances, I may well go under.

3rd September

The weather's now wonderful, after such a dreadful summer. The last few days have been warm, with bright sunshine.

Every day I go off to work to this *Hooter* of mine, and every day is a complete and utter waste of time.

The pattern of my life is such that, although I have little money, I continue to live beyond my humble means. I eat and drink well, but there's not enough money to buy things.

Not a day goes by without a damn drink, without beer. Today, for example, I was in the tavern on Strastnaya Square with Alexei Tolstoy, Kalmens* of course, and the lame "captain", who, when compared with the count, seemed like a shadow.

The relatives left for Saratov today.

A telegram arrived this afternoon: there's been a terrible earthquake in Japan. Yokohama destroyed, Tokyo on fire, coast inundated, hundreds of thousands of dead, the Emperor's palace destroyed, fate of the Emperor himself unknown.

And today I caught a glimpse of another telegram saying that Italy had attacked Greece – don't know the precise details yet.

What is going on in the world?

Tolstoy has been talking about how he started to write. First in verse. Then imitations. Then he turned to portraying the life of landowners, taking the theme to its limits. It was the war that inspired him to begin writing.

Sunday, 9th September

Went to see Tolstoy at his dacha again today and read him my story 'Diaboliad'.* He thought it was very good and will be taking it to St Petersburg, where he wants to publish it in *Zvezda** with his own introduction. But I'm not happy with the story myself.

It's cold already. Autumn. Yesterday I got really angry with Kalmens's constant pressurizing and rejected his offer of 500 roubles, leaving me in a tight spot. Had to borrow a billion from Tolstoy (his wife's suggestion).

Tuesday, 18th September

Among the entries and scrappy record of events in my diary I haven't once referred to events in Germany.

Here's what's going on: there has been a catastrophic fall in the value of the German mark. Today's newspapers, for example, report that one dollar is equivalent to 125 million marks! The government is headed by a certain Stresemann, dubbed by the Soviet newspapers as the German Kerensky.* The Communist Party is going all out to incite revolution and stir up trouble. At major Party gatherings Radek* is declaring categorically that the German revolution has already begun.

It's true: there's nothing to eat in Berlin now, and there are clashes in several cities. Two things are possible: either the Communists will win and then we will be at war with Poland and France, or the fascists will win (German Emperor and so on) and Soviet Russia's position will deteriorate. Either way, we are on the brink of huge events.

Not well today. Very little money. Had a letter from Kolya a day or two ago; he's ill (anaemia), feeling depressed and miserable. Wrote to *On the Eve* in Berlin asking them to send him 50 francs. I hope the swine will do this.

A. Erlich came to see me today and read me his story. Komorsky and Davy.* Chatted over a glass of wine. I still don't have an apartment – I'm only half a human being.

25th September

Heard yesterday that a conspiracy has been uncovered in Moscow. Among others arrested have been Bogdanov, the chairman of the Supreme Economic Council! And Krasnoshchekov,* the chairman of the Industrial Bank! And Communist Party members. The conspiracy was led by a certain Myasnikov, who had been expelled from the Party and who had settled in Hamburg. Also involved were some factory heads of committees (metallurgists). It's not known what all these people intended, but I have been told by one Party lady that it was a "left-wing" conspiracy – against NEP!*

Pravda and other newspapers have started sabre-rattling with regard to Germany (even although there is clearly no hope of a revolution there, since the Stresemann government has begun negotiations with the French). In connection with this, it seems that the chervonets on the black market has fallen below even the State Bank rate.

*Qui vivra – verra!**

30th September

Probably because I'm a conservative to the... wanted to write "to the core", but that's hackneyed... anyway, in a word, I'm a conservative who's drawn to his diary around anniversary time. What a pity I can't remember the exact date in September I arrived in Moscow two years ago. Two years! Have there been many changes during this period? Of course there have. Nevertheless this second anniversary finds me still in the same room and inwardly everything's just the same.

Apart from anything else, I'm ill.

Firstly, the political situation – always the same ghastly, unnatural political situation. Germany's still in upheaval. But when the Germans put a stop to the passive resistance in the Ruhr the mark began to rise. On the other hand, there's civil strife in Bulgaria. They're fighting... the communists! Wrangel's troops are joining in,* on the side of the government.

I'm absolutely certain that these minor Slav countries are in just as chaotic a state as Russia, and represent magnificently fertile ground for communism.

Our newspapers exaggerate events in every way possible, although, who knows, perhaps the world really is dividing into two parts – communism and fascism.

Nobody knows what will happen.

Moscow is, as ever, like some marvellous cesspit.

Outrageous prices, but not so much for these new roubles as for gold. Today's rate for the chervonets is 4,000 roubles in the 1923 currency (four billion old roubles).

As always, and now even more so than ever, it's quite impossible to buy any clothes.

Leaving aside my imaginary and actual fears, I can say there's only one thing that's really wrong about my life: the lack of an apartment.

My writing is progressing slowly, but at least it's moving forward. I'm sure that's the case. The only problem is that I'm never absolutely certain that what I've written is any good. It's as if there's some fog obscuring my brain and preventing me from writing – precisely when I need to describe what I so profoundly and genuinely can understand and sense with my heart and my brain (I'm certain of it).

Friday 5th October

First of all, political events.

In Bulgaria the communists have been totally defeated. Some of the rebels have been killed; others, including the ringleaders Kolarov and Dimitrov,* have fled across the border into Yugoslavia. The Bulgarian government (Tsankov)* is demanding that they be handed over. According to totally reliable reports, the Bolsheviks (if it's true that the rebels were indeed Bolsheviks) have finally been crushed by Wrangel's forces.

As for Germany, in place of the expected communist revolution a clear and broad-based fascism has emerged. The Stresemann cabinet has resigned, and a working cabinet is being formed. The fascist nucleus is headed by Kahr,* acting as dictator, and Hitler; together they're forming some "Union" or other. All this is taking place in Bavaria, from where the Kaiser will one fine day evidently emerge. But the mark is continuing to fall. The official rate in today's *Izvestiya** is 440 million marks to a dollar, but the unofficial rate is 500.

Izvestiya also has a leading article by Vilensky-Sibiryakov* saying there is unrest everywhere and that the Whites are once again thinking about intervention. Trotsky's letter to the artillery units of the Western Siberian military district is even more graphic, stating plainly that, in the event of something happening, "he is relying on the soldiers of the Red Army, its commanders and political commissars".

Aftershocks are continuing in Japan. There's been an earthquake on Formosa.

So much going on in the world!

Thursday night, 18th October

Am taking up my diary today aware of its importance and necessity.

We can no longer be in doubt we're on the brink of momentous and, in all probability, dire events. The word "war" hangs in the air. For two days now orders have been pasted all round Moscow relating to the call-up of young men (affecting, most recently, those born in 1898). They're talking about a so-called "muster of territorials". It's all temporary and it has a certain academic character, but nonetheless it gives rise to completely understandable rumours, fears and alarm... Konstantin arrived from St Petersburg today.* His trip to Japan now won't take place of course, and he's returning to Kiev. Konstantin has been telling me that it seems that all the 1890 cohort in the St Petersburg Military District have been called up! Orders relating to the training of territorials have been pasted up in Tver and Klin. And I heard today that there are even more serious signs of war. It seems that the journal *Krokodil** is preparing to go to the Front.

The situation is as follows. There is unrest not only in Germany, but now in Poland as well. In Germany Bavaria has become the centre for fascism, and Saxony for communism. Although it would be quite wrong to say that this is communism as we know it in Russia, the Saxon government nonetheless includes three communist ministers: Brandler, Heckert and Böttcher.* *Izvestiya* headlines: "Bloody clashes in Berlin"; "Food unrest", etc. The mark has fallen to an incredible level. A few days ago the dollar was worth several billion marks! There's no news today about the mark – it's probably a little higher.

According to *Izvestiya*, a miners' strike has flared up in the Dąbrowski region of Poland and has spread through the whole (?) country. Workers' organizations subjected to terror etc.

The world may well be on the edge of a general conflict between communism and fascism.

If events unfold, the first thing that will happen will be war between the Bolsheviks and Poland.

From now on I will start keeping a precise record of events.

Several days ago there was an explosion in Moscow, in a hunters' shop on Neglinny. Huge disaster. The house destroyed and large numbers of casualties.

Went to the doctor today about the pain in my leg. He made me
feel very depressed when he found me in such a state. I shall have
to take serious care of myself. The most monstrous thing is that
I'm afraid to take to my bed, because at the lovely newspaper
where I work I am being undermined, and they might ruthlessly
get rid of me.

The Devil take them, damn it.

The chervonets, by the grace of God, is worth 5,500 million
roubles (5 ½ billion) today. One French roll costs 17 million, a
pound of white bread 65 million. Yesterday ten eggs cost 200 million. Moscow is noisy. Tram No. 24 (to Ostozhenka) has started
running again.

No sight or sound of my 'Notes on a Cuff'. That's clearly the end
of that.

19th October
Friday night

The political situation remains the same. No major changes.

Had a horrible day today. The nature of my illness is evidently
such that I'll have to take to my bed next week. Am anxiously
trying to decide how I can ensure that the *Hooter* does not get rid
of me. And secondly, how I can turn my wife's
summer coat into a fur coat?

Have had a chaotic day, racing about everywhere. This was partly
due to time spent (afternoon and evening) at the *Workers' Copeck.**
Two of my satirical articles have disappeared. It's possible that
Koltsov* (the *Copeck* editor) took them for his own use. I could
neither find the originals, nor find out what had happened to them.
In the end I gave up trying.

Tomorrow Gross (the director of the *Copeck*'s financial department) will give me an answer regarding an advance for my article
– three chervonets maybe.

All my hopes rest on that.

Have been getting very little from *On the Eve* recently (they're publishing my four-part article on the exhibition). Waiting for an answer from *Nedra* about 'Diaboliad'.

Generally speaking, I've enough for food and bits and pieces, but I have nothing to wear. Certainly, if it weren't for the fact that I was ill, I wouldn't be so afraid for the future.

So then, let's put our trust in God and live. That is the best and only way.

Late this evening went to see my uncles.* They've mellowed. I'd given Uncle Misha my story 'Psalm', and he had read it a day or two ago and started asking me about it, what I'd been trying to say, etc. They are now paying greater attention to the fact that I am a writer and beginning to understand me more.

Autumn's rainy, slushy period is just beginning.

22nd October
Monday night

Today's *Izvestiya* includes a speech by Trotsky* to the provincial congress of metalworkers given a couple of days ago. Here are some excerpts:

"The German Communist Party is growing month by month.

"Two potential areas of future strife have been noted in Germany: fascist Bavaria and proletarian Saxony and Thuringia…

"The general situation throughout Germany is becoming more and more unstable from day to day, and from hour to hour.

"We are on the brink of open conflict…

"Some comrades are already impatiently saying that war with Poland is inevitable. I don't agree. I think just the opposite: there are many factors indicating that there won't be war with Poland…

"We don't want war…

"War is an equation with many unknown variables...

"The German revolution does not require material assistance..."

In general, it's clear that the future is uncertain.

Something remarkable and rather awkward happened at work at the *Hooter* today. The "Initiative" group of non-Party members proposed a meeting on the question of aid for the German proletariat. When N. opened the meeting, the communist P. stood up and, clearly agitated, declared menacingly that it was quite unprecedented for non-Party members to convene their own meetings! He demanded that the meeting be closed and replaced by a general meeting. N. paled and declared that would only happen if the workers' cell agreed.

After that it was all quite simple. The non-Party workers voted unanimously that the Party members present should invite their colleagues to join them and added ingratiating remarks. The other Party members then appeared and, for their part, passed a resolution that Party members give twice as much as non-Party members (non-Party members one day's wages, Party members two days' wages), thereby spitting in the non-Party donkeys' faces.

When it came to the vote for membership of the editorial board, my name was put forward with general support. Whereupon I. Kochetkov stood up and immediately proposed an alternative. Quite what he has against me I don't know.

"Call-up of territorials" apparently implies general mobilization – at least that's what the dressmaker Tonya told me when she came to measure me for a shirt, saying that the 1903 cohort had gone into barracks for eighteen months. When I asked her who we would be going to war with she replied:

"With... Germany. We're going to fight the Germans." (!!!)

The chervonets is now 6,200 to 6,350!

Slush. Slightly foggy.

26th October
Friday evening

I'm unwell, and that's not very pleasant, because it might mean I'll have to take to my bed. And that, as things stand, could harm my position at the *Hooter*. Am therefore in a rather depressed frame of mind.

Came back early from the *Hooter* today. Went to bed in the afternoon. On my way back called in at *Nedra* to see P.N. Zaytsev.* My story 'Diaboliad' has been accepted, but they're only giving me 50 roubles a sheet. And I won't be getting the money before next week. It's an idiotic, pointless story, but Veresayev (one of the *Nedra* editors) likes it a lot.*

When I'm ill and alone I give in to sad and envious thoughts. I bitterly regret that I gave up medicine, thereby condemning myself to an uncertain existence. But, as God is my witness, I only did this because of my love of writing.

Writing is difficult at the moment. With my views, expressed as they are voluntarily or involuntarily in my works, it is difficult to get published and earn a living.

And being ill under such circumstances is extremely unfortunate.

But I must not get depressed. Have just finished *The Last of the Mohicans,* which I recently bought for my library. What old-world charm this sentimental Cooper possesses! Just like a David singing and singing his psalms and inspiring in me thoughts of God.

Strong, courageous people may well not need him, but the thought of him makes life easier for people such as myself. My illness is complicated and prolonged. I'm a completely broken man. And that can prevent me from working – that's why I'm afraid, and that's why my hope is in God.

Today, back from work, I waited at the baker's next door for Tasya (who has the keys). The baker started talking about politics. He considers the actions of the authorities to be criminal (bonds etc.). He told me that two Jewish commissars had been beaten up at the Krasnopresnensky Soviet building by a group of conscripts because of their offensive and threatening behaviour, including the use of a revolver. Don't know if that's true. According to the baker, the conscripts were in an extremely nasty mood. He also complained at the increase in hooliganism by young people in the villages. The man has the same thoughts as everyone else – he's a clever chap, he knows perfectly well that the Bolsheviks are crooks, don't want war and have no idea about the international situation.

What a dark, primitive, unhappy nation we are.

The chervonets is worth 6,500 roubles. One can be consoled by the fact that the dollar is worth 69 billion marks. There have been clashes in Hamburg between workers and police. The workers were beaten up. Germany will have to live through nothing like what happened to us. That's the general opinion. According to Sokolov-Mikitov,* whom I saw at *On the Eve* today, Lidin,* just arrived back from Berlin, maintains that *Izvestiya* and *Pravda* are writing a lot of lies about Germany.

That's undoubtedly true.

What is interesting is that Sokolov-Mikitov has confirmed my supposition that Alexander Drozdov* is a swine. He once telephoned Drozdov as a joke, saying that he was Markov the second,* that he had the means to start a newspaper and invited him to participate. Drozdov accepted eagerly. This was immediately before Drozdov joined *On the Eve*.

My gut feelings about people never let me down. Never. A group of really nasty people is forming at *On the Eve*. I can congratulate myself that I'm one of them. Oh, I know: it will be very difficult for me later, when I have to scrape the accumulated dirt from my name. But I can say one thing with a pure heart: iron necessity has forced me to publish there. Had it not been for *On the Eve*, neither my 'Notes on a Cuff' nor many other pieces of true literary worth would ever have seen the light of day. One would have to be exceptionally heroic to remain silent for four years, to remain silent without a hope of ever being able to open one's mouth in the future. And, sadly, I am not a hero.

But I'm more courageous now – yes, much more courageous – than I was in '21. And if it weren't for my illness, I would be able to contemplate the dark, misty future with much greater confidence.

No letter from Kolya. Any correspondence with Kiev is hopeless.

27th October
Saturday evening

This evening there was a glow in the sky. I was in Starokonyushenny Alley at the time. People rushed out to look; it turned out that the Exhibition was on fire.

After seeing the doctor on Starokonyushenny I ran to Prechistenka. Usual talk, but the sense of both anger and hope was greater than normal.

I'm feeling confused. I was unpleasantly struck by the apparent dryness in the doctor's manner when he greeted me. But also excited that things are improving. Help me, O Lord.

Just seen a suite of bedside furniture at Syoma's, not expensive at all. Tasya and I decided to buy it, provided they would agree to defer payment until next week. We'll find out tomorrow. I'm hoping against hope that next week *Nedra* will be paying me for 'Diaboliad'.

29th October
Monday night

The heating was on for the first time today. Spent the entire evening sealing the windows. This first day of heating was especially noteworthy for the fact that the famous Annushka left the kitchen window wide open all night. I really don't know what to do with the wretches who live in this apartment.

I have a severe nervous disorder connected with my illness, and such things drive me mad.

The new furniture from yesterday is now in my room. In order to pay on time we had to borrow five chervonets from Mozalevsky.*

Mitya Stonov and Gaidovsky* came round this evening, invited me to join the journal *Town and Country*. Then Andrei.* He was reading my 'Diaboliad' and said that I had created a new genre and an unusually fast-moving plot.

It had only been the Moscow Agricultural Pavilion on fire at the Exhibition, and it had been quickly put out. Definitely arson, in my opinion.

6th November
Tuesday evening

Kolya Gladyrevsky* has just gone; he's treating my illness. After he'd left I read Mikhail Chekhov's poorly written and second-rate book on his great brother.* I'm also reading Gorky's brilliant *My Universities.*

I'm now full of thoughts, and have just begun to realize clearly that I need to start being serious about things. And, what's more, that writing is my entire life. I'll never return to any sort of medicine. I don't like Gorky as a person, but he's such a huge, powerful writer, and he makes such terrifying and important points about writing.

Today, at about five, I was at Lezhnev's,* and he said two things of significance to me: firstly, that my short story 'Psalm' (published in *On the Eve*) was magnificent, as "a miniature" ("I would have published it"), and, secondly, that *On the Eve* was universally despised and loathed. That doesn't frighten me. What does frighten me is the fact that I'm thirty-two, and the years I have wasted on medicine, my illness and my weakness. I've already had two operations on the idiotic tumour behind my ear. <...> They've written from Kiev to say I should begin radiotherapy. Now I'm afraid that the tumour will spread. And I'm afraid that this blind, stupid, detestable disease will interrupt my work. If I'm able to carry on, I'll write something better than 'Psalm'.

I'm going to start studying from now on. My voice may sometimes trouble me, but it cannot be anything other than prophetic. Quite impossible. And I cannot be anything other than a writer.

   Let's wait and see, learn and be silent.

1924

Bulgakov's Diary

8th January

There's a bulletin in today's newspapers about the state of Trotsky's health. It begins as follows: "On the 5th November last year L.D. Trotsky was ill with influenza…" and ends as follows: "…to take time off, with a full release from all his responsibilities, for a period of not less than two months." Any further comment on this historic bulletin would be superfluous.

And so, on 8th January 1924, Trotsky was kicked out. May God help Russia: He alone knows what the future holds for her! May God help her.

Spent the evening at Boris's.* Have just got back with Taska. Great fun. I drank wine, and my heart was fine.

The chervonets is worth 3.6 billlion.

22nd January

Syomka has just (half-past five in the evening) told me that Lenin has died. There has been, he says, an official communiqué to this effect.

Monday, 25th February

Pyotr Nikanorovich gave me the latest *Nedra* this evening. It includes my story 'Diaboliad'. This was while I was reading extracts from my *White Guard* at Vera Oskarovna's.

It evidently made an impression on this group. Vera Oskarovna asked me if I would give further readings at her place.

So this is the first time one of my works has appeared not in a newspaper but in an *anthology*. Yes. But what torture it's been! What torture!

My 'Notes on a Cuff' is dead and buried.

Tuesday, 15th April

Hottest topic of the day is the telegram that Poincaré* sent last week to the Soviet government, in which he went so far as to interfere in the trial of the Kiev regional "Centre of Action" (a counter-revolutionary organization), with a serious request not to carry out the death sentences.*

The newspapers include responses and reactions to this telegram by professors from Kiev and elsewhere. The tone of these responses is sycophantic and their source is quite clear.

In the newspapers there's a rant by a certain Professor Golovin (an ophthalmologist) – he had contrived to make an extremely reactionary speech at a gathering of ophthalmologists.

The staff at the *Hooter* were being filmed today. I left, because I don't want to be filmed.

Numerous arrests in Moscow of individuals with "distin-guished" names. More deportations. Saw D. Kiselhof today, full of fantastic rumours, as usual, claiming that a manifesto from Nikolai Nikolayevich* is going round Moscow. The Devil take all Romanovs! Just what we need!

There's a campaign under way to re-elect the boards of housing committees (sling out the bourgeois and replace them with workers). The only block where this will not be possible is ours. We don't have a single bourgeois on the board, so there's no one to replace.

It's a hard, cold spring. Little sun as yet.

16th April
Wednesday night

Just returned from the opening of the railwaymen's congress at the Assembly of Nobility (now Union House). The entire editorial board of the *Hooter*, with very few exceptions, was there. My job, with others, was to correct the shorthand report.

In the circular hall, divided by a thick curtain from the Hall of Columns, there was the clatter of typewriters and the bright electric lights of the chandeliers glowing in their frosted white shades. Kalinin,* in a dark-blue shirt, round-shouldered, mispronouncing his Rs and his Ls, appeared and said something or other. In the dazzling floodlights they were filming everywhere.

After the first session, there was a concert. Mordkin and the ballerina Kriger* danced together. Mordkin is handsome, flirtatious. Performers from the Bolshoi sang, including, amongst others, Viktorov,* a Jew, a dramatic tenor with a repellently piercing but huge voice. A certain Golovin,* a baritone from the Bolshoi, also sang. It turns out that he is a former deacon from Stavropol. Joined the Stavropol Opera and within three months was singing the part of the Demon* – and then, a year or so later, found himself with the Bolshoi. Incomparable voice.

Thursday, 17th April

At half-past seven Zinoviev* appeared at the congress. He walked quickly through the circular hall, enquiring with false modesty where he could leave his coat, passed through into the presidium room, where he took his coat off and climbed onto the platform. He was greeted by a round of applause that interrupted the previous speaker, who was mumbling something or other. Then the floodlights went on again and they started filming him. I may have come into the picture myself.

Zinoviev spoke for a long time, and I heard part of his speech. He spoke about the international situation, roundly abusing Ramsay MacDonald* and calling the British bankers money-grubbers. An interesting speech. He made a number of jokes that went down well with the audience.

He wore a little jacket that made him look like an orchestral violinist. Thin voice, with a lisp, and a barely noticeable accent.

One point emerged from his speech: the current conference in London will evidently break down. The British are demanding the restitution of confiscated foreign property, independent courts and the banning of propaganda.

Monday, 21st July

Copper 5- and 2½-rouble pieces have appeared. Tried in vain to save them up: they just melt away, and you can't do anything with them! In general there's an abundance of silver, especially noticeable in the shops at the Moscow Agricultural Industry Pavilion, where they're giving a lot of silver as change.

Spent the evening as usual at Lyubov Yevgenyevna's* and Deinka's.* We spoke Russian this time, about all kinds of nonsense. Left in the rain, feeling sad and somehow homeless.

Ilf and Yuri Olyesha* have arrived from Samara. Samara has two trams. The front of one says "Revolution Square – the Prison", the other "Soviet Square – the Prison". Something of the sort. In a word, all roads lead to Rome!

In Odessa they asked a young lady of high-born origin:

"Have you been subjected to a purge?"

She replied:

"I am a virgin."

It's interesting chatting to Olyesha. He's caustic and witty.

Friday, 25th July

What a day! Spent the morning at home writing a satirical piece for *Red Pepper**. Then the daily process began of dashing from one editor to another in search of money, without seeing any chink of light ahead. Saw the unspeakable Furman* from the newspaper *Dawn of the East**. Two of my pieces were returned. I had great difficulty getting Furman to hand the manuscript back, since I owed them the twenty roubles they'd already paid me. I had to write him a note that I would return the money no later than the 30th. Then I handed in one of these articles to *Red Pepper*, together with the one I had written earlier that morning. I'm sure they'll be rejected. And then, in the evening, Sven* rejected my article for *Splinter**. Was at his apartment, and somehow managed to get a promissory note for 20 roubles, for tomorrow. Nightmarish existence.

To cap it all, I rang Lezhnev in the afternoon to learn that there was no point in negotiating with Kagansky* concerning the publication of *The White Guard* as a separate edition, as he hadn't got any money at the moment. This was a new surprise. I now regret that I didn't take the thirty chervonets at the time. I'm sure *The White Guard* won't now be published.*

In short, the Devil only knows what's going on.

It's late, about 12; have been with Lyubov Yevgenyevna.

Saturday, 2nd August

Heard yesterday that Kalinin's carriage has been struck by lightning (he was somewhere in the provinces). The coachman was killed, Kalinin totally unscathed.

A demonstration took place today on the occasion of the tenth anniversary of the "Imperialist" war. Didn't take part. Returning home from the *Hooter* I saw policemen in uniforms and civilians marching towards Strastnaya Square, led by a band. Horsemen in caps, in strict formation and wearing red armlets. Two of them had their trousers/breeches hitched up, and underneath I could see the ties of their drawers.

The bookseller Yaroslavtsev has finally published his "Renaissance" anthology. It includes the first part of my 'Notes on a Cuff', severely mangled by the censor.

S. told me that a regiment of the GPU* joined the demonstration with the band playing 'These Girls Adore Everything'.

Monday, 4th August

The well-known satirical journal *Red Pepper* has surpassed itself several times. In particular, in its penultimate number, it had a sketch under the heading "Results of the 13th Party Congress". The sketch depicted a fat NEP lady being laced up by a maid, and the NEP lady saying more or less as follows: "What are you tying it so tightly for? Hasn't the 13th Party Congress just restricted us enough already?" Something like that. There was an uproar in the Moscow Party committee. The upshot was that they closed the *Red Pepper* and its sister journal *Splinter*. They will be replaced by just one insubstantial journal. A certain Verkhotursky (the editor of *Evening Moscow*,* apparently) has been entrusted with the editorship. Today I was at the meeting which discussed the new journal's title and subject matter. Sharp move to the left: the journal will have to be orientated towards the working class, and its title must reflect its working-class orientation. Sven tried to argue for the title *Punch* proposed by someone, but it was no use. It will be called *The Vice* or *The Brace*, or something like that. When they discussed the subject matter of the first sketch, entitled "European Balancing Act" (depicting, of course, a juggler and so on), Verkhotursky said: "Yes, and it would be good if there could be workers visible in the background, waiting to come in and smash the entire bourgeois circus to smithereens."

Caught a glimpse of Yeremeyev,* former editor of *The Worker*, at the *Hooter* today. He's turned into a sailor, with his dark jacket covered in red stripes. He's going to be the editor of *The Joker*,* with Sven as his assistant.

Wednesday, 6th August

There's a report in today's newspapers that the Anglo-Soviet conference has collapsed. The communiqué is written in dry, official
language: "The discussion broke down on the question of satisfy-
ing the claims of former private property owners... Since it was
clear that it was impossible to reach agreement on the question of
former major property owners, the conference was declared closed."

Finita la commedia, as they say. It would be interesting to know just
how long the Union of Socialist Republics can survive in this situation.

Saturday, 9th August

Buses have appeared on the streets of Moscow. Route: Tverskaya
Street – Centre – Kalanchevskaya Street. Just a few for the moment.
Very nice buses. Large and yet stylish. Coloured brown, with yellow
window frames. Single-decker, but enormous.

Today <...>

Haven't seen the newspapers, but apparently the Anglo-Soviet
agreement has been signed.

Latest joke: "The Chinese for Jew is 'tam'. 'Tam-tam-tam-tam', to
the tune of the 'Internationale' means 'many Jews'."

16th August
Saturday evening

It seems that recently Rakovsky* <...> but recent reports indicate that in England a strenuous campaign has begun against any
such agreement, and it's quite possible that it won't be ratified by
Parliament.

There has been an unexpected announcement about the agreement: a telegraphed report about the break-up of the talks, followed
by an announcement that it had been signed.

In Britain they're saying things that, from the British point of view, make absolute sense: you can't give the Bolsheviks any money, when these very same Bolsheviks are dreaming only of Britain's destruction! Stands to reason.

The English will get into trouble! [...]

Yesterday there was a nebulous report about an uprising in Afghanistan, assisted by "British agents".

Galya Syngayevskaya* arrived today. She has nowhere to live. Tatyana found her somewhere to spend the night for the time being, at Zina Komorskaya's.* I will feed her. People say she is an exceptionally talented dancer.

Took an extract from *The White Guard* to *The Contemporary*.* They probably won't take it.

At Frankel's publishing house today (the place where Lyubov Yevgenyevna works as a typist), even some Jewish employee said that the brochures, *People of the Revolution*, the brainchild of I.M. Vasilyevsky,* were unsuitable...

Blyumkin will be the author of *Dzerzhinsky*. The same astounding man, it seems, who assassinated Mirbach.*

The insolent swine.

Saturday, 23rd August

The Conservative British press is conducting an energetic campaign against the Anglo-Soviet agreement, and there are grounds for supposing that Parliament <...>

Although I make no claims at all to be a mentor, any conversations in the corridor have got to stop. The workers' correspondents are coming, and they look on the newspaper as some holy of holies...

I have become so used to such behaviour that it makes no impression on me.

Olyesha showed me the reviews in *Zvezda*. The comment on 'Diaboliad' was that it was "written with great humour".

Moscow is full of dust – from all the building work, it seems.

In Kislovsky Alley they've started work again on that huge building which I had looked at in the winter for the *Hooter*. Evidently,
it's not going to fall down!

Lemke's *250 Days at Headquarters** is on sale everywhere, with
people yelling, "Secrets of the Romanovs."

Tuesday, 26th August

Wasted the whole day at Kubuv*. Appointment with Professor Martynov*
about the revolting tumour behind my ear. He says he doesn't believe
it's malignant and has arranged for it to be X-rayed. Briefly saw N. in
the evening, and then spent the rest of the evening with S.

Thursday, 28th August

Lyubov Yevgenyevna called in just now with the news that Boris
Savinkov* has been arrested on the border. He came here apparently
in order to commit a terrorist act.

Friday, 29th August

Can't make head or tail of the Savinkov story. Today's government
communiqué was astonishing. It turns out that he had already been
tried in Moscow and condemned to death, but because he had
repented and acknowledged Soviet power, the court had requested
the Central Judicial Commission to reduce the sentence.

It's reported that Savinkov was caught together with Chepedaleva.*

Wednesday, 3rd September

Upheaval in China. Counter-revolutionaries, supported by the British,
have risen up against Sun Yat-sen's* southern (left-wing) administration.

Just been with the writer Lidin. His room has been placed on the register.

"Where on earth am I going to write then?" he asked the people from the municipal authorities.

"You can write here," they replied.

Lidin told me about one citizen who had happened to meet a girl from a good family in the street and had married her only so that she could move into his room. I myself heard of another such case today: a Jew named Ravvinov asked in the "Rainbow" shop whether someone could recommend him a woman – any woman, didn't matter who. A woman was recommended and he immediately married her in a registry office and even agreed to give her supper, as long as she moved in (his room was over 12 yards wide).

Friday, 12th September

Bright and sunny today.

Some news: a day or two ago a group of completely naked people (men and women) appeared in Moscow with ribbons over their shoulders proclaiming "Down with shame". They got onto a tram. The tram stopped, the public indignant.

Civil war is raging in China. I'm not following this topic in the newspapers – I only know that "imperialist predators" are involved, and that therefore a "Hands off China" society has been formed in Odessa (!).

Friday, 26th September

Just got back from seeing a performance of *Aida* at the Bolshoi with Lyubov Yevgenyevna. Incredible shouting by the tenor Viktorov.

Spent the whole day on the lookout for money, so that Lyubov Yevgenyevna and I can get ourselves a room. Borrowed some from Yevgeny Nikitich.* Gave him a receipt.

For the last few days it's been sunny and warm in Moscow. Details have been coming in about the St Petersburg flood which struck the great and ill-fated city some days ago. Nearly as widespread as the flood of 1824.

Sunday, 12th October

They're burying Bryusov* today. Crowds of people are queuing near the literary institute named after him. Horses are standing waiting with red plumes. Among the rows of waiting people are members of the intelligentsia and semi-intelligentsia. Many young people of the communist, workers'-education-Meyerhold type.

Saturday, 18th October

Things at the *Hooter* as tortuous as ever. Spent the day getting hold of 100 roubles at *Nedra*. Big difficulties with my grotesque story *The Fatal Eggs*.* Angarsky* underlined about twenty passages which I would have to change because of the censors. The story's ending is botched, because I wrote it too hastily.

Was at the Zimin Opera (now the Experimental Theatre) this evening. Saw the new production of the *Barber of Seville*. Magnificent. Walls and furniture shifting about the stage.

Night of 20th to 21st December

Have once again abandoned my diary. And this, to my great regret, is because there have been many very important events during the last two months. The most important of these of course is the split within the Party arising from Trotsky's book *The Lessons of October*,* the concerted attack on him by all Party leaders headed by Zinoviev, Trotsky's banishment to the south under the pretext of illness, and then – silence. The hopes of the Whites abroad and of counter-revolutionaries here at home that this Trotskyism/ Leninism business would lead to bloody conflict or a revolution within the Party have not of course been realized – as I knew would be the case. Trotsky has been eaten up, and that's an end to it.

Joke:

"How are you, Lev Davydovich?"

"Don't know; haven't seen today's newspapers yet."

(The reference is to the daily bulletin on the state of his health, couched in completely laughable language.)

England has given us a real kicking. The treaty's been torn up and the Conservative Party is once again waging an implacable economic and political war on the USSR.

Their minister for foreign affairs is Chamberlain.*

Zinoviev's famous letter,* with its unambiguous appeals to the English workers and armed forces to rise in revolt, is unreservedly viewed as genuine not only by the Foreign Office but evidently by England as a whole. With England it's all over. The slow-witted Brits are beginning, albeit belatedly, to understand that Monsieur Rakovsky and the couriers with their sealed packets represent a hidden but very real threat to Britain's future stability. Now it's the turn of the French. Monsieur Krasin has raised the red flag with a flourish on the embassy building on the Rue de Grenelle. The question is posed sharply and clearly: either Krasin and his plenipotentiaries will start a manic propaganda campaign in France while at the same time seeking a loan from the French, or the French will cotton on to the real meaning of the flag with the hammer and sickle in a quiet quarter of Paris… The second is much more likely. Their press is already beginning a violent assault not only on the Bolsheviks, both Muscovite and Parisian, but also on the French premier Herriot,* who granted these Bolsheviks access to Paris. I have no doubt that he is a Jew. Lyuba confirmed this for me when she said she had spoken to people who knew Herriot personally. That would explain everything.

Monsieur Krasin's arrival in Paris was marked by a totally absurd, Russian-style event: some half-witted woman, part journalist, part erotomaniac, approached Krasin's embassy with a revolver, with the intention of shooting. She was immediately arrested by a police inspector. She didn't shoot anybody, and it is in general a trivial, disgusting affair. I had the pleasure of meeting this Dickson woman* in Moscow in either 1922 or '23, in the lovely surroundings of the *On the Eve* publishing house, on Gnezdnikovsky Alley. A large, completely mad woman. She was granted permission to leave the country by "daddy" Lunacharsky,* after pestering him to death.

The big news in Moscow is that 30% vodka is for sale, appropriately dubbed by the general public as Rykov's tipple.* It differs from imperial vodka in that it is 10% weaker, nastier and four times more expensive. One bottle costs 1 rouble 45 copecks. Also on sale is "Armenian Cognac", advertising itself as 31% proof. (From the Shustov Factory of course.) Worse than the old brandy, weaker, costing 3 roubles 50 copecks a bottle.

After several days of frost, Moscow is now sinking in thawing mud. There are boys everywhere on the street selling Trotsky's book *The Lessons of October*. A quite dazzling stunt: while the newspapers have been publishing resolutions condemning Trotsky, the State Publishing House has magnificently succeeded in selling the entire edition. Oh, you immortal Jewish brains. There have, it is true, been rumours that Schmidt* has been kicked out of the State Publishing House precisely for allowing the book to be published, and that it was only later that people realized it would be impossible to ban it – and even more harmful since the general public don't understand the slightest thing about the book and is supremely indifferent towards it, whether it relates to Zinoviev, Trotsky, Ivanov or Rabinovich.* It's just "Slavs arguing among themselves".

There's mud everywhere in Moscow, but there are more and more streetlights. Strangely, there are two things happening the city: life is getting better, while simultaneously being in a state of utter gangrenous decay. In the centre of Moscow, starting at the Lubyanka, the water company has been testing the soil to investigate the possibility of an underground railway line. That's life. But the underground will never be built, because there is no money. That's gangrene. A road-traffic plan is under development. That's life. But there isn't any traffic – there aren't enough trams, and laughably there are only eight buses for the whole of Moscow. Apartments, families, academics, work, comfort and practical proposals are all gangrenous. Nothing progresses. Everything is gobbled up by the hellish maw of Soviet red tape. Every step taken, every move made by Soviet citizens is a torment, taking up hours, days, sometimes even months. Shops are open. That's life. But they're also going bust, and that's gangrene. It's the same with everything else. The state of literature is appalling.

Have been living in Obukhov Lane for about two months now, right next to K.'s apartment, with whom are connected such wonderful, important memories of my younger days – in 1916 and the beginning of 1912. I'm living in some totally unnatural hovel but, strange as it may seem, I feel a little more "defined" as a person. The reason for this is <...>

Tuesday night, 23rd to 24th December

Today is the 23rd, according to the new calendar,* which means that tomorrow is Christmas Eve. Christmas trees are on sale at the Church of Christ the Saviour. I left the house very late today, at about two o'clock in the afternoon, firstly because my wife* and I slept for a very long time as usual. We were woken at half-past twelve by Vasilyevsky, who had arrived from St Petersburg. Once again I had to let the two of them go off together on their business. But I left at an even pace, as my route is now a completely straight line. I dictated the last entry in my diary to my wife, ending with a joke. I had wanted to talk about this straight line in the previous entry. I found the conversation at the barber's very consoling. I was shaved by an accomplished young girl. I was mistaken about her – she is only seventeen, and she is the barber's daughter. She herself started talking to me, and for some reason during our conversation the quiet mirrors of Prechistenka Street remained perfectly still and calm.

It's always a joy for me to see the Kremlin. It consoled me, with its rather sombre appearance. It's a winter's day today. I've always found it lovely.

Had a very disturbing time at work and wasted some three hours to no purpose (they'd withdrawn one of my articles). Spent the whole time trying to recoup my strength. I should have called in at a number of other places, but wasn't able to as I stayed at the *Hooter* almost until five o'clock, while R.O.L.,* in the presence of Aron,* Pototsky* and one other person, gave his usual speech addressed to me concerning the form the *Hooter* should take. Even now, when it's my turn to speak, I'm still unable to control myself and I begin gesturing in a feeble, clownish manner. While I talked, I wanted to wave both my arms about, but I only waved my right arm, remembering the railway carriage in January 1920 and the little bottle of vodka with its grey strap and the lady who took pity on me because of my terrible twitch. As I looked at R.O.'s face I had a double vision: the man I was talking to, while I myself was remembering... no, not double, but triple: seeing him, and at the same time the railway carriage which was taking me somewhere where I didn't need to go, and then also the image of me lying shell-shocked under the oak tree and of the colonel who had been wounded in the stomach.

> Immortality – that calm and radiant shore,
> Towards which all our paths must bend.
> Rest now, those whose life is no more,
> Peace for all pilgrims, patient till the end.*

Unless I forget – and so that posterity should not forget – I am putting on record when and how he died. He died in November 1919 during the Shali-Aul campaign,* and his last words to me were as follows:

"There's no need to console me – I'm not a child."

I had suffered from shell shock half an hour after him. And so I had this triple vision. Firstly, that November night-time battle, through which I could see the railway carriage, with me now talking about the battle, and then that blasted room at the *Hooter*. "Blest he whom battle's overwhelmed."* Battle only overwhelmed me in a minor way, and I shall have to accept my share.

In the hallway of that damned *Hooter* building, as we were all going our own ways out into the winter fog, Pototsky said to me: "Well done, Mikhail Afanasyevich." That was good to hear – although of course I haven't done anything at all to be proud of, so far.

To allow myself a little congratulation: with regard to France, I have been proved totally prescient. Near Paris the police have carried out a raid on the communist school which, in the words of the Paris correspondent Rappoport, "was engaged in the peaceful study of Marx and Engels". Apart from this, the fishermen are on strike somewhere, and *les Camelots du Roi* (Royalist thugs) have been parading past Krasin's refuge and shouting.

Apparently, if I'm not mistaken, some trouble has started in Amiens. Krasin has won the first round in France. The chaos has begun.

Didn't manage to get any money from anywhere today, so came home feeling sour and depressed. Was greatly irritated by the thought of their trip together, and my only consolation was my straight line. As always, it is the shortest distance between two points, and as soon as it comes to mind I'm completely calm. At home I fell into a terrible rage; after two weeks' practice I was immediately able to explain such behaviour to myself, like the dog with the owl,* and locked it away. Mustn't talk about politics under any circumstances.

Vasilyevsky has become terribly weak. He used to have a sixth sense, but he's begun to lose it in the USSR. That will be disastrous of course. His head is full of projects, one of which is absolutely brilliant. None of them do it the American way: something only has to be said once, and I've understood. I *have* understood. I've mentally tried to hypnotize him so that he does it, but I am a dilettante in such things and cannot guarantee success.

He has brought and shown me two of the books produced by his publishing house. One of them, in the series Leaders and Statesmen

of the Revolution, has been written by Mitya Stonov* (*Kalinin*).
The other by Bobrishchev-Pushkin (*Volodarsky*).* It's difficult to
retain one's sanity – Bobrishchev writing about Volodarsky. But
the old fox has got a better sixth sense than Vasilyevsky. This can
be explained by the difference in their blood. He has contrived to
hide his real name – not behind just one pseudonym, but behind
two at once. The old prostitute walks along Tverskaya Street
expecting to be mugged at any moment. He doesn't walk very well.

Vasilyevsky says the authorities have seized his apartment. When
all's said and done, it hasn't been a successful move. But you'll
understand nevertheless. Here we have an old, convinced Jew-basher
and full-blooded anti-Semite writing a book in praise of Volodarsky,
calling him a "defender of the freedom of the press". The mind grows
numb. Vasilyevsky writes about all of this in an especially animated,
senile kind of jauntiness. At one terrifying moment he reminded me
of old man Arsenyev.* They all consider that the game has been so
hopelessly played and that they're throwing themselves into the water
with their clothes on. Vasilyevsky published one of the books under
a pseudonym. As far as the opening move is concerned that's quite
all right. And the only mistake of all these Pavel Nikolayeviches and
Pasmaniks ensconced in Paris* is that while they're still completing
the first set, there is a second, totally different game being played
as a logical consequence of the first. Whatever combinations might
arise in this second set, Bobrishchev will not survive.

I've forgotten whether *The Wanderer Playing on Muted Strings**
is a play or a novel.

It was Vasilyevsky who told me what Alexei Tolstoy had said:

"I'm not Alexei Tolstoy any more. I'm the natural-born workers'
correspondent Potap Dermov."

Dirty, dishonest clown.

And it was also Vasilyevsky who told me what Demyan Bedny*
had said in a speech to an audience of Red Army soldiers:

"My mother was a whore."

Had dinner at Valentina's in a state of hopeless rage. This criminal
from Povarskaya Street was living right opposite me. There's a

huge difference between him and a bedbug, and the Jewish girls are mistaken in likening him to one. He's just a troglodyte, the lowest of the low. A huge difference: it's not pleasant to squash a bedbug. Troglodytes don't understand that. There's nobody like someone close to you. And people close to you can do more damage than strangers, damn it!

To dictate diary entries is perhaps not the highest act of trust, but it's still an act of trust.

There's a report today that yet another provincial correspondent has been killed – Sigayev.* Either I have lost my sixth sense, in which case I'll end up on the slippery slope, or this is the prelude to a totally unbelievable opera.

So many impressions have piled up in just one day that it's possible to convey them only piecemeal, with the intention to group them all together later. Just as during the defence of Sevastopol, a day is equivalent to a month, and a month to a year. But where are my marines?...

Of all the things that Vasilyevsky has told me, the most monstrous has been his story about Frankel, now a Moscow writer but formerly a rabbi (probably still is, but keeps it hidden), who travelled in an international sleeper from St Petersburg to Moscow. It's one of those large centres in Moscow which is now feeding scores of Jews working in the book business. He has a scruffy but well-equipped office in the very centre of Moscow that's humming the whole time like a beehive. People are constantly assembling and dashing in and out of the courtyard in Kuznetsky Alley. It's like breast cancer. You can't tell where the money of one person ends and the money of the next begins. He travels to St Petersburg very frequently, and it's typical that he should be accompanied by a respectful crowd of people. He's evidently still at work, giving advice about printing techniques. He's a clever man.

Still really angry. To calm myself down I'm rereading a satirical article by a St Petersburg writer of the 1870s. He's describing a musical event in Pavlovsk, portraying the Jewish musician in scornful terms, with an accent.

God give me strength!

I'm now working perfectly well – a wonderful situation to be in, something that's quite normal for other people, but that for me, alas, has become a luxury. It's because I've relaxed a little. But basically the main thing is that I'm getting better and my strength is returning to me, even if slowly. I'll start exercising with massage in the New Year, as I used to do in 1916 and '17, and will be in shape by March.

There's just one ridiculous, annoying thing: my damned stomach and nerves. I write about my state of health only so that I can subsequently reread what I've written and find out whether I've done what I've said I'd do.

Vague rumours are flitting around, and I've managed to latch on to a couple of their tails. What a swine!

Night of 26th to 27th December

Just returned from spending the evening at Angarsky's, the editor of *Nedra*. There was one topic of conversation that is everywhere at the moment: the censorship, attacks on it, talk of "literary truth" and "falsehood". Present were Veresayev, Kozyrev, Nikandrov, Kirillov, Zaytsev (P.N.), Lyashko and Lvov-Rogachevsky*. Several times I was unable to restrain myself from saying how difficult it was to work now, attacking the censor and so on, all things that I shouldn't have said.

    The proletarian writer Lyashko, who instinctively has an insurmountable dislike of me, objected to what I was saying with barely concealed irritation.

"I don't understand what 'truth' comrade Bulgakov is talking about. Why does he need to depict just the faults? He should give all points of view, etc. etc."

And when I said that the present epoch is the epoch when accounts need to be settled, he replied with loathing in his voice:

"That's rubbish."

I didn't have time to reply to this presumptuous comment as everyone got up from the table at that moment. There's no salvation from scum like that.

Severe frost. The plumber thawed the frozen pipes this morning. But then, at night, as soon as I had got back, the electricity failed everywhere.

Angarsky has only just returned a day or two ago from abroad. Both in Berlin, and apparently in Paris, he showed to absolutely everyone the proofs of my *Fatal Eggs*. He says that everybody liked it enormously and that someone in some Berlin publishing house will translate it.

What concerns me more than all these Lyashkos is the question whether I am a real writer or not.

There is an echo of the conversation at Angarsky's in the sensational letter/pamphlet of Bernard Shaw which appeared in yesterday's *Izvestiya*.* Radek attempted a reply with an article, 'Mr Pickwick on Communism', but it is feeble. The pamphlet includes the following phrase: "Stop talking about international revolution – that's just for the cinema."

Night of 28th December

I'm writing this at night, because practically every night my wife and I don't get to sleep until three or four in the morning. That's our idiotic routine now. We get up very late, at twelve, sometimes at one, sometimes not even until two. We got up very late today and, instead of going to the damned *Hooter*, I changed my route and went to get a shave at the barber's on my favourite street, Prechistenka. And then I went to my regular dentist, Zinushka. She's treating two of my teeth, which I reckon will last for ever. She doesn't rush my treatment; I keep my appointments regularly; she inserts cotton wool soaked now in iodine, now in oil of cloves, and I'm very pleased that I never feel any pain and that she doesn't dig around in my root canals with a needle.

I didn't get to her until after three. Moscow had become dark and the lights were on. From her windows I could see Strastnoy Monastery and the illuminated clock.

What a magnificent city Moscow is! I didn't see my lovely, my only beloved Kremlin today.

After the dentist I went to *Nedra*, where that strange man Angarsky is carrying out some purge of his employees. Thanks to him I was given ten roubles.

And so I walked along Kuznetsky Bridge, just as I had done scores of times over the last few winter days, visiting several shops on the way. I needed to buy this and that. I bought the inevitable bottle of white wine of course, and half a bottle of Russian vodka, but for some unknown reason took special care over the purchase of tea. At the newspaper seller's I happened to see the fourth number of *Russia*** with the first part of my *White Guard* – that is to say not the first part, but the first third. When I got to the second newspaper seller on the corner of Petrovka and Kuznetsky Bridge, I couldn't hold back any longer and bought a copy. I alternate between seeing the novel as weak and then very strong. I can't seem to make sense of my feelings any more. What struck me above all for some reason was the dedication. That's how things have worked out. There she is: my wife.

This evening, at Nikitina's,* I read my story *The Fatal Eggs*. On the way there I'd had the childlike desire to show off and to dazzle, but returning home my feelings were more complex. What is it? A satire? A piece of cheek? Or, perhaps, a serious piece of work? In that case it's something half-baked. Anyway, there were about thirty people present, and not only was there not a single writer among them, but there was a general lack of understanding about the essential nature of Russian literature.

I'm afraid that for all these achievements I might get dragged off to "places that are not so far away".* But my wife greatly helps me to rid myself of such thoughts. I've noticed that she sways when she walks. With everything else that's going on in my head, it's all very silly, but it seems I'm in love with her. I wonder about one thing: would she have settled in so comfortably with just anyone, or am I somehow special?...

Today's political news is not for me. All these *Nikitina Sabbaths, all this stagnant, Soviet, servile rubbish, with a thick admixture of Jews.*
 Not for the diary, and not for publication: I'm overwhelmed by my feelings for my wife. That's both good and desperate, and delightful, and at the same time hopelessly complex: I'm a sick man right now, while, for me, she...
 I watched her today as she got changed before we went to Nikitina's, watched her greedily...

No political news, none. Instead, just political thoughts.

All this Change of Landmarks stuff has entered me like a splinter (what's it got to do with me?). And the fact that this devilish woman has sucked me in like a cannon in a swamp is an important issue. But on my own, without her, I can no longer think straight. Evidently, I've got used to her.

Monday, 29th December

The vodka's called a "Rykov" or a "Semi-Rykov". "Semi-Rykov" because it's 30%.
 At the damned *Hooter* again, and then spent the evening at Lydia Vasilyevna's.* We arranged what we'd do for the New Year.
 Lezhnev is discussing with my wife the possibility of getting *The White Guard* from Sabashnikov* and handing it over to him. Lyuba refused – she's a high-spirited and quick-witted woman, and I heaped the entire burden onto her shoulders. I don't want any

contact with Lezhnev, and it would be awkward and unpleasant to negotiate with Sabashnikov. We're up to our ears in debt.

Night of 2nd to 3rd January 1925

If you were to add a "Semashkovka" to a "Rykovka", you'd get a fine bottle of "Soviet Commissar".

"Rykov drank on the occasion of Lenin's death for two reasons: firstly, from grief, secondly, for joy."

"Trotsky is now written 'Troy' – the Central Committee has dropped out of his name."*

All these anecdotes were told me in the evening by that sly, freckled fox Lezhnev when I was sitting with my wife, working on the text of the agreement concerning the continued publication of *The White Guard* in *Russia*. My wife sat reading a novel by Ehrenburg,* while Lezhnev tried to cajole me into agreeing. We didn't have a copeck between us. Tomorrow an unknown Jew named Kagansky should be paying me 300 roubles and the rest in the form of promissory notes. With these promissory notes we should be able to get by. The Devil knows if that's right, however! I wonder if they'll bring the money tomorrow. I won't let go of the manuscript.

No newspapers today, so there's nothing new to report.

Here's an amusing story: I had no money for a tram, so I decided to go home from the *Hooter* on foot. The middle of the River Moskva was not frozen, for some reason, and there were crows standing on the ice and on the snow along the river banks. Lights on the far side of the river. As I was passing the Kremlin and drawing level with the tower on the corner, I stopped and glanced upwards at the Kremlin and was just thinking "How long, Lord!" to myself, when a figure dressed in grey and carrying a briefcase darted behind me and gave me a searching look. Then the figure attached itself to me. I let him go on ahead of me, and we walked for a quarter of an hour, coupled together. When he spat from the parapet, I did the same. Managed to get away from him at the foot of the Alexander monument.

1925

Bulgakov's Diary

3rd January

Received 300 roubles from Lezhnev today as advance payment for my novel *The White Guard*, which will be appearing in *Russia*. The rest will be paid in a promissory note.

Was in the Green Lamp this evening with my wife. I talk more than I should, but I cannot refrain from talking. The mere sight of Yuri Potekhin,* who had come because of Chekhov's notebook* and who started insolently declaring that "we are all people without ideology", acted on me like the sound of a bugle at a cavalry charge.

"Stop lying!"

If the worst comes to the worst our literature may possibly be Communist, but it won't be of the Sadyker/Change of Landmarks persuasion.* Oh, those jolly Berlin bastards! All the same I'm afraid that disaster might have struck *The White Guard*. This very evening at the Green Lamp, Auslender* started to say, "During the reading…" and then grimaced. But I like him, goodness knows why.

I'm in a terrible state: I'm falling more and more in love with my wife. How annoying: for the last ten years I've kept on turning away from anyone close to me… a woman is just a woman, after all. But now I allow myself to be humiliated by even the slightest twinge of jealousy. She's sweet and lovely. And large.

Didn't read the newspapers today.

4th January

St Petersburg will be empty.

St Petersburg was flooded yesterday: Vasileostrovsky, Peterburgsky, Moskovsko-Narvsky and Central Regions are under water. Late in the evening the water started to recede.

A note has come from England signed by Chamberlain, which makes it clear that the British government has no wish to say another word about the Zinoviev letter. Relations with Britain are intolerably foul.

There's a report from Kiev that the entire work of the Union of Sewing Industry Workers is gradually being translated into Hebrew, in view of the fact that the workforce is 80% Jewish.

That even makes me happy.

My story 'Bohemia' appeared in the first edition of *Krasnaya Niva** today. It's my first venture into the specifically Soviet petty journalistic sewer. I reread the piece today and I like it very much, but I was terribly struck by one aspect, for which I am totally responsible. It's imbued with a feeling of unapologetic poverty. We had become too used to being hungry and were not ashamed of it, but now it seemed as if I was ashamed. There was a sense of grovelling about it. For the first time since that famous autumn of 1921, I think I'll give myself a little pat on the back – but only in my diary. I wrote one passage totally in the pre-revolutionary orthography, with the exception of one or two phrases ("I was offended", for example).

Everything is bottom up and face down in mud. All of Moscow is swimming in thawed mud, and I spent the whole day just going around inviting guests. We want to dance at Nadya's.*

Saw the lovely Lyamins* and gave them the copy of *Russia* which contained *The White Guard*.

In the interval between foxtrots some sweet Jewish girls grabbed hold of me and started on about women's correspondence. They pressed and pressed me, and they were absolutely right. I responded in kind, but I won't do a damn thing about it, of course. She definitely won't send them. Like a lump in the throat. And, indeed, I'm just like a cobra. They pressed me so hard that in the course of just one day I became thin and my entire face sagged to one side. I'll think and think for three days and nights and then I'll come up with something. Whatever happens, I'll be the one in charge, and no one else.

5th January

The weather in Moscow is something quite extraordinary: in the thaw everything has melted, and the mood amongst Muscovites precisely mirrors the weather. The weather suggests February, and there's February in *people's hearts*.

"How's this all going to end?" a friend asked me today.

Such questions are asked in a dull, mechanical way, hopelessly, indifferently, any way you like. Just at that moment there was a group of drunken communists in my friend's apartment, in a room right across the corridor. In the corridor itself there was a foully pungent smell – one of the Party members, my friend told me, was asleep there like a pig, completely drunk. Someone had invited him, and my friend hadn't been able to refuse. Again and again he went into their room with a polite and ingratiating smile on his face. They kept shouting to him to join them. He kept coming back to me, cursing them in a whisper. *Yes, right: somehow this must all stop. I believe it will!*

Went specially today to the publishers of the *Atheist*.* It's situated in Stoleshnikov Alley or, rather, in Kozmodemyanovsky, not far from the Moscow City Council building. M.S. was with me* and he delighted me from the first.

"What, aren't they smashing in your windows?" he asked the first girl we came across, sitting at a desk.

"What do you mean?" (*confused*). "No, they aren't" (*threateningly*).

"What a pity."

I wanted to kiss him on his Jewish nose. It turned out that there were no copies from 1923 left. All sold, they reported proudly. We managed to get hold of the first eleven back numbers from 1924. Number 12 had not yet appeared. When she found out that I was a private individual, the young lady, if that's the right way to describe her, gave them to me reluctantly.

"I should really be giving this to a library."

Apparently they have a print run of 70,000, and it's a total sell-out. There are some unspeakable swine in the office who keep on leaving the room and coming back in again; and a small stage, curtains, scenery... On a table on the stage there's some sacred book, a bible perhaps, with a couple of heads bent over it.

"Just like a synagogue," said M. as we were leaving the building.

I was very interested to know just how much this had all been said for my special benefit. It would be wrong of course to exaggerate, but I have the impression that some of the people who have been reading *The White Guard* in *Russia* use a different tone of voice when speaking to me – with a kind of oblique, apprehensive deference.

I was very struck by M.'s reaction to the extract from *The White Guard*. It could be described as rapturous, but even before this I'd had this feeling growing inside me, a process that had been going on for some three days. I will be terribly sorry if I'm mistaken and if *The White Guard* is not an exceptional piece.

When I skimmed through the copies of the *Atheist* at home this evening I was shocked. The salt was not in the blasphemy, although that was huge, of course, if you're looking at it just from the outside. The salt was in the idea, an idea that can be historically proved. Even Jesus Christ was being depicted as a crook and a scoundrel. It's not difficult to understand who's responsible for this. The offence is immeasurable.

L.L.* was here this evening and said that there are Trotskyites in this world. Joke: As Trotsky was leaving the country people said to him: "The farther you go, the quieter you'll be."

At the *Hooter* today I felt for the first time, with a sense of horror, that I can't write any more satirical articles. Physically impossible. "It's an outrage against me and against my whole being."

Most of the notes in the *Atheist* are signed by pseudonyms.

"But I will explain that owl."*

Friday, 16th January

The day before yesterday I was at P.N. Zaytsev's to attend a reading by Andrei Bely.* The room was crowded with people. Nowhere to sit. S.Z. Fedorchenko* was there. Straight away she seemed to grow softer and more emotional.

Bely was wearing a black jacket. He seemed to me to be posing and playing the clown quite intolerably.

He was reminiscing about Valery Bryusov. It all made an unbearable impression on me... Some rubbish or other... about the Symbolists... "Bryusov's a seven-storey house."

"One day we were walking along the Arbat... Suddenly he asks" – here Bely started to imitate Bryusov's intonation – "'Tell me, Boris Nikolayevich, what do you think? Did Christ come down to only one planet or to many others as well?' Firstly, what kind of Balaam's ass am I to start pontificating on such matters? And, secondly, I sensed some sort of trap...'"

And, in general, he talked and talked for an intolerably long time, now and then throwing in amusing anecdotes... something to do with bracken... about Bryusov being the "face" of the Symbolists, but also at the same time someone who loved to behave in a foul way...

I left without waiting until the end. After 'Bryusov' there was to have been an excerpt from Bely's new novel.

Merci.

25th February
Wednesday evening

I'm facing an insoluble problem.

That's all.

10th May

To M.A. Voloshin*

Highly esteemed Maximilian Alexandrovich,

N.S. Angarsky has passed on to me your invitation to Koktebel. I am
extremely grateful to you. Please would you let me know whether
there would be a separate room for me and my wife in July/August.
It would be lovely to visit you. Please accept my greetings.

M. Bulgakov

15th October

To Vasily Luzhsky*

Highly esteemed Vasily Vasilyevich,

Yesterday's meeting, at which I had the honour to be present, showed me that there are some difficulties associated with my play.* There were questions concerning its staging at the Maly Theatre, about the coming season, and finally about the play's basic form, essentially touching on the creation of a new play.

While I am perfectly prepared, working hand in hand with the director, to make amendments to the play, I nevertheless don't feel I can bring myself to rewrite it.

As a result of the profound and pointed criticism levelled at the play at the meeting I have become extremely disillusioned with it (though I welcome criticism), and I am not convinced that the Maly is the right theatre for it to be staged.

And finally, there is only one answer to the season question as far as I am concerned: it must be this season, and not the next.

I would therefore ask you, highly esteemed Vasily Vasilyevich, to discuss the following question at your management-board meeting as a matter of urgency, and to give me a definite answer:

Does the First Arts Theatre agree to include the following unconditional points in the play's contract:

That it should be staged *only at the Bolshoi*.

During *the current season* (March 1926).

That there should be amendments to the play, but not a fundamental rewriting?

If these conditions should prove unacceptable to the Theatre, I shall reserve the right to ask permission to consider the negative answer as a signal that the play *The White Guard* is no longer bound by the agreement.

Respectfully yours, M. Bulgakov

18th October

To the All-Russian Union of Writers

Respected comrades
In reply to your invitation to the literary exhibition, I am sending you my 'Diaboliad'.

With regard to my portrait:

Not having a particularly distinguished record either in the field of Russian literature or in any other field of activity, I consider that it would be premature to place a portrait of me on public display.

And, in any case, I haven't got one.

Respectfully yours,
M. Bulgakov

Bulgakov's Diary

13th December

Haven't been following the newspapers for about a month. Heard in passing that Budyonny's wife had died.* Then there was a rumour that it was suicide, and then, it turns out, that he murdered her. He'd fallen in love with someone, and she was in the way. He's remained totally unpunished.

It's being said that she threatened to expose his cruelty towards his soldiers in pre-revolutionary days, when he was a cavalry sergeant-major.

[*There are no further extant diary entries after this date. Bulgakov's apartment was raided by the OGPU in May 1926 and his diaries confiscated. This may have discouraged the author from continuing to record his thoughts in his private notebooks.*]

1926

To OGPU*

From the Writer Mikhail Afanasyevich Bulgakov,
Resident of Moscow, Chisty (Bolshoi Obukhovsky) Alley, No. 9,
Apartment 4.

Declaration

During the search by representatives of OGPU that took place in my
apartment on 7th May 1926 (order No. 2287/45) the following items
were taken with a corresponding entry in the record: two copies of
my story *A Dog's Heart* from the typewriter and three notebooks
containing my handwritten memoirs entitled 'My Diary'.

In view of the fact that I urgently need both *A Dog's Heart* and
the 'Diary' in order to continue my work as a writer, and also that
the diary contains material of a very intimate and personal nature,
I request that you return them to me.

Mikhail Bulgakov

4th June

To the Council and Management Board of the Moscow Arts Theatre

I hereby have the honour to inform you that I do not agree with the removal of the Petlyura scene* from my play *The White Guard*.

My reason: the Petlyura scene is an organic part of the play.

Neither do I agree that the play should be renamed *Before the End*.

Neither do I agree that the play should be reduced from four acts to three.

I agree to discuss with the Theatre's council the possibility of another name for *The White Guard*.

If the Theatre does not agree to the above, I request that the play *The White Guard* be removed from the repertoire as soon as possible.

Mikhail Bulgakov

26th July

*To Alexei Popov**

Hello, my dear director!

Your letter of 16th July came yesterday when I was in Kryukov, near Moscow. There has evidently been some misunderstanding. I had supposed that I had sold the Studio a *play*, whereas the Studio supposed that I had sold them a *sketch* which they (the Studio) could alter as they saw fit.

I would be very grateful for an answer. You are a director: how is it possible to turn a four-act play into a three-act play?! [...]

Zoyka's Apartment,* in short, is a four-act play. It's im-poss-ible to turn it into a three-act play.

I will not write a new three-act play. I'm ill (firstly), exhausted (secondly) and, thirdly, people who have seen the rehearsal quite rightly say to me:

"Don't listen to them (the theatre management, if you'll forgive me!) – they're the ones who are at fault."

Fourthly, I had supposed that the position would be as follows: I would write plays and the Studio would put them on. But it doesn't put them on. Oh, no! It hasn't got time to put plays on! It has a whole mass of other things to do, such as thinking up schemes for adaptations. Evidently, I will be the one who has to put the plays on! But I don't have a theatre! (*Regretfully!!*)

And so I agreed that there should be amendments. But absolutely not that there should be only three acts. I am now sitting working at an amended version – a sick, persecuted, worn-out man, wracked by headaches [...]

Well, all right. I'm amending *Zoyka's Apartment* because, sadly, I love the play and want it to be a success. [...]

Finally, can you please tell me whether the Vakhtangov Theatre* will be putting on *Zoyka's Apartment* or not? Or are we going to be amending and amending it until 1928? But however much we amend the play, I cannot force the actors and actresses to perform the Alla I've written, the Zoyka I've created, the Alleluia which I've composed. You, Alexei Dmitrievich, will have to do that.

I hope you haven't been offended by the somewhat confused tone of this letter. I'm writing this in great haste (on my way to something in Moscow) and am exhausted.

In a couple of days I'll give the Studio typist my new *Zoyka's Apartment* so that she can type it out. If I'm still alive. If it turns out to be worse than the first version then the responsibility for this will be on all of us! (*And first and foremost the Council.*)

I'm writing to you without any clenching of teeth. You've put a lot of work into this. So have I.

Greetings.

Yours, Mikhail Bulgakov

11th August

To Alexei Popov

Esteemed Alexei Dmitrievich!

Yes, I am indeed "exhausted". In May there were all kinds of surprises unconnected with the theatre, and also in May there was such a rush with my *White Guard* at the Moscow Arts Theatre Studio* (an official preview); June was a series of constant petty jobs because I was getting no income at all from a single one of my plays, and July was spent rewriting *Zoyka's Apartment*. And in August everything came together at once. But it's not a question of "lack of trust". What would be the point of that? The theatre forces are fresh. You are the director, you have wit and energy (I mean that quite sincerely). There's just one thing: you don't see my characters in the same way as I do – and yes, you want them to relate to each other not *quite* as I have done. But the difference between us is small! And agreement between us is very possible.

As far as the Council is concerned, it is clearly infallible! I, on the other hand, am a fallible person, capable of making mistakes, and I therefore pay the greatest attention to everything that emanates from you.

I hope we won't be threatened by debate, conflict or confusion. I want a good outcome as much as the Studio does, and certainly not a catastrophe! [...]

In any event, we'll be able to sort out the question of the final acts. And this means a great deal. You and I will agree on a lot. The actors' and director's heads won't swell up (mine has already burst). I would be very pleased if the play could start as soon as possible.

If you would like to reply to this letter, please do so as soon as you can, and let me have your thoughts. Perhaps you will be able to put the third and fourth acts together in the form of two scenes (one act). (Why do you have such a burning desire to have three acts?!)

I shall look forward to your reply...

PS: Forgive this scrappy letter, written in haste: I'm overwhelmed by *Zoyka's Apartment*.

22nd September

From the Record of an Interrogation at OGPU

Depositions on the facts of the case

I began work as a writer in the autumn of 1919, in Vladikavkaz,* then under the control of the White forces. I wrote short stories and articles for the White newspapers. In my *works I adopted a critical and hostile attitude to Soviet Russia.* I had no connection with the Information Agency, and was never asked to work for them. I was in White territory from August 1919 through to the end of February 1920. *My sympathies were entirely on the side of the Whites, whose retreat filled me with horror and incomprehension.* When the Red Army arrived I was in Vladikavkaz, since I was ill with a recurrence of typhus. When my health improved I began to work for the Soviet authorities, in charge of the literary section of the Commissariat of Education. Before my arrival in Moscow I hadn't published a single substantial piece of work. After my arrival I started working in the literature section of the Political Enlightenment Commissariat as a secretary. At the same time I began work as a reporter for the Moscow press, in particular for *Pravda*. My first major work, 'Diaboliad', appeared in the journal *Nedra*, articles started appearing frequently and regularly in the *Hooter*, and I published short stories in various journals. Then I wrote the novel *The White Guard*, followed by a story, *The Fatal Eggs*, published in *Nedra* and in an anthology of short stories. In 1925 I wrote another story, *A Dog's Heart*, which has not been published anywhere. Before this I had written the story 'Notes on a Cuff'.

I hereby declare this to be a true record of my verbal statement.

M. Bulgakov

<...>* 'Diaboliad' and *The Fatal Eggs* have been published. Only two thirds of my novel *The White Guard* have been published; the

other third remains unpublished because the journal *Russia* has been closed down.

My story *A Dog's Heart* has not been published for censorship reasons. I think that this story turned out to be much darker and angrier than I had envisaged while writing it, and I can understand why it has been banned. The dog-turned-human-being Sharik came to be seen as a negative character, from Professor Preobrazhensky's viewpoint, as it had fallen under a factional influence. I read the work to Comrade Angarsky, the editor of *Nedra*, at the Nikitina Saturday meetings, to a group of poets gathered at Pyotr Nikanorovich Zaytsev's and at the Green Lamp. There were about forty people at the Nikitina Saturday meetings, about fifteen at the Green Lamp, and about twenty at the poets' meeting. It should be noted that I was invited to read this story at a number of different places more than once, and that each time I refused the invitation, since I realized that the its satirical element was too pointed and that it was therefore attracting too much attention.

Question: Can you tell us the names of those people in the Green Lamp group?

Answer: I refuse to answer on ethical grounds.

Question: Do you consider that there is a political aspect to *A Dog's Heart*?

Answer: Yes it does have moments of political significance, attacking the current regime.

M. Bulgakov

I am unable to write about peasant life because I don't like the countryside. It seems to me to be much more closely aligned to the kulak way of life than is generally considered.

I find it difficult to write about working-class life. Although I understand such a way of life far better than peasant life, I nevertheless don't understand it very well. And, indeed, it doesn't interest me very much, the reason for this being that I am so busy. I am keenly interested in the way of life of the Russian intelligentsia. I love the intelligentsia and consider it a weak but nevertheless very important social group in the country. The fates of its members are close to my own, and their experiences are dear to me.

In other words I can only write about the life of the intelligentsia in the Soviet Union. But I have a satirical frame of mind. My pen produces things which ordinary communist circles evidently sometimes find sharply provocative.

I always write things from a pure conscience, and just as I see them! I am attracted towards the negative aspects of life in the Soviet Union, because I can instinctively see that they contain much material that I am able to use (I am a satirist).

22nd September 1926
Mikhail Bulgakov

1927

28th November 1927

To the All-Union Society of Cultural Links with Abroad (ASCL)

I would be grateful if you would translate the attached "letter to the editor" into the relevant foreign languages and publish it in the newspapers of the following cities: Riga, Revel,* Berlin, Paris and Vienna.

I would ask you to be so kind as to send me copies of the translations.

M. Bulgakov

Letter to the Editor's Office

Mr Editor, I would be grateful if you would publish the following letter.

I have just learnt that a Mr Kagansky,* together with others whose names are not yet known to me, has turned up abroad. Brandishing a document purporting to be a power of attorney from me, they have begun to make use of my novel *The White Guard* together with my play *The Days of the Turbins* for their own purposes and financial gain.

I am writing to inform you that there is not, nor can there be, any such power of attorney in the possession of this Mr Kagansky or any of the other individuals going about making claims of a dubious nature by word of mouth.

This is to inform you that I have never handed over copies of my plays *The Days of the Turbins* or *Zoyka's Apartment* either to Mr Kagansky or anyone else making claims to this effect. If they do possess copies of these works, then they have either

72

been copied illegally or acquired without the consent of the author or sent abroad, again without the consent of the author. There may exist draft manuscripts or proofs of the unfinished novel *The White Guard* published in the USSR that have been acquired illegally.

I would therefore ask you not to have any dealings with Mr Kagansky or any other individuals going about making dubious claims, relating to the staging of *The Days of the Turbins*, to the filming or staging of my novel for the cinema or the theatre, or to any translations of it into a foreign language or its publication in Russian.

I would ask anyone who knows the whereabouts of Kagansky or any of the other individuals mentioned above to let me know where they are. [...]

I would also ask anyone in Berlin who knows the name of the individual or the publishing house responsible for the publication of the translation of *The Days of the Turbins* without my permission to write and inform me of the same.

My address: Moscow, Bolshaya Pirogovskaya Street, 35a, Apartment 6.

Telephone: 2-03-27.

I would be grateful if foreign newspapers would reproduce this letter.

Mikhail Afanasyevich Bulgakov

1928

21st February 1928

*Addendum to the Application of M.A. Bulgakov
to the Department of Administration,
Moscow City Council*

Purpose of Travel Abroad

I wish to travel so that I can call to account Zakhar Leontievich Kagansky, who has claimed while abroad to have acquired from me the rights for *The Days of the Turbins*, on the basis of which he has published the play in German, secured the rights for America and so on and so forth.

Kagansky (together with other individuals) has moved at top speed to take advantage of my name as a writer, thereby placing me in an extremely difficult position. That is why I need to go to Berlin.

I wish to go to Paris to conduct negotiations with the Théâtre des Mathurins concerning the production of *The Days of the Turbins*, as well as with the Société des Auteurs Dramatiques, of which I am a member.

I request that permission be granted for my wife to accompany me as my interpreter. Without her it will be extremely difficult for me to carry out all that I have to do (I don't speak any German).

In Paris I intend to get to know the city so that I can best stage the production of my play *Escape** that has now been accepted by the Moscow Arts Theatre (Act 5 of *Escape* takes place in Paris).

My trip abroad will definitely take no longer than two months, after which I have to be in Moscow (for the production of *Escape*).

I hope that permission to travel abroad on the important business that I have so conscientiously set out here will not be refused.

M. Bulgakov, 21/2/1928
Moscow
Bolshaya Pirogovskaya Street 35a, Apartment 6
Telephone: 2-03-27

PS: The refusal to grant me permission to travel abroad would seriously jeopardize my future work as a playwright.

27th September

To *Yevgeny Zamyatin**

Dear Yevgeny Ivanovich!
I have delayed replying to your letter this time precisely because I wanted to reply to it as soon as possible.

Over the course of two weeks I have added thirteen more pages of 'The Première'* to the seven that have been lying untouched in my top drawer. And yesterday, in the very same stove in my apartment by which you have sat many times, I burnt all twenty closely written pages, after correcting any mistakes.

It's good I came to my senses in time.

There can be no talk at all about sending a work such as this for publication while those close to me are still alive.

I'm glad I didn't send it. Please forgive me for not doing as I promised I would. I can say with certainty that you wouldn't have published it under any circumstances.

That's the end of 'The Première'.

And, more generally, it seems that all my incursions into the field of belles-lettres have stopped.

But that's not the problem; the problem is that I have neglected my business correspondence.

I'm simply a hopeless case.

As well as the love I feel for you after your congratulations I also have a feeling of (reverential) awe.

You congratulated me two weeks before permission was given for *The Crimson Island* to be staged.*

In other words you are a prophet.

As for the permission, I don't know what to say. I've finished *Escape* and submitted it.

But, in the meantime, permission has been given for *The Crimson Island*.

Total mystery.

Who? What? Why? What for?

My brain has become enveloped in the densest fog.

I hope you will keep me in your prayers!

Greetings also to Lyudmila Nikolayevna.*

The old boy* has been staying with us. We reminisced about our trip to the coast. Oh, what a ravishing city Leningrad is!

Yours,

Mikhail Bulgakov

8th October

To the Ladyzhnikov Publishing House in Berlin

I hereby give permission to the Ladyschnikow Publishing House for the translation of my play *Zoyka's Apartment* into German, the inclusion of this play in their list and the protection of my rights as an author on the conditions set out in the letter from the Ladyschnikow Publishing House that was sent to me on 3rd October 1928.

I would like to inform you that I have never granted the rights to this play either to Mr Livshits or to Mr Kagansky. The play has not been published in Russia.

I consent to the Ladyzhnikov Publishing House prosecuting those individuals who have been illegally exploiting my work *Zoyka's Apartment*, according to the conditions set out in the letter of 3rd October 1928 from the Ladyzhnikov Publishing House which agreed to accept the responsibility for any legal expenses.

I will send the legal power of attorney as soon as it has been prepared.

With the sincerest respect,

Mikhail Bulgakov

Mikhail Afanasyevich Bulgakov
Bolshaya Pirogovskaya Street 35a, Apartment 6, Moscow.

1929

July

To the General Secretary of the Party Y.V. Stalin.
The Chairman of the Central Executive
Committee M.I. Kalinin,
The Head of the Main Committee
for the Arts A.I. Svidersky,*
A.M. Gorky,*

From the writer Mikhail Afanasyevich Bulgakov
(Moscow, Bolshaya Pirogovskaya Street, 35a, Apartment 6,
telephone: 2-03-27)

Declaration

This year marks the tenth anniversary of the start of my career as
a writer in the USSR. Of these ten years I have devoted the last four
to the theatre, writing four plays. Of these, three (*The Days of the
Turbins*, *Zoyka's Apartment* and *The Crimson Island*) have been
produced on the stages of state theatres in Moscow, but although
the fourth (*Escape*) was accepted by MAT it was banned during
the process of preparing it for the stage.

I have now heard that further productions of *The Days of the
Turbins* and *The Crimson Island* have been banned. Last season, on
the order of the authorities, *Zoyka's Apartment* was taken off after
its two hundredth performance. This theatre season, therefore, it
turns out that all my plays have been banned, including *The Days of
the Turbins*, which had been performed about three hundred times. ·

On the day of the dress rehearsal of *The Days of the Turbins*
in 1926 I was ordered to go to OGPU, accompanied by an OGPU
agent, and subjected to interrogation.

79

Several months previously my apartment had been searched by representatives of OGPU, during which three notebooks of my diary were taken away, together with the only copy of my satirical story *A Dog's Heart*.

Before this, the second edition of my story 'Notes on a Cuff' had been banned. My anthology of satirical stories *Diaboliad* had been banned, as had the publication of my collected satirical articles and any public readings of my *Adventures of Chichikov*.* The publication of my novel *The White Guard* in the journal *Russia* was interrupted when the journal itself was banned.

While offering my works for publication I became the focus of greater and greater attention on the part of critics in the USSR, during which not only did not a single one of my works, whether of prose or of drama, ever receive a positive review, but quite the opposite: the more my name became known in the USSR and abroad, the more enraged the press reviews became, finally taking on a violent and abusive nature.

All my works have met with a monstrously unfavourable critical response, and my name has been demonized not only in the periodicals but also in such publications as the *Great Soviet Encyclopedia* and the *Literary Encyclopedia*.

Unable to defend myself, I have submitted a number of requests for permission to go abroad, even if only for a short period, but these have been refused.

My works *The Days of the Turbins* and *Zoyka's Apartment* have been stolen and taken abroad. One of the publishing houses in Riga completed the writing of my novel *The White Guard*, publishing under my name a book with an illiterate conclusion. The fees from my foreign publications have begun to be misappropriated.

Then my wife Lyubov Yevgenyevna Bulgakova* asked for permission for a second time to go abroad on her own in order to sort out my affairs, with me offering to remain as a guarantor for her.

We were refused.

I have asked OGPU several times for the return of my manuscripts and have either been refused or have had no reply to my requests.

I have asked for permission to send my play *Escape* abroad in order to protect it from being stolen beyond the borders of the USSR.

This has been refused.

At the end of my tenth year as a writer my strength has broken, and I am no longer able to exist. Persecuted, knowing that it is no longer possible for my stories to be published or my plays to be staged in the USSR and driven to a state of nervous breakdown, I am turning to you and asking for you to intercede on my behalf with the government of the USSR TO DEPORT ME FROM THE USSR, TOGETHER WITH MY WIFE L.Ye. BULGAKOVA, who joins me in this request.

M. Bulgakov

30th July

To the Head of the Main Committee
for the Arts A.I. Svidersky

From the writer Mikhail Afanasyevich Bulgakov
(Moscow, Bolshaya Pirogovskaya Street, 35a, Apartment 6,
telephone: 2-03-27)

Declaration

This year marks the tenth anniversary of the start of my career as a
writer in the USSR. In this period, during which I have not once travelled beyond the borders of the USSR (the article on me in the *Great
Soviet Encyclopedia* states wrongly that I was once in Berlin), I have
written a number of satirical stories, together with four plays, three
of which have been subjected many times to censorship corrections,
have been banned and then revived on the stages of state theatres in
Moscow, while the fourth, *Escape,* was banned during the process
of preparing it for the stage of MAT and has not seen the light at all.

I have now learnt that performances of the remaining three plays
have also been banned.

That means that, in the forthcoming season, not one of these
plays, including my favourite *The Days of the Turbins*, will be
performed.

I have to tell you that, in the process of submitting my works
for publication and subsequently for performance, they were all
without exception subjected to censorship in one form or another,
while, in addition, my satirical story, *A Dog's Heart*, was taken from
me by representatives of the State Political Administration during
a search of my apartment in 1926.

As my works began to be published, the critics began to pay
more attention to me, and I came face to face with an appalling
and striking phenomenon:

At no time did a *single* positive review about my work *ever or anywhere* appear in the USSR press, with the exception of one review that appeared and then rapidly disappeared again without trace at the beginning of my writing career, and your and Gorky's reviews of my play *Escape*.

Not a single positive review. On the contrary: the more my name has become known in the USSR, the worse and more terrifying the attitude of the press towards me has been.

I have been called a conduit for harmful and false ideas and a representative of the petty bourgeoisie, and my works have been portrayed in totally negative and insulting terms. Throughout my career as a writer there have been calls for my works to be removed and banned, and there has even been open abuse.

The entire press has been intent on putting an end to my writing career and, by the end of the ten years, its efforts have been crowned with complete success: I am able to claim with suffocating, verifiable certainty that I can no longer exist as a writer in the USSR.

After the staging of *The Days of the Turbins* I requested permission for me and my wife to go abroad for a short period – and was refused.

When some individuals managed somehow or another to take my works abroad and to make illegal use of them there, I asked that my wife be granted permission to travel abroad *on her own* – and this was refused.

I have asked for the return of my diaries that were taken from me during a search of my apartment – and have been refused.

Now my position has become clear: not a single line of work will be published, not a single play will be performed, I am unable to work in this atmosphere of absolute hopelessness, my annihilation as a writer will be followed by complete and definite physical collapse.

I am therefore asking you in all sincerity to convey the following declaration to the government of the USSR:

I ask the government of the USSR to take heed of my intolerable position and to grant me, together with my wife Lyubov Yevgenyevna Bulgakova, permission to travel abroad for whatever period that will be found to be necessary.

Mikhail Afanasyevich Bulgakov

24th August

To Nikolai Bulgakov

[...] I am also extremely grateful to you for your willingness to help me with my literary affairs. I expected nothing less.

As for the fact that I'm a poor correspondent – what can you do?! I'm telling you now, dear brother of mine, that I'm in a bad way.

All my plays have been banned from being performed in the USSR, and not a single line of my prose works is being published. The year 1929 has seen my total annihilation as a writer. I have made one final effort and sent a request to the government of the USSR, asking for permission for me and my wife to go abroad for an undefined period.

In my heart, there is no hope. There's been one ominous sign: they haven't given permission for Lyubov Yevgenyevna to go abroad on her own, despite the fact that I was to remain here (that was some months ago).

There is a dark rumour snaking around me now that I am a totally doomed man.

If my request to the government is declined, then the game is over. It will be time to put away my pack of cards and blow out the candles.

I shall have to sit about in Moscow without writing anything, since people can't seem to stand what I write; they can't even bear the sight of my name.

I can tell you without the slightest faintness of heart, brother of mine, that my death is simply a matter of time – unless, of course, there is a miracle. But miracles rarely happen.

Please write and tell me whether you understand what I'm saying in this letter, but on no account are you to include *any expressions of consolation or sympathy*, to avoid worrying my wife.

So there's a more generous letter for you.

It's a shame that I have felt so tired and overcome by indifference this spring. There is a limit, after all... [...]

3rd September

To *the Secretary of the Central Executive Committee of the USSR A.S. Yenukidze**

In view of the fact that my works have clearly become totally unacceptable to Soviet society; in view of the fact that the complete banning of my works in the USSR has condemned me to total annihilation as a writer; in view of the fact that this fact has now led to material catastrophe (my lack of savings, my inability to pay taxes, my inability to make a living, starting from next month – all this can be proved with documentary evidence).

In a state of extreme exhaustion, worn out by the failure of all my efforts, I am turning to the supreme organ of the Soviet Union – the Central Executive Committee of the USSR – with the request to grant me and my wife Lyubov Yevgenyevna Bulgakova permission to travel abroad for a period which the Soviet government should see fit to grant me.

> Mikhail Afanasyevich Bulgakov
> (author of a number of plays, including
> *The Days of the Turbins* and *Escape*).

To A.M. Gorky

Highly esteemed Alexei Maximovich!

I have submitted a request to the government of the USSR to grant me and my wife permission to leave the borders of the USSR for any period of time which the government may see fit to specify.

I would be very grateful if you, Alexei Maximovich, would support my request. I wanted to convey everything that is happening in my life in a detailed letter, but I am overwhelmed by exhaustion and a sense of hopelessness. I am unable to write anything.

Everything has been banned; I am ruined, persecuted and totally alone.

What is the point of keeping a writer in a country in which his works cannot exist? I ask for a humane resolution – to allow me to leave.

Respectfully yours,

M. Bulgakov

I earnestly request that you let me know that you have received this letter.

2nd October

To the Executive Committee
of the All-Russian Union of Writers

From Mikhail Afanasyevich Bulgakov

Declaration

I am writing to request that you expel me from the membership of
the All-Russian Union of Writers.

Mikhail Bulgakov
2nd October 1929
Moscow

1930

To Nikolai Bulgakov

[...] Now about me: all my works of literature and all my plans have crumbled to nothing. I have been condemned to silence and, very probably, to total starvation. In the second half of 1929, under impossibly harsh conditions, I wrote a play about Molière.* The leading experts in Moscow considered it the best of my five plays. But everything seems to indicate that they won't allow it to be staged. My torments concerning it have been going on for some six weeks now, despite the fact that we're talking about Molière and the seventeenth century, and despite the fact that it doesn't touch on contemporary life.

If this play fails, I shall have no means of salvation – as it is, *my situation is catastrophic*. I have no help, no defence. I'm telling you in all sobriety: my ship is sinking, and the water's already up to the bridge. I must drown courageously. Please take careful account of what I'm saying.

If it is at all possible for you to send on my fee (bank? cheque? whatever's best), please do so: *I don't possess a single copeck*. I hope of course that, to avoid any unpleasantness, this will be an official transaction.

21st February

To Nikolai Bulgakov

Dear Kolya,

You ask whether I might be interested in your work. Yes, extremely interested! [...] I am pleased and proud that, in the most difficult conditions, you have begun to make your way in life. I remember you as a young man, have always loved you and am now firmly convinced that you will become a scientist. [...]

Many of my acquaintances have asked me about our family, and I have always been consoled by the fact that I am able to speak about your talents.

But there's one thought that weighs on me: we will evidently never see each other again in our lifetime. My fate has been chaotic and terrible. Now I am being reduced to silence; for a writer, this is equivalent to death.

I have a question for you in turn: are you interested in my work as a writer? Please write and tell me. If it does interest you in any way at all, please pay, if at all possible, particular heed to what I'm about to say – although careful reading of your letters, combined with instinct and experience, tells me that your interest and attention are already engaged.

I have tried to carry out my task as a writer as I should, under impossibly harsh conditions. Now my work has come to an end. I see myself (or so I suppose) as a complex machine whose products are no longer needed in the USSR. My Molière play has proved this to me all too clearly. And it is still doing so.

At night I wrack my brains in torment trying to think up some means of salvation. But I can't see anything. Who else is there, I wonder, whom I can petition?...

Now about something more immediate: please be kind – put up with me worrying you a little longer (I won't need, I should imagine, to impose on you for much more). From the sum of money that Vladimir Lvovich* gave you from my fee, please send me some more, again through the bank. I need any amount, however insignificant. I don't know how much he gave you. Don't send me the whole lot, but I just badly need money for tea, coffee, socks and stockings for my wife. If it's not too much trouble, please would you send me a parcel with tea, coffee, two pairs of socks and two pairs of lady's stockings (size 9) (on no account anything silk). I don't know what this will cost. Preferably as follows: a parcel in the first instance, and if there is any money left over, then ten dollars to me through the bank and keep the rest for yourself for expenses. If my calculations are wrong, then just send the parcel.

If *Vanya** *is short of money* send me the parcel and then some of the money to him.

Please work out for yourself what's best!

On 15th March the first payment to the finance office will fall due (income tax for last year). I reckon that, unless there's some sort of miracle, there won't be a single item left in my small, totally damp apartment (incidentally, I have suffered many years from rheumatism). I won't mind so much about the junk. And as for the chairs and the cups, well, to hell with them! But it's the books I'm worried about! I've not got a very good library, but nonetheless life for me without books would be tantamount to death! When I work, I work very seriously – there's so much I need to read.

Nothing I've written starting with the words "On 15th March" is anything to do with business, and none of it means that I'm complaining or asking for help here – I simply say these things for my own amusement.

You will have to become reconciled to the thought that I'll be writing more frequently (but probably, as I say, not for long). I have not, it's true, mastered the art of letter-writing: however much you thrash about, the words don't flow off the page, and I'm never able to express my thoughts correctly.

I shall look forward very much to hearing from you. Take heart, stay cheerful, and don't forget about your brother Mikhail. If you can find the time, think about Mikhail Bulgakov...

2nd April

To OGPU

I would be grateful if you would ensure that my letter of 28.3.1930, enclosed with this letter, is sent on to the government of the USSR for their consideration.

M. Bulgakov

28th March

To the Government of the USSR

From Mikhail Afanasyevich Bulgakov
  (Moscow, Bolshaya Pirogovskaya Street 35a, Apartment 6)

I wish to address the government of the USSR as follows:

1.

Now that all my works have been banned I have heard from many people who know me as a writer, all offering the same advice:

I should write a "communist play" (my inverted commas) and then write to the government of the USSR with a penitential letter in which I renounce my previously held views expressed in my literary works, together with an assurance that henceforth I will write as a fellow traveller devoted to the idea of communism.

The aim: to save myself from persecution, poverty and inevitable final ruin.

I have not followed this advice. I would scarcely be presenting myself to the government of the USSR in a favourable light, were I to write a mendacious letter which was nothing more than an unsavoury and, what's more, a naive political about-face. And I have not even made any attempt to write a communist play, fully aware that I would never be able to do such a thing.

My strong desire to put an end to my literary torments forces me to write this honest letter to the government of the USSR.

2.

On looking through my collection of newspaper cuttings I have discovered that, during the ten years of my career as a writer, there have been 301 reviews of my work in the Soviet press. Three of these reviews were complimentary, and 298 hostile and abusive.

These 298 reviews represent the mirror image of my literary career.

In one review, in verse, the hero of my play *The Days of the Turbins*, Alexei Turbin, was called a "SON OF A BITCH", while the play's author was characterized as being "AS SENILE AS AN OLD DOG". I have been referred to as a "literary VULTURE ", picking over the remains of the vomit "PUKED UP by a dozen guests".

And again:

"…MISHKA Bulgakov, my mate. WHAT AN EXPERT WRITER HE IS, IF YOU'LL FORGIVE THE EXPRESSION, PICKING HIS WAY THROUGH STALE RUBBISH… Why, do I ask, do you have such an UGLY MUG, mate… I am a man of delicate sensibilities, just take a basin and CRACK IT OVER HIS SKULL… The man in the street no more needs the Turbins than a DOG NEEDS A BRA… We've got a fine one here, THIS TURBIN, THE SON OF A BITCH, NO SALES OR SUCCESS FOR HIM, LET'S HOPE…" (*The Life of Art*, No. 4, 1927).

They have written of a "Bulgakov who will never change, a NEO-BOURGEOIS PIECE OF FILTH, spitting his poisonous but feeble saliva onto the working class and its communist ideals" (*Komsomolskaya Pravda*, 14/10, 1926).

They have written that I like the "ATMOSPHERE OF A DOG'S WEDDING around some auburn-haired wife of a friend" (A. Lunacharsky, *Izvestiya*, 8/10, 1926), and that a "STENCH" emanates from my play *The Days of the Turbins* (Shorthand report of an Agitprop meeting in May, 1927), and so on, and so on…

I am quoting all this, I hasten to add, by no means in order to complain about such criticism or to enter into any kind of polemical discussion. I have something far more serious in mind.

From the documents in my possession, I can demonstrate that, throughout the ten years of my career as a writer, the entire USSR press, together with all those institutions which have been entrusted with the role of overseeing the repertoire, have unanimously and with EXTRAORDINARY FURY demonstrated that the works of Mikhail Bulgakov cannot exist in the USSR.

And I hereby declare that the USSR press is TOTALLY CORRECT.

3.

Let my play *The Crimson Island* serve as the starting point of my letter.

Without exception, every review in the Soviet press has maintained that this was a "third-rate, toothless and squalid" play, and that it was a "malicious slander on the revolution".

On this point there was total unanimity, until it was suddenly broken, in the most astonishing fashion.

In the *Repertory Bulletin* (No 12, 1928) there was a review by a P. Novitsky which said that *The Crimson Island* was an "interesting and witty parody" featuring the "ominous figure of the Grand Inquisitor suppressing artistic creativity and cultivating ABSURDLY SERVILE AND FAWNING DRAMATIC STEREOTYPES, thereby eradicating the personality of both actor and writer" – and that, in *The Crimson Island*, there is a reference to a "dark and evil force that nurtures HELOTS, TOADIES AND SYCOPHANTS".

The review went on to say that "if such a dark force exists, then the INDIGNATION AND MALICIOUS WIT OF THE DRAMATIST, SO ACCLAIMED BY THE BOURGEOISIE, HAS BEEN JUSTIFIED".

Where is the truth, might I ask?

What then, in the final analysis, is *The Crimson Island*? "A squalid third-rate play" or "a witty lampoon"?

The truth is to be found in Novitsky's review. I won't attempt to judge whether my play is witty, but I admit that it indeed possesses an ominous shadow, and that that shadow is cast by the Main Repertory Committee. It is precisely this committee which nurtures helots, sycophants and frightened lackeys, and it is precisely this committee which is killing creative thought. It is destroying Soviet drama and won't stop until this is achieved.

I have not expressed such thoughts in a whisper or in a corner. They can be found in a dramatized lampoon that I have put on the stage. On behalf of the Repertory Committee, the Soviet press called *The Crimson Island* a vicious slander on the revolution. This is just nonsensical babble. There are many reasons why the play is not a vicious slander on the revolution, but, for lack of space, I'll point out only one: the hugely momentous scale of the revolution means that it would be IMPOSSIBLE to write a vicious slander on it. The lampoon is not a slander, and the Repcommittee is not a revolution.

But when the German press writes that *The Crimson Island* is "the first summons for the freedom of the press in the USSR" (*The Young Guard*, No. 1, 1929), it is speaking the truth. I admit this. It is my duty as a writer to fight against censorship, whatever form it may take, and whatever authority it may represent, just as it is to call for freedom of the press. I am a fervent believer in such a freedom and I maintain that if any writer were to think of showing that he didn't need it, then he would be like a fish declaring publicly that it doesn't need water.

4.

There you have one of the characteristics of my creative endeavour, and it alone is quite sufficient for my works not to exist in the USSR. But all the other characteristics present in my satirical stories are connected with this one: the black and mystical colours (I am a MYSTICAL WRITER) with which I depict the innumerable unsavoury aspects of our everyday life; the poison that permeates my language; the feelings of profound scepticism for the revolutionary process that is taking place in this backward country of mine, in contrast to my beloved concept of the Great Evolution; and, most importantly of all, the portrayal of the terrible features that characterize my people, features which gave rise long before the revolution to the deepest sufferings of my master Mikhail Saltykov-Shchedrin.*

It goes without saying that the Soviet press has never seriously thought about taking any of this into account, occupied as it is with making unconvincing statements to the effect that M. Bulgakov's satire is "SLANDEROUS".

Only on one occasion, just as I was beginning to make a name for myself, did a comment appear with just a suggestion of high-minded astonishment:

"M. Bulgakov WISHES to become the satirist of our age" (*The Bookseller*, No. 6, 1925).

The verb "to wish", alas, has been used incorrectly, in the present tense. It should be used in the pluperfect tense: M. Bulgakov HAD BECOME A SATIRIST, precisely at a time when any idea of genuine satire (reaching into forbidden areas) was absolutely inconceivable in the USSR.

The honour of expressing this criminal idea in the press has not fallen to me. It has been expressed with complete and utter clarity in the article by V. Blyum* (*Lit. Gaz.* No. 6), and the idea of this article has been brilliantly and precisely summarized in the single phrase:

EVERY SATIRIST IN THE USSR INFRINGES UPON SOVIET SOCIETY.

Am I thinkable in the USSR?

5.

And finally, here are my other characteristics as reflected in my ruined plays *The Days of the Turbins* and *Escape*, and in my novel *The White Guard*: the persistent portrayal of the Russian intelligentsia as the finest stratum in our country. In particular, the portrayal of an aristocratic family of the intelligentsia, who through the will of immutable historical fate finds itself thrown into the ranks of the White Guard during the civil war, in the tradition of *War and Peace*. Such a theme is entirely natural for a writer who himself is intimately part of the intelligentsia.

Yet despite the author's best efforts to LOOK DOWN
DISPASSIONATELY ON REDS AND WHITES ALIKE, such por-
trayals result in him, together with his characters, being dubbed in
the USSR an enemy White-Guardist, and once he has been called
that, as everyone will understand, he can no longer consider his
existence viable in the USSR.

6.

My literary self-portrait is complete. At the same time it is a political
portrait. I am unable to say just what depths of criminality might
be found in it, but I would like to make one request: please don't
look for anything else beyond what it says. It has been done in the
most conscientious way.

7.

Now I have been annihilated.

Such an annihilation has been greeted by Soviet society with rapture
and referred to as an "ACHIEVEMENT".

Noting my annihilation, R. Pikel* has expressed the following
liberal thought (*Izvestiya*, 15/9/1929):

"We do not mean by this that the name of Bulgakov has been
deleted from the list of Soviet dramatists."

And he has reassured the condemned writer with the following
words: "We are talking here about his previous dramatic works."

Reality, however, in the form of the Repertory Committee, has
shown that R. Pikel's liberalism has no foundation.

On 18th March 1930 I received a document from the Repcommittee
laconically stating that it has FORBIDDEN THE PRODUCTION of
a new, not an earlier play of mine, *The Cabal of Hypocrites* (*Molière*).

I shall simply say this: all my work in the archives, my fantasy,
a play which has evoked innumerable testimonials from qualified
theatre specialists, a dazzling play – all this has been buried under
two lines of an official document.

R. Pikel is mistaken: it is not just my past works that are dead,
but my present and all my future ones as well. With my own hands
I have personally thrown the draft of a novel about the Devil,* the

draft of a comic work and the opening of a second novel, *The Theatre*,* into the stove.

All these things are hopeless.

8.

I ask the Soviet government to take into account the fact that I am not a politician, but a writer, and that everything I have written has been for the Soviet stage.

I ask the government to direct its attention to the following two reviews about me in the Soviet press.

They both come from people who are implacably hostile to my works, and are therefore very valuable.

The first was from 1925:

"A writer has appeared who HAS NOT EVEN DISGUISED HIMSELF IN THE COLOURS OF A FELLOW TRAVELLER" (L. Averbakh ,* *Izvestiya*, 20/9/1925).

And then in 1929:

"His talent is as evident as the socially reactionary nature of his work" (R. Pikel, *Izvestiya*, 15/9/1929).

I would ask it to note that, for me, the impossibility of writing is equivalent to being buried alive.

9.

I REQUEST THAT THE GOVERNMENT OF THE USSR AS A MATTER OF URGENCY ORDER ME TO LEAVE THE BORDERS OF THE USSR, ACCOMPANIED BY MY WIFE LYUBOV YEVGENYEVNA BULGAKOVA.

10.

I appeal to the humanity of the Soviet authorities to ask that you magnanimously set me free, as a writer who cannot be of use in his own homeland.

11.

If what I have written has not been sufficiently persuasive and if I should be condemned to a lifetime of silence in the USSR, then

I ask the Soviet government to give me specialized work in the theatre and assign me to a permanent post as a director.

I am emphatically and specifically requesting a CATEGORICAL ORDER, AN OFFICIAL ASSIGNMENT, precisely because all my efforts to find work in the only area in which I, as an exceptionally qualified expert, might be of use to the USSR, have resulted in utter failure. My name has become so odious that any proposals on my part for work are met with a sense of CONSTERNATION, despite the fact that my specialist knowledge of the stage is so well known by the vast majority of actors, theatre managers and theatre directors in Moscow.

I am offering myself to the USSR as a completely honest and totally trustworthy specialist theatre director and actor, who will conscientiously undertake the production of any play, from the plays of Shakespeare right up to the present day.

I ask that I be appointed as an assistant director with MAT 1 – the very best theatre school, headed by K.S. Stanislavsky and V.I. Nemirovich-Danchenko.

If I can't be appointed as a director, then I would ask for a permanent position as an extra. And if that is not possible, then as a backstage workman.

And if even that is not possible, then I ask the Soviet government to decide what I should do as it thinks necessary, but to decide in one way or another because, AT THIS PRESENT MOMENT, I, a dramatist, the author of five plays, having made a name for himself both in the USSR and abroad, am faced with destitution, homelessness and death.

1931

To the General Secretary of the Central Committee of the All-Russian Communist Party (Bolsheviks), Yosif Vissarionovich Stalin

Highly esteemed Yosif Vissarionovich!
"The longer I live the greater the desire in me to be a contemporary writer. But at the same time I have come to realize that, when portraying contemporary life, it is impossible to be in that calm and constructive frame of mind which is necessary for me to produce work that is both of outstanding quality and harmonious.

"Present-day reality is too alive, too changeable, too irksome; *the writer's pen shifts imperceptibly towards the satirical.*

"...It has always seemed to me that some great act of self-sacrifice lies ahead of me and that in order to serve my fatherland *I shall have to find sustenance from somewhere a long distance away.*

"...I only know that the reason I am going is not at all so that I can enjoy being abroad, but rather in order to survive, as if sensing in advance that I would come to know the true value of Russia only when I was beyond its borders, and that I would come to love her only when I was far away from her."

– Nikolai Gogol*

I fervently ask you to intercede on my behalf with the government of the USSR to send me abroad on leave for the period from 1st July to 1st October 1931 inclusive.

I am writing to say that, after one and a half years of silence, new creative ideas have started welling up inside me with irresistible force, and that these ideas are wide-ranging and powerful. I therefore ask the government to give me the possibility of realizing them.

Since the end of 1930 I have been suffering from a serious form of neurasthenia, together with panic attacks and heart-related anxiety, and now I have come to the end of the road.

I have all these ideas, but I lack physical strength and any of the conditions that are so necessary in order to carry out my work.

I am fully aware of the causes of my illness.

In the wide field of literature in the USSR I have been the only existing literary wolf. I was advised to dye my skin. Absurd advice. A wolf may have his skin dyed or be shorn, but he'll never be a poodle.

I have been treated as if I were a wolf – a wolf who has for many years been hunted and then attacked by dogs in a fenced-in courtyard.

I am not resentful, but I am very tired and, at the end of 1929, I collapsed. After all, even a wild beast can become tired.

This wild beast has declared that he is no longer a wolf, or a writer. He renounces his profession. He is falling silent. And this, to be honest, is cowardice.

The silent writer doesn't exist. If he has fallen silent, that means he's not a real writer.

And if a real writer has fallen silent, he will perish.

My illness has been caused by the years and years of being hounded, and then falling silent.

In the course of the last year I have achieved the following:

In the face of very severe difficulties I have turned Gogol's *Dead Souls* into a play;

I have worked as a director during rehearsals of this play at MAT;

I have worked as an actor at these rehearsals, taking the parts of actors who have fallen ill;

I have been appointed as a director at MAT for all this year's special events and celebrations of the revolution;

I have worked in TRAM in Moscow,* switching from my daytime work at MAT to evening work at TRAM;

I left TRAM on 15th March 1931, when I felt that my brain was refusing to function and that I was no longer of any use to TRAM;

I have started work on a production at the Health Education
Theatre (I will have finished this by July).

And, at night, I have started to write.

But I am worn out!

I am exhausted.

At the moment all my impressions have become dulled, my
creative ideas are wreathed in black, and I have been poisoned by
anxiety and my customary irony.

While I was writing, everybody – Party members and non-Party
members alike – was constantly impressing on me that, from the
moment I started writing and publishing until the end of my life,
I would never see other countries.

If that is the case, then my horizons are closed, I have been
deprived of the highest kind of literary education, and of the possibility of deciding the greatest questions for myself. The psychology
of a prisoner has been instilled in me.

How am I to sing my country's praises?

Before writing to you I weighed up all the possibilities. I need to
see the world and then, having seen it, come back. That's the key.

I am writing to tell you, Yosif Vissarionovich, that I have been
very seriously warned by leading figures from the arts world who
have travelled abroad that I would find it impossible to remain there.

I have been warned that, if the government opens the door for
me, then I must take extra care not to slam this door behind me
accidentally and close off my way back, so as not to be overtaken
by a catastrophe worse than the banning of my plays.

In the general opinion of everyone who has taken a serious interest in my work, I could not exist in any other country other than
my own, the USSR, because it has been the source of my creativity
for eleven years.

I am sensitive to such warnings, the weightiest of which has
come from my wife, who has been abroad and who told me, when
I asked to be deported, that she wouldn't want to remain abroad
and that I would die from homesickness in less than a year.

(I myself have never been abroad. The statement in the *Great
Soviet Encyclopedia* that I have is false.)

"The Soviet theatre has no need of this Bulgakov" was the sententious judgement of one critic when I was banned.

I don't know if the Soviet theatre needs me, but I need the Soviet theatre just as much as I need air.

I ask the government of the USSR to allow me to go abroad before the autumn and to give permission for my wife, Lyubov Yevgenyevna Bulgakova, to accompany me. I am requesting this last point because I am seriously ill; I need to be accompanied by someone close to me. When I am alone I suffer from panic attacks.

If anything arises from this letter needing further explanation I will be able to give it to whoever asks me to go and see them.

But, in conclusion, I would like to tell you, Yosif Vissarionovich, that my dream as a writer is that you yourself invite me to see you in person.

I say this, believe me, not only because I can see that this would be of such advantage to me, but also because of our telephone conversation of April 1930 which is so sharply etched on my memory.

This is what you said: "Perhaps you really do need to go abroad..."

Such conversations have been few and far between in my life. Inspired by what you said I have been working willingly and conscientiously as a director in Soviet theatres for a year.

M. Bulgakov

22nd–28th July

To V.V. Veresayev

Dear Vikenty Vikentevich!
I received your letter of 17th July today, having just got back from Zubtsov, where I have been swimming and writing for twelve days. I was very pleased to get it. [...]

But why do we see each other so rarely? During that dark year, when I was so crushed by everything and I had only one card left to play – to put an end to everything, by shooting myself – you came and raised my spirits. The cleverest sort of writer's sympathy!

But that's not all. Our meetings, our conversations, you yourself, Vikenty Vikentevich, are all so interesting and dear to me!

Thank you for relieving me of the burden of inhibition.

The cause is to be found in my lifestyle. There are many ways of occupying one's time. Mine, for example, is unnatural. It consists of an extremely dark anxiety, of focusing on trivial things which shouldn't be occupying me at all, utter hopelessness, neurotic fears and fruitless endeavours. I have a broken wing.

I've stopped meeting people and writing letters. This is just the most recent example. It's truly monstrous, isn't it? Official letters arrive, and you need to answer them, don't you? But I take ages to reply to them, and sometimes I haven't replied at all.

Do you think that, whenever I've been unable to come and see you because the theatre has taken up so much of my time, I haven't tried to write to you? Let me assure you that I have begun to write to you several times. But I can't manage to write as much as five lines. I'm afraid to write! I burn what I've written in the stove. [...]

I am in torment over the dispiriting realization that I have not been able to talk to the General Secretary. This is so horrible, like a dark grave. I desperately want to see other countries, even if it is only for a short time. I get up in the morning with this thought, and I go to sleep with it.

For a year I have been wracking my brains, trying to understand what happened. After all, I wasn't hallucinating when I heard his words, was I? He did say "Perhaps you really need to go abroad…", didn't he?

Yes, he did say that! What has happened? And I know he wanted to receive me!

27th July. To continue: while talking to me about some other literary matter of mine, a certain very well-connected person with a famous literary name said in a not entirely assured tone:

"You have an enemy."

Even at the time this phrase set the alarm bells ringing. A serious enemy? That's not good. Things are difficult enough for me as it is now, but at that time I couldn't cope with life at all. I am not a child, and I understand what is meant by the word "enemy". In my position it means *lasciate ogni speranza*.* It would be better to stock up with some potassium cyanide! I began to search my brain. There are scores of people in Moscow who can't say my name without grinding their teeth. But that's all in the petty literary or theatrical world – it's all very feeble, like having one foot in the grave.

There must be a genuinely powerful enemy somewhere – but how, in what way, could he have appeared in my life?

And then suddenly it came to me! I remembered who it might be! It was Alexei Turbin, Kalsoner, Rook and Khludov (from *Escape*). These were the people who were my enemies! It's not for nothing that, when I am lying in bed unable to sleep, it is they who come to me and say: "You have given birth to us, but we will be a barrier to any further progress. Lie there and dream on, with closed lips."

So there we are: my main enemy, it transpires, is myself.

There are two theories going around Moscow. According to the first theory, which has numerous supporters, I am someone who is under constant and unflinching observation, during which every line, thought, phrase and step I take are noted. It's a flattering theory, but it possesses one enormous flaw.

When I ask, "Why, then, if this is all so significant and interesting, am I not allowed to write?" the ordinary Muscovite
comes up with the following answer: "That's just it: since
you write whatever you please, you must burn in the crucible
of deprivation and unpleasantness, and when you have been
finally reduced to molten liquid, your pen will begin writing
words of praise."

But this is the complete reversal of the formula "existence determines consciousness",* for it is totally impossible, even physically,
to imagine that someone whose life has consisted of nothing but
deprivation and unpleasantness should suddenly burst out in words
of praise. I therefore reject such a theory.

There is another theory. Although it has hardly any supporters,
I am one of their number.

According to this theory, there's nothing at all! Neither enemies,
nor crucible, nor observation, nor the desire for praise, nor the
phantom Kalsoner or Turbin – nothing! None of this is interesting to anybody, none of this is necessary – and, anyway, what's
all the fuss about? Someone's had some plays staged; they've been
taken off – so what? Why should this person, some Tom, Dick or
Harry, write declarations and petitions to the Central Executive
Committee, to the Commissar of Enlightenment and everyone
else – and about going abroad, what's more?! What difference
will it make to this person? None. Neither good nor bad. There
simply won't be any answer. And that's right, that's logical! For
if you were to reply to every Tom, Dick or Harry then you'd have
a regular tower of Babel.

So that's the theory, Vikenty Vikentevich! But the thing is that
it's absolutely useless. The theory's useless because, just a little
over a year ago, at the height of my despair, it was demolished
when I was fortunate enough to receive a telephone call from the
General Secretary. Please believe me when I say that he spoke to me
powerfully, clearly, elegantly and in a statesmanlike way. The hope
glowed in my writer's heart that all I needed to do now would be
to see him and to learn my fate.

28th July. But a thick curtain has descended. A year and more has gone by. There is no way of course that I could have written another letter.

Nevertheless, this spring, I did write another letter and sent it off. I went through torments trying to write it. When you are dealing with the General Secretary only one approach is possible: to tell the truth, without equivocation. But just try to set it all out in a single letter. You'd need to write forty pages. Best of all, it's true, would be to send a telegram: "Dying in a state of nervous exhaustion. Give me something new to think about for three months. Will be back!"

That's all. And the reply too could be by telegram: "Send him abroad tomorrow."

When I thought about getting a reply like this my weary heart started to beat fast and a light appeared in my eyes. I imagined the sun's rays over Paris! So I wrote a letter, in which I quoted Gogol. I tried to convey everything that was going through my mind and heart.

But the ray of light vanished. There was no reply. My feeling now is of darkness. Someone tried to console me by saying "it can't have reached him". But that can't be it. Somebody else, with a practical mind, lacking any fantasy or rays of sunlight, subjected the letter to expert analysis. And was not at all satisfied with it. "Who will believe that you are so ill that you must be accompanied by your wife? Who will believe that you will come back? Who will believe it?"

And so on and so forth.

I've hated those words – "who will believe it?" – ever since I was a child. Wherever there's this "who will believe it?" I am no longer alive, I no longer exist. I myself could ask scores of such questions: "Who will believe that Gogol is my teacher? Or who will believe that I have such great thoughts? Or who will believe that I am a writer?" And so on.

I'm not expecting anything good to happen now. But there is one thought that torments me. The time has come, that is, to think about more important things. But before deciding such important and terrible things, I would like now to be granted a holiday from all this – or, at least, some information. Would it at least be possible to have some information?

If I don't stop now, I'll never send this to you. If we don't see each other in the near future, I will write to you again about my play.

Vikenty Vikentevich, I have become anxious, scared, superstitious, and I keep on having premonitions of some disaster or other.

I wish you good health and rest. Greetings to Mariya Germogenovna.* I shall look forward to your coming to see me, hearing the doorbell ring. Lyubov Yevgenyevna is in Zubtsov.

Yours, Mikhail Bulgakov

PS: I've reread it and realize the letter's a confounded mess! Sorry!

30th August

To K.S. Stanislavsky

Dear Konstantin Sergeyevich!
This spring I received a proposal from one of the Leningrad theatres
(the Red Theatre) asking for a play on the theme of a future war.
The theatre gave me leave to explore and develop this theme as I
wished, without imposing any framework on me.

I have written a four-act play, *Adam and Eve*.*

Total iron necessity has compelled me to offer this play to the
Vakhtangov Theatre in Moscow, and they immediately signed a
contract with me, not altering a single word of the play.

I was very sorry that the play was not offered to the Arts
Theatre. There were many reasons for this, reasons that were
insurmountable. There can be no doubt whatsoever that MAT
would not have arrived at a blind agreement with me without
knowing the play; we would have had to start negotiating in the
autumn, and I was *physically* unable to wait until then. But apart
from that, MAT contracts invariably contain the harsh and, for
me, terrible clause that in the event of the play being banned
then the author will have to return the advance (as it is, I am
already returning a thousand roubles paid to me for *Escape*).

I live constantly under the threat of being banned. So, as far as I
am concerned, it's an impossible clause! Besides, MAT only gives
an advance for the author's fees, but not for production rights –
and, for me, already burdened by having to pay back advances
because my plays are banned, it would be unthinkable to accept
such money.

That's why my play went straight to the Vakhtangov Theatre.

During my recent negotiations with the Leningrad Bolshoi
Dramatic Theatre, with which I have been linked for a long time,
I agreed – again there and then – to write a play for them based
on Tolstoy's novel *War and Peace*.

I am writing to tell you this, Konstantin Sergeyevich – since, if you would like to include *War and Peace* in the Arts Theatre programme, I would be extremely glad to offer it to you.

I would be really pleased if you were able, as a matter of urgency, to raise the question of the possibility of *concluding an agreement in relation to* War and Peace.

I repeat: my agreements are now ruled by iron necessity. I consider it my duty to inform you that, in concluding terms with the Leningrad Bolshoi Dramatic Theatre, I agreed to give them the right to stage the première. There was nothing else I could do!

But, in my personal opinion, this will not lead to any disaster.

With love and respect,

Mikhail Bulgakov

31st December

To K.S. Stanislavsky

Dear Konstantin Sergeyevich!

I wanted to write this letter on the day after the rehearsal of the party scene in *Dead Souls** but, firstly, I was too shy and, secondly, I wasn't able to get in touch with the Theatre that day (had a cold).

I'm writing this informal letter to you to express the sense of delighted admiration which I have been feeling throughout these last few days. In the space of three hours, in front of my eyes, you managed to transform that crucial scene, which had become bogged down and which was not going anywhere, into something that was alive. The magic of the theatre does exist!

This awakes in me my very best hopes and cheers me up when I am unhappy. I find it difficult to express what it was that most delighted me. I honestly don't know. The high point perhaps was what you said about Manilov:* "You mustn't say anything to him, you mustn't ask him about anything, he'll pester you straight away." Such a striking formulation, in precisely the theatrical sense. As an example of how things should be done, it was the sign of a consummate master!

I have no qualms concerning Gogol when you are at the rehearsals. He will come alive through you. He will come alive in the first scenes of the play accompanied by laughter, and he will leave in the final scene wrapped in great thoughts. He will come alive.

Yours,

Mikhail Bulgakov

1932

To Pavel Popov*

Dear Pavel Sergeyevich!

Here, at last, is a reply to your most recent letter.

Insomnia, now my faithful mistress, comes to my aid and starts wielding a pen. Lady friends, as you know, can betray you. Oh, how I would love this mistress to betray me!

So, my dear friend, you ask what you should eat as a starter. Ham. But that's not all. You need to eat it at dusk sitting on an old, worn sofa surrounded by old, familiar objects. There should be a dog sitting by your chair, and no trams should be audible. It's now after 5 a.m. here, and they're already beginning to screech as they leave the depot. The whole damned building is shuddering. I mustn't tempt fate, however; come the summer, and I may have to leave, as the lease is coming to an end.

Someone came here once for the first time in his life, looked around the apartment and said it was inhabited by a good spirit. I suppose he liked the books, the cat and the boiled potatoes. He wasn't very observant. My hole is inhabited by some very unsavoury company: bronchitis, rheumatism and the black queen – neurasthenia. I can't throw them out. Not on your life! I need to go away and leave them.

But where would I go?

Where, Pavel Sergeyevich?

I should imagine, however, that you're not getting much pleasure from reading this letter, and so I'll turn to other things.

I wonder whether you already know, and whether the news has reached you in Leningrad and Tyarlevo? No? Let me tell you then: on the afternoon of 15th January there was a telephone call from the Theatre to say they would be putting on *The Days of the Turbins* again very soon. Sad to say, I felt overwhelmed by the news. I felt physically unwell. There was an initial rush of joy, but this was immediately followed by a feeling of sadness. It's my heart, my heart!

Earlier on the same day as the telephone call there was a really ominous sign. We have a new domestic working here, a girl of about twenty, globular in shape. From the very first it became clear that she possessed the calculating miserliness of a peasant, had a speech defect, a rich talent for figures, considered the existence of domestic pets, dogs and cats as unnecessary ("got to feed them too, damn it!") and was tormented by the thought that she might have to wait before getting married. But, apart from all that, she had a secret, a secret that tormented her. Finally, this secret was revealed; first my wife and then I, somewhat later, guessed what it was: she was tragically stupid. Not, it turned out, in a simple way, but in the effect her stupidity had on others, reducing acquaintances to fits of delighted laughter. And this was crowned by such obstinacy as I had never seen the like in my life before. Short lectures on various topics, for which I became responsible, led to brilliant results – with both our heads finally becoming thoroughly confused. I avoided giving any lectures on drama, thinking in my naivety that the girl's interests didn't include the theatre. But I had omitted to take into consideration that, apart from my university, there were six cooks in our apartment block, six Marusyas, Grushas and Nyushas.

28th January. To continue: if the girl didn't fully attend a drama course in the kitchen, at least she was present at Mikhail Bulgakov's lectures on the history of drama. She liked these, since – as is well known – drama is the sister of bookkeeping.

And it's precisely while the most complicated tasks are being decided in the landlady's salon – exactly what kinds of financial operation are to be performed on Mikhail Bulgakov next summer – that in the kitchen they're fretting over simpler calculations: how many metres of calico should one buy as part of the bride's dowry, if it should turn out that the generous playwright's plays were to make it onto the stage!

29th January. I'm afraid this letter's getting rather long. But, in my total isolation, my pen has long since become rusty. After all, I'm not totally dead yet, and I wish to speak in words that are genuinely my own!

And so, around midday of the 15th, this girl came into my room and – completely unrelated to anything that had been going on before or to anything that was to come – declared prophetically in a firm voice:

"That tubing play of yours goin' to be on. You be getting thousands."

Then she vanished from the house.

And, a few minutes later, the telephone rang.

I can say with certainty that nobody from the Theatre had telephoned the girl, and that there aren't any telephones in the kitchen. So what had happened? I presume it was truly a magical event.

To continue: at the Theatre, Pavel Sergeyevich, everybody was enthusiastic about the play, and my heart was uplifted!

And then it has made quite a splash in the city. Honest to God, what is going on?

30th January. There have been three unfortunate consequences. The first can be summarized in the formula: "Congratulations! You'll be a rich man now!" Once is all right – twice is all right. But, by the hundredth time, it becomes really irritating. What an uncultured lot we are! What a way to congratulate someone! Particularly since to congratulate me in this way has the long-term effect of seeming to sound like the most idiotic mockery. When I think about the coming summer and what's going to happen to my apartment, I am overcome by a feeling of horror.

Secondly: "I shall be mortally offended if I don't get a ticket for the première." It's a form of medieval torture.

And thirdly, worst of all: the Moscow public, it seems, frantically wants to know: What does this all mean? People have begun to torment me with this question. They've found the source! Then these people have decided to explain what it means themselves, seeing that neither the author nor anyone else either wished or was able to do this. And then, Pavel Sergeyevich, they launch into such lengthy explanations that the light dies in my eyes. And then, to cap it all, a very familiar figure with a pointed nose and a mad expression in his eyes* dashes in to see me in the middle of the night demanding to know what it all means.

"It means," I reply, "that the city's inhabitants and, above all, its literary figures are acting out Chapter 9 of your novel which I, O great master, have adapted for the stage in your honour. As you yourself have said: 'People's heads are full of rubbish, confusion, turmoil and impurity of thought... deriving from extraordinary natures that are filled with constant doubt and endless fear.' Please protect me with your armoured greatcoat."

And when he wrapped his coat around me I could hear, less distinctly, the sound of theatrical rain, and my name echoing around, together with that of Turbin, and then, "Shalyapin is coming, and Kachalov has had his leg amputated"!!* (Kachalov really is ill, but nevertheless you can't take the leg away from people's artists such as Kachalov! And anyway Shalyapin apparently isn't coming, and they've stupidly cut off the telephone at the Bolshoi. It's their tongues that should be cut off!

But all the same, Pavel Sergeyevich, what does it mean? As if I knew!

I do know: in the middle of January 1932, for reasons which are unknown to me and which I can't begin to discern, the government of the USSR ordered MAT to do something very extraordinary: to revive *The Days of the Turbins*.

For the play's author this means that for him – that is the author – part of his life has been returned to him. That's all.

19th March

To Pavel Popov

[…] The Leningrad Bolshoi Dramatic Theatre has sent me a letter saying that their artistic-political council has banned *Molière*. The Theatre has released me from all my contractual obligations.

(a) The play has been stamped with a "B" by the Main Repertory Committee, permitting unrestricted production.

(b) The Theatre has paid the author a fee for the production rights.

(c) Work on the play has already begun.

What's going on?

First of all, it comes as such a blow to me that I can't begin to describe it. Too difficult, and it would take too long.

I have staked everything on the première taking place on the Fontanka* in April, or thereabouts. But my card has lost, and the summer has flown by like smoke… in a word, what more is there to say?!

You're the only person I'm telling what a blow this has been to me. Please don't tell anyone else, otherwise people will start twisting it and may well cause me further harm.

It also means, to my horror, that the Main Repertory Committee's stamp is valid for all plays with the exception of mine.

I consider it my pleasant duty to inform you that this time I have no complaint to make concerning any organ of state. The stamp exists – here it is. It's not the state, in the form of any of its control organizations, that has taken off the play; the state is not to blame for the Theatre taking it off.

So *was* it the Theatre that took off the play? Really! Why then should it pay me 1,200 roubles and send a member of its board hotfoot to Moscow to finalize a contract with me?

Finally, the information came crashing through from Leningrad. It turned out that it wasn't any government organization that had taken off the play. *Molière* had been killed off by a completely unexpected individual! By a private, unofficial individual, an amateurish and insignificant individual, for completely non-political reasons. This person is a playwright by profession. He turned up at the Theatre and frightened it into removing the play.

At first, when I was told about this playwright turning up at the Theatre, I burst out laughing. But I stopped laughing very quickly. There was, alas, no doubt: several different people told me the same story.

What on earth was going on?

I'll tell you: on the Fontanka, in broad daylight, someone stabbed me in the back with a Finnish knife in the presence of a silent group of people. The Theatre swears, moreover, that it shouted for help, but no one came dashing to its aid.

I don't dare doubt that it did indeed shout for help, but it didn't shout very loudly. It should have shouted for help by telegram to Moscow, even to the People's Commissariat for Enlightenment.

A couple of sympathetic faces have just leant over me. They see a citizen swimming in his own blood. "Shout!" they say. But I'm not comfortable with the thought of shouting while lying down. It's not the business of a playwright!

I have a request, Pavel Sergeyevich: maybe you've seen some reference to this matter in the Leningrad newspapers, expressed in a caricature perhaps, or some comment or other. If you have, please do let me know!

Why do I ask? I don't know myself. Probably simply to take embittered pleasure in looking in the eye the snake in the grass one more time.

When, one hundred years ago, the commander of our Russian order of writers was killed,* they discovered a serious gunshot wound on his body. And when, in a hundred years' time, they remove the clothes from one of his descendants before sending him off on his long journey, they will find several scars from a Finnish knife. And they'll all be on his back.

Weapons change!

I'll be continuing this letter later, if you have no objection. I'm feeling very low.

Yours,
Mikhail Bulgakov

24th April

To Pavel Popov

Dear Pavel Sergeyevich,

And so, here are my notes. I suggest that the best thing to do when you've read them is to throw them in the fire. The stove has already been lit by my beloved publishers. What I like about the stove is the fact that it accepts everything, consuming with equal willingness laundry receipts, unfinished letters and even, shame upon shame, poems! Ever since I was a child I haven't been able to stand poems (I'm not talking about Pushkin – Pushkin is something other than poems!), and any I have written have always been satirical, evoking revulsion on the part of my aunt and grief on the part of my mother, who dreamt only of one thing: that her sons should become railway engineers. I don't know whether, lying in her grave, she is aware that her youngest son is now a solo balalaika player in France, her middle son is a bacteriologist, again in France, and that her eldest has had no desire to become anything. I should imagine she is aware of this. And I see her at times, in the midst of bitter dreams (she has appeared to me in my dreams three times recently. Why is she disturbing me like this?), with the lampshade, the piano keys and the score of *Faust*,* and I want to say to her, "Come with me to the Arts Theatre. I will show you a play. And that is all I can offer you now. Peace, Mama?"

The play was staged on 18th February.* Men could be seen standing all the way along from Tverskaya Street to the Theatre mumbling mechanically, "Any spare tickets?" It was the same along Dmitrovka.

I was backstage, not in the auditorium. The actors' excitement was infectious. I began moving from place to place, my arms and legs felt light and weightless. Bells were ringing everywhere, one moment there were dazzling floodlights, the next it was pitch-black except for the light from the stagehands' torches,

and the play seemed to be proceeding at a dizzying pace. After
a mournful song from Petlyura's men, there was a blaze of light
and, in the semi-gloom I watched Toporkov* running onto the
stage and standing on the staircase, panting... He was forcing
air into his lungs, and there was no way he was going to part
company with it. Everywhere you could sense the shadow of the
year 1918, reflected in dashing up the High School staircase and
undoing the collar of one's greatcoat with weak hands. Then
suddenly the shadow came to life, hid its fur hat, took out a
revolver and disappeared back into the High School (Toporkov
played Myshlayevsky brilliantly). The actors were so excited
that their faces turned pale under their make-up, their bodies
were covered in sweat and their eyes were tortured, wary and
inquisitive.

When Petlyura's troops, stretched to the limit, started chasing
after Nikolka, a stagehand fired a revolver right by my ear, thereby
bringing me to my senses in an instant.

The round stage was cleared, a piano appeared and the young
baritone sang an epithalamium.

At that moment a messenger appeared in the form of a beautiful woman. Recently, I have refined a particular ability to the
nth degree, an ability which makes life very difficult: the ability
to know beforehand what it is that anyone coming up to me
wants from me. Evidently my nerve casings have now totally
worn away, and living with my dog has taught me always to
be on guard.

In a word, I know what people are going to say to me and, sadly,
I know that what they are going to say to me will be nothing new.
There will be nothing unexpected, I'll know everything. I only had
to glance at her tense, smiling lips to know that she would ask me
not to go onto the stage.

The messenger said that K.S.* had rung and asked where I was
and how I felt...

I asked her to thank him and said that I felt fine, that at the
moment I was backstage and that I wouldn't respond to any calls
from the audience to go onto the stage.

At this the messenger beamed – oh, how she beamed! She said that K.S. would take this to be a wise decision.

But there wasn't any particular wisdom in such a decision. It was a very simple decision. I didn't want to take any bows or any curtain calls, I didn't want anything at all other than to be left in peace, for Christ's sake, so that I could have a hot bath and stop thinking all the time about what I'm to do with my dog in June when the lease on the apartment has ended.

In general, I knew for certain that I didn't want anything.

The curtain rose and fell twenty times. Then the actors and acquaintances bombarded me with questions. Why hadn't I taken any curtain calls? Why such affectation? And so it turns out that if you take curtain calls, that's affectation, and if you don't take curtain calls, that's also affectation. I simply don't know what I should do. [...]

30th April

To Pavel Popov

Dear Pavel Sergeyevich!
Thank you for your lovely letter of the 26th. I am extremely grateful for the newspaper cutting. As a result, I have Citizen Vishnevky's* complete dossier in every particular detail on my desk. This Vsevolod Vishnevsky is the very man who took my *Molière* off the stage in Leningrad, thereby apparently depriving me of any possibility of buying an apartment this summer. And it was he who was responsible for a whole number of further exploits relating to other playwrights and theatres – in Moscow as well as in Leningrad. These exploits are of such a nature that I simply don't wish to talk about Vs. Vishnevsky. But I need nevertheless to say one or two words about *The Days of the Turbins*. Vs. Vishnevsky was the only person to note the fact of the play's revival in the press. What he had to write, moreover, cannot really be summarized; it needs to be given in its entirety. I will here cite just one extract: "Everyone watches the play, shaking their heads and remembering the Ramzin affair..."* Only someone in a delirious fever, it seems, could link the characters of *The Days of the Turbins* with the participants in the Ramzin affair.

But I do believe I know what I am talking about (if that's a self-opinionated remark, so be it!). This is not actually delirious talk, but something quite rational. The spiritual essence of a totally sane individual. This individual is taking the first modest steps to removing my scenery from the stage. It's possible that these steps may turn out to be stupid. Oh, but that's beside the point!

I would like to say just one thing: during the year, in the field of Russian drama, a flower in the form of Vishnevsky has appeared, the like of which even an expert botanist such as myself has never seen before. Many others have spotted it too, and a number of them have vowed that, given a little time, it will be pulled up by its roots.

But I really don't mind. Enough about him. Oblivion! He can go to hell!

Back then to my reminiscences. My heart is beating anxiously, and I'm in a hurry to get them down on paper. […]

7th May

To Pavel Popov

It seems you're jumping the gun with regard to my *Dead Souls*, dear Pavel Sergeyevich! You're ruining my plan. But all right, if that is what you want. But afterwards, I shall go back to *The Days of the Turbins*.

And so, dead souls… in nine days' time I shall be 41. That's a monstrous thought! But true nevertheless.

And so towards the end of my work as a writer I have been forced to do stage adaptations. Such a dazzling finale, isn't it?! I look along my bookshelves and, horrified, ask myself whom I shall have to adapt tomorrow: Turgenev, Leskov, *Brockhaus-Efron*? Or Ostrovsky?* But luckily he, Ostrovsky, set his own work for the stage, evidently foreseeing what would happen to me in 1929–31. Briefly…

1. *Dead Souls* cannot be adapted for the stage. Accept that as axiomatic from someone who knows the work well. I have been told that there are 160 adaptations in existence. That may not be the exact figure but, in any case, a staged version of *Dead Souls* is out of the question.

2. But then why did I agree to do this?

But I didn't agree to do it, Pavel Sergeyevich. I haven't agreed to do anything for a long time – fate has grabbed me by the throat and I am unable to control anything I do. As soon as I was appointed to MAT, I was taken on as an assistant director for *Dead Souls* (the senior director Sakhnovsky, Telesheva* and me). All it needed was just one glance at the notebook containing the stage adaptation written by someone commissioned for the purpose and everything began swimming before my eyes. I realized that, even on the very threshold of the Theatre, I had been plunged into a disaster: I had been appointed to produce a non-existent play. That was a good start, wasn't it? There's not much more to be said. After many tortuous enquiries, something became clear which I had already known for a long time, but of which others, unfortunately, weren't aware: in order to adapt something for the stage, it needs to be written first. To cut a long story short, the task of writing the adaptation fell to me.

My first idea was that the action should take place in Rome (stop looking at me like that!). At one time Gogol saw Russia from "a beautiful distance", and so that is how we shall see it.

My Rome idea was annihilated as soon as I submitted my overall plan for the adaptation. And the loss of my Rome made me unutterably sad!

3. All right: if there was to be no Rome, then there would be no Rome.

In other words, Pavel Sergeyevich, I had to cut! Simply cut! And I broke Gogol's poem* into little pieces. Literally cut it into shreds. The first scene (or prologue) takes place in an inn either in St Petersburg or Moscow, in which, quite by chance, the secretary of the Council of Trustees gives Chichikov the idea of buying up dead serfs and mortgaging them (look at Volume 1 of the novel, Chapter 11). And so Chichikov goes off to buy serfs. But in a totally different order from the poem. The questioning of Selifan, Petrushka, Korobochka and Nozdryov takes place in Scene 10, called the "Chamber Scene" on the rehearsal sheets. This is followed by the story about Captain Kopeykin,* and then the appearance of Captain Kopeykin himself, at which point the public prosecutor dies. Chichikov is arrested, thrown into prison and then released by the chief of police and a colonel in the gendarmerie, who rob him of everything he possesses. He leaves. "Let's go, Pavel Ivanovich!"

What a business!

And what about Nemirovich's* reaction when he'd read it! As you can see, it's not the 161st adaptation, it's not even an adaptation at all, but something quite different. (You can't of course say everything in a letter but, for example, whenever Nozdryov appears he's always accompanied by Mizhuyev, who follows him everywhere like a shadow. The words are time and again conveyed through the lips of people who are quite different from those in the poem, and so on.)

Vladimir Ivanovich's reaction was one of horror and outrage. There was a huge argument, but nonetheless work on the play continued, and it continued for about two years!

4. So, did they succeed in carrying out this plan? Don't worry, Pavel Sergeyevich: no, they didn't succeed. Why not? Because, to my horror, Stanislavsky was ill for the entire winter and was unable to work at the theatre (as for Nemirovich, he was abroad).

Goodness knows what's happening on the stage at the moment. The only hope is that K.S.* will be up and about in May and will be able to see what's happening himself.

When will *Dead Souls* open? In my opinion, never. If it should open in its present form, the Bolshoi stage will witness a big disaster.

What's the problem? The problem is that, in order to stage Gogol's captivating, fantastic ideas you need to have a talented director at the theatre.

That's the problem, Pavel Sergeyevich!

But who cares? Who cares? And, once more, who cares?!

Until my next letter.

6th September

*To V.G. Sakhnovsky**

Top secret. Urgent.
At 3.45 I am getting married in the Registry Office.* Please allow
me to leave in ten minutes' time.

1933

To Nikolai Bulgakov

Dear Kolya!

I hope you are alive and well. You will of course already have become used to the fact that I only write occasionally to you. And I don't know anything about what's been happening with you recently. I trust that Ivan and his family are alive and well too.

At the moment I am completing something big – a biography of Molière.

I would be very obliged to you if you could find a spare moment to take a look, if only briefly, at the memorial to Molière (the Molière Fountain) in the Rue de Richelieu.

I need to have a short but precise description of this memorial in its present form, including the following details:

The material and colour of Molière's statue.

The material and colour of the women at the foot of the memorial.

Whether or not there's running water in the fountain (coming out of the lions' heads).

A description of the location (the present-day streets, crossroads, the direction in which Molière is looking and which building he's facing).

If at all possible, please tell me the names of the French Molière specialists who are in Paris at the present time. It would be good to have one or two names of genuine, not amateurish Molière experts, together with their addresses.

If you could do this for me it would make my difficult work much easier.

I'm also writing to tell you that an enormous and important change has taken place in my life. Lyuba and I have got divorced, and I have married Yelena Sergeyevna Shilovskaya. Her son, six-year-old Sergei,* is living with us.

As always, of course, I promise to write to you about my life in detail. I think that, after 1st February, I will be able to do this, because I shall be helped in this by severe exhaustion. 1st February is the date by which I must submit my *Molière*, and then I think I shall have to stop writing for a very long time.

I've come to the end of my strength. I'll be able to manage the rehearsals at the Theatre, but that's all. And then my faithful companion, Yelena Sergeyevna, will help me sort out my correspondence.

Yelena Sergeyevna is going around with the idea that she will make me get better in six months. I don't believe this in the slightest but, because of her presence, I'm prepared to look at the future through rose-coloured spectacles.

I am dictating this letter to my wife, because it is easier to work in this way, rather than writing by hand myself.

And so, I embrace you and Ivan. May your fates be kind to you both.

By the way, I forgot to ask: I know there have been reviews of *Dead Souls* (my adaptation of Gogol's novel) in Paris; if you come across any references in the press – in French, Russian or whatever – please would you cut them out and keep them.

I would like to have a photograph of you. And of Ivan. Please send them to me.

I embrace you once again. Please don't forget me.

I'm at the same address: Bolshaya Pirogovskaya Street, 35a, Apartment 6.

8th March

To Nikolai Bulgakov

To my great joy I have finally finished *Molière*, and have submitted the manuscript on 5th March. I found it an incredibly exhausting task – a task which sucked all the vital juices out of me. I can no longer remember exactly which year I started work on the play and how long I have been living in the transparently clear and magical world of Paris of the seventeenth century. And now it looks as if I shall be parting from it for ever.

If you should ever happen to go to the corner of Rue de Richelieu and Rue Molière, remember me. Greetings to Jean-Baptiste Molière from me!...

10th April

To *the Zamyatins*

And so Lyubov Yevgenyevna and I have got divorced and I am now married to Yelena Sergeyevna Shilovskaya. Please love and cherish her as I do. There are now three of us living on Pirogovskaya Street – me, her and her six-year-old son Sergei. I have spent the winter sitting by the stove, reading fantastically interesting stories about the North Pole and elephant hunts, shooting from a toy pistol and constantly going down with flu. At the same time I completed a biography of your fellow Parisian Jean-Baptiste Molière* for the *Life of Remarkable People* series. Tikhonov* has been praising the biography.

So you've married *Anna Karenina*, have you? My God! The very word "Tolstoy" fills me with horror! Having written an adaptation of *War and Peace* for the stage I can't pass by a bookshelf with a book by Tolstoy on it without shuddering. May all adaptations be cursed, now and for evermore!

You ask me when I'm planning to come to the West? Just imagine: in the last three months many people have asked me that question...

12th April

To Alexander Tikhonov

Dear Alexander Nikolayevich!

N.A. Ekke* has given me your comments on my book on Molière. I have read it through and considered what you have said. Things don't look very good. It's not a question of your detailed observations, which I found striking in content as well as tone [...]. It's the fact that the book that I have written has been totally annihilated, and that it is to be replaced by a new book which would be about something totally contrary to what I have written in my own book.

In order to do as you propose and have as the book's narrator a "serious Soviet historian" rather than an "easy-going young man", I myself would have to become a historian. Yet I'm not a historian, but a dramatist studying Molière during a given period. But, as someone in this position, I maintain that I am able to see *my* Molière clearly. From my point of view *my* Molière is the only true Molière, and the particular way I have chosen to convey him to the reader has not been a random process, but the result of careful thought.

You yourself must understand that, as the author of the book, I simply cannot rewrite it in a totally different form. For goodness' sake!

I regret therefore that I cannot rewrite the book and refuse to do so. But what then are we to do?

In my opinion, Alexander Nikolayevich, we have a brilliant way out of this. The book is not suitable for the series, so it's not necessary to publish it. Let's bury it and forget about it!

Respectfully yours,

M. Bulgakov

13th April

To Pavel Popov

[...] Well, my Molière days have begun, starting with Tikhonov's critique, containing, my dear Patya, so many pleasant things. The narrator of the biography is described as "an easy-going young man", who believes in magic and witchcraft, possesses dark sensibilities, is fond of fireside stories, makes use of dubious sources and, worst of all, has royalist tendencies!

But that's not all. According to T. my book contains "fairly obvious hints about our Soviet reality"!!

When Ye.S. and K.* read what the editor had to say they were enraged, and Ye.S. even wanted to dash off and have it out with him. Clutching at her skirt, I only just managed to dissuade her from such impulsive behaviour. Then I composed a letter to him. But after a great deal of thought I considered it would be better not to get into a fight. I simply bared my teeth at the tone of the critique, but I didn't bite. In short this is what I did: in reply to T.'s observation that I should replace my narrator with a "serious Soviet historian", I said that I wasn't a historian and refused to rewrite the book.

In the same letter Tikhonov said that he had sent the manuscript to Sorrento.*

I want therefore to bury Jean-Baptiste Molière. That will be easier and less stressful for everyone. I am completely indifferent to the fact that bookshop windows will not be decorated with a cover of my book. Essentially I am an actor, and not a writer. Besides, I am very fond of peace and quiet. [...]

19th May

To Pavel Popov

Dear Pavel!
I've heard that you're going away on holiday. Also, Kolya tells me that you tried to ring me but there was no answer. I hope you'll be able to grab a moment and pop in to say goodbye. Bring the ill-fated *Molière* with you.

And what about me? The wind is stirring in the leaves by the skin clinic, and my heart stops beating when I think of rivers, bridges, oceans. There is a gypsy sighing in my heart. But it will pass. I can already foresee that I will be spending the entire summer on Pirogovskaya Street writing a comedy (for Leningrad). It will be hot, noisy and dusty, and I shall drink mineral water. [...]

2nd August

To Vikenty Veresayev

[...] First of all I would like to tell you about my visit to Leningrad. MAT was putting on *The Days of the Turbins* there, in two theatres. The performances were very successful, to full houses, as a result of which I heard from all sides that I had grown rich. And the royalties I will be getting from there will indeed be very respectable.

And so we arrived in Leningrad, aware just how difficult it would be actually to get hold of such riches.

It was Yelena Sergeyevna, not me, who, armed with my authorization, descended on the second of these theatres – the Narvsky House of Culture. The theatre manager twice promised that he would be sending on five thousand roubles from my royalties. As you will have guessed, as of this moment we haven't received five copecks.

So, once again, I find myself in the familiar territory of the dead theatre season. Yelena Sergeyevna sends off telegrams via the All-Russian Drama Committee and manages by some magic to extract small advances, while I dream only of the happy day when she has complete success and I am able to pay you back the rest of what I owe you, and remembering what you have done for me, my dear Vikenty Vikentevich.

Oh, what memories I will have of those years 1929 to 1931!

I would have been on my feet earlier, moreover, if I didn't have to leave this hellhole on Pirogovskaya Street! The Nashchokinsky apartment is still not ready. It's a year late. A year! And I have been torn in half.

But that's enough of that!

What will you be doing after your *Sisters*?* Yelena Sergeyevna has such interesting things to say about that book! We have spent a long time talking about it.

As well as that, I have been sitting up for two nights reading your Gogol.* My God! What a character! What an amazing figure!

There is a devil inside me. When still in Leningrad, and now back here, suffocating in my tiny little rooms, I have begun to scribble out anew page after page of the novel I destroyed three years ago. Why am I doing this? I don't know. To amuse myself! Let it fall into oblivion! In any case, I shall doubtless abandon it soon.

Please give my greetings, and those of Yelena Sergeyevna, to Maria Germogenovna.

I hope you have a good holiday. With very best wishes,

Mikhail Bulgakov

13th August

To Nikolai Bulgakov

Dear Kolya!

I wonder if you would be able to help me with one matter, by acting as my attorney? A certain Mme Reinhardt, an actress [...] has translated my play *Zoyka's Apartment* [...] into French, and has put forward the idea to me of staging it in French in a number of theatres [...]

I am signifying my agreement to this, stating that our contract should run for two years for dramatic productions, and for one year for films, starting from the première of the first dramatic performance.

I know of course how busy you are, but I would ask if you could become my attorney in this matter and, as recompense for your efforts on my behalf, to deduct for yourself 25% of the total sum of money that I receive.

And there's something else: in 1928 I gave permission for the Ladyzhnikov Publishing House in Berlin to publish *Zoyka's Apartment* in German translation and to secure for itself the rights to perform the play outside Russia. [...]

According to my information, this publishing house is no longer in existence. And, moreover, from December 1928 to this day, I have not once heard from them concerning *Zoyka's Apartment*. Could you please find out whether I am correct in supposing that there is nothing to prevent me from concluding an agreement with Maria Reinhardt. This is in order to avoid any conflicts or misunderstandings. [...]

I am enclosing a note empowering you to conduct negotiations with Reinhardt and to receive any resulting monies. Please would you go and see her?

In my next letter I shall send a complete copy of Reinhardt's letter to me in French.

I have received Vanya's letter with the poems attached. I shall be writing to him and to you again. For now I'm simply rushing to complete this letter on the Reinhardt matter.

I am troubling you with this because I have no one else to turn to. I embrace you and ask you to reply to this letter as soon as possible.

Yours, Mikhail Bulgakov

(M. Bulgakow)

Mikhail Bulgakov (1891–1940)

Afanasy Bulgakov,
Bulgakov's father

Varvara Bulgakova,
Bulgakov's mother

Tatyana Bulgakova,
Bulgakov's first wife

Lyubov Belozerskaya,
Bulgakov's second wife

Yelena Shilovskaya,
Bulgakov's third wife

Nikolai Bulgakov,
Bulgakov's brother

The Bulgakov family in Bucha, Ukraine, August 1913,
with Mikhail Bulgakov on the top left

Bulgakov and his second wife Lyubov with Nikolai Lyamin and Sergei
Topleninov (above); Bulgakov and his third wife Yelena in 1936 (below)

Yelena Bulgakova, 1936 (above); Mikhail and Yelena during a trip to Kiev in 1934 (bottom left); a postcard of the writer dedicated to Yelena in 1939 with the following words: "This is how someone might look who has had to spend several years in the company of Aloysius Mogarych and Nikanor Ivanovich [characters from *The Master and Margarita*] and others. I present this photograph to you, Yelena, in the hope that you might make me look more cheerful. Fondest love and kisses. 16th May 1939. M." (bottom right)

Bulgakov with Sergei Shilovsky ("Seryozha") and Sergei Yermolinsky (above);
Bulgakov in the final days of his life, February 1940 (below)

Bulgakov's residences on Bolshaya Sadovaya St. (above) and Nashchokinsky Pereulok (bottom left); an unfinished letter to Stalin (bottom right)

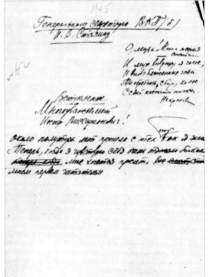

...ейший — Иван Николаевич, верьте вам в Христе. Тома ... Сера ... ас
...умалишался.

— Начальник белой магии, — пробормотал Иванушка.

— Необходимо быть последователем, они ... са ... не это ... — Будьте добры, он ... Руфаво, наступите ... не это ...рет, он ... остры ... на изображение Христа на песке.

— Просто странно, ... видит ...мо?

— Да не полно я! — ... Иванушка.

— Боитесь, — кротко сказал Воланд.

— И не думаю!

— Боитесь!

Иванушка, ... , посмотрел на ... и ...

... подсел к Иванушке:

— Помилуйте, доктор! Ни вхаки

A manuscript page from *The Master and Margarita*

13th August

To Marie Reinhardt

Madame!

I am writing this letter to signify my agreement granting you the right to translate my play *Zoyka's Apartment* into French and for its performance in French… on the basis of the conditions suggested by you in your kind letter of 5th July 1933 – that is 4% to me as author's royalties for each performance in a theatre, and 50% of the monies that you will receive from cinema showings of the French version.

I suggest that our agreement should be valid for two years (from the date of this letter) for performances in the theatre, and for one year for the cinema – starting from the première of the first performance in a Paris theatre.

I consider it my duty to inform you that, in accordance with the permission given by me on 7th October 1928, the I. Ladyzhnikov Publishing House published the German translation of *Zoyka's Apartment* in Berlin, with a note confirming translation and performance rights for the play and including the securing of performance rights beyond the borders of the USSR.

In view of the fact that, since that date, I have heard nothing about the play from the Ladyzhnikov Publishing House, and that moreover, according to my information, the publishing house no longer exists, I assume that there is no barrier to finalizing an immediate agreement with you.

But I would ask you to take measures to clarify this issue so as to avoid any misunderstandings or legal disputes.

In case I am mistaken and the Ladyzhnikov Publishing house does possess the rights to *Zoyka's Apartment*, perhaps we shall need to finalize the contract through them?

At the same time as this letter I am writing to my brother, Dr Nikolai Afanasyevich Bulgakov, who lives in Paris… requesting

him to come and see you to discuss all the details, including the
Ladyzhnikov issue. I would ask you to look upon N.A. Bulgakov
as my legal representative, and to hand over to him any monies
that are owing to me as a result of our agreement.

I would be very pleased if you could send me the French text of
Zoyka's Apartment, and if you would keep me informed about
the play's progress.

Please accept my best regards,

M. Bulgakov

30th August

To Nikolai Bulgakov

Dear Kolya!

Your letter of 25th August arrived this morning. First of all I would like to thank you most warmly for answering so quickly and in such detail. Now to reply to your various points:

1. You have set out the position very clearly.

2. I am enclosing with this letter a copy of my letter of 8th October 1928 to the Ladyzhnikov Publishing House. As you can see, it's just a letter rather than a contract that has been laid out clause by clause. Furthermore, as you will also see, the letter does not include any reference to a duration – the result, no doubt, of haste on my part.

Note: Zakhar Leontievich Kagansky is the very same person who engaged in a whole series of underhand ploys abroad with regard to my novel *The White Guard* and my play *The Days of the Turbins*. Then, as I had been forewarned by the Ladyzhnikov Publishing house, he started to behave in the same way with the translation and publication of *Zoyka's Apartment*. Hence the reference to him in my letter. While on the subject I warn you that Kagansky is a professional crook, active not only in Berlin but, as far as I know, also in Paris and perhaps in other cities as well.

3. All of you in Paris will have to decide yourselves what to do about Kagansky. For my part I will attempt to consult a lawyer tomorrow; perhaps I'll be able to find out something here.

4. I willingly grant you all foreign rights to *Zoyka's Apartment*, and I shall ask tomorrow for my signature on the power of attorney to be witnessed. As soon as it has been witnessed I will send it on to you.

5. You ask if it's possible for me to send you the text of *Zoyka's Apartment*. No, I think that this will not be possible.

6. *Zoyka's Apartment* is clearly being distributed abroad in one of the versions which people have circulated by means that are unknown to me, possibly via Riga or Berlin. I don't know what state this version is in. It's possible, of course, that it's in a mess.

7. It's absolutely imperative to operate the other way round: as soon as possible Reinhardt must send me copies of her French translation (by registered post, of course), or a copy of the Russian text which she used for her translation. I shall look forward to receiving that.

8. If it should prove impossible to send these (although I don't know why that should be so), or if there should be a delay in sending them, I really need you to write to me enclosing some key examples from the Reinhardt translation (a list of the dramatis personae, an indication of the number of scenes and acts, the beginning and conclusion of scenes), so that I can form some picture of her translation. I shall look forward to receiving these as soon as possible.

9. I strongly recommend that you obtain a copy of the text of the Ladyzhnikov *Zoykas Wohnung* from Berlin. You may be able to compare the versions.

10. As far as the sketches for the costumes and scenery are concerned, this, in my view, will be impossible, because it is forbidden to photograph or copy the Vakhtangov Theatre production in Moscow. Something different will be needed: the author's precise instructions concerning the costumes and the scenery. I can give these to you if you need them.

That's all for now. As you can see, I am replying to your letter on the day it arrived. Now you must wait for my next letters. Tomorrow we shall ask for my signature to be witnessed. [...]

4th October

To Nikolai Bulgakov

[...] I am replying to the particular points in your detailed, clear and lovely letter.

1. Thank you for copying out the text.

2. I'm still waiting for the *adaptation française*. The version you sent is an uncorrected copy, containing a number of distortions and numerous misprints. It would of course be good, if at all possible, to get a copy of the Russian text before the adaptation, but if that is not possible then there's nothing you can do about it. I will immediately arm myself with one of my own copies of *Zoyka*, on the assumption that it will be identical to the one you have, and I'll send you the corrections, trying to clarify the messy bits without distorting the sense. [...]

3. Thank you for the copy of the agreement and its Russian translation. If you find you don't have the time to translate something in future, send it as it is and I can translate it.

4. I am pleased to hear of your membership of the Société.

5. I have spoken to the solicitor. His opinion is that I no longer need to consider myself as bound to Ladyzhnikov, and I have NOT SENT them the legal power of attorney. [...]

I need to write to Ladyzhnykov letting them know that I have given you the power of attorney and asking them to cancel the agreement. I will do this.

6. Re Fischer:* it turns out that they're right in their claim that they already have an agreement relating to *Zoyka's Apartment*. [...]

[...] Not a peep out of Ladyzhnikov whether they've transferred the distribution rights of *Zoyka's Apartment* to Fischer; in fact I've heard nothing from them about anything. Please bear all of this in mind. I shall of course write to Fischer immediately letting them know that you have the power of attorney, asking them to

sort out the question of the Czech Republic with you, and saying
that I shall be referring all those correspondents concerned with
Zoyka's Apartment to you. [...]

7. I am pleased to hear of the discussions with the theatres.

8. The list of dramatis personae, character descriptions, costumes
and social situation will follow immediately with my next letter.

9. Please, dear Nikol, as soon as you get this letter, would you
tell Professor d'Hérelle* that I would be extremely pleased to see
him here [...]. I would be very happy to meet your boss, with
whom you are connected through your scientific work, and to hear
something about you. Even if his time is taken up with official visits
and scientific exchanges, I think he will undoubtedly find the time
to see me while he's here. [...] Both my wife and I speak French.

In general I'm going through a French phase at the moment. I'm
reading about Molière (while still continuing to study him), and I
recently chatted to Herriot, who's visiting MAT and who's been
to a performance of *The Days of the Turbins*. [...]

1934

To Pavel Popov

Dear Pavel,

Thank you for your letter of the 6th.

One of Kolya's friends has been saying all kinds of unpleasant things about me, including the fact that I am tainted by an "unhealthy urbanism". I was of course immediately told about this.

Yet, despite this urbanism, I have appreciated birchwood forests, bubbling samovars and jam. To sum up: a very pleasant letter, and you yourself are a clever person. Make sure you have a rest!

This winter seems really endless. You look out of the window and you want to spit. The grey snow on the roofs never seems to go away. I'm fed up with it all! Winter!

The new apartment is gradually getting into shape. But I've been finding the carpenters as tedious as the winter. Constantly coming and going, banging everywhere.

I've hung up a lantern in the bedroom. As for the study, to hell with it! All such studies are useless.

I've already forgotten about Pirogovskaya; a sure sign that it wasn't a good place to live. Yet a lot of interesting things went on there. [...]

Now what about *Molière*? Well, at least we're rehearsing it. But slowly, and not very often. And, between you and me, I'm feeling rather depressed about it. Lyusya cannot talk about what the Theatre is doing to my play without feeling irritated. I myself have long since stopped feeling upset about it all. If it weren't for the fact that I need a new play to be performed in order to carry on living, I would have stopped thinking about it altogether. If it's performed, then that's fine – if not, then so what? But, however infrequent the rehearsals, I throw myself into them life and soul. You can't do otherwise if you've got theatre in your veins!

But I have to work more on other stuff. We're rehearsing *The Pickwick Club** on stage. But when it's going to be performed, and when I shall be able to let you admire my red judge's robes, I don't know. This play, no doubt, will get bogged down too. Sudakov has burst into the station with *The Storm*,* crashing across the points and steaming full speed ahead. We need *The Storm* as much as a cat needs trousers, but nevertheless Sudakov is an outstanding personality. If you ever write a play, then do your best to get Sudakov as its director. After Sudakov comes the explosive talent of Mordvinov, with Kirshon* at his beck and call. As well as other things I'm involved in preparing the MAT singers for a concert and, from time to time, dashing off a comedy, scene by scene. Who's benefiting from all this? And why am I doing it? Nobody seems able to explain. I may even get to love my own work.

Please write to me again from Yasnaya.* It's so good to see your envelope on my desk, among all the other envelopes which I rip open with a curse. Letters from abroad, and from handsome men who are interested in my plays.

If you come, we'll be able to listen to gypsy waltzes. Incidentally, did you manage to wrest the guitar from the talons of that... forgotten his name... that man who was at the show?

Please kiss Anna Ilinichna's* hand from me and ask her to kiss me on the forehead. Lyusya sends very warm greetings, and I embrace you.

Yours, M.

26th April

To Vikenty Veresayev

Dear Vikenty Vikentevich!
I'm dictating this letter lying down, as I'm not very well. As you can see, we've had a telephone installed, but for the time being I am resorting to the post rather than to the telephone, since you can say more by post. I can't go anywhere, as I'm totally overwhelmed by work. I spend every day, with few exceptions, rehearsing, and my evenings and nights finally dictating a play which I first conceived long ago. I used to dream that I would submit it to the Satire Theatre, with which I have a contract, as soon as I had finished it, but then I would immediately forget about it and begin writing the stage version of *Dead Souls*. But it didn't turn out as I had thought.

I read the play to the people at the Satire Theatre, and they said that the beginning and end were fine, but that the middle part of the play was no good at all. So, instead of forgetting about it, I lie around with neuralgia and think what a rotten dramatist I am! Just an absolute mishmash in my head: on the one hand, we have Chichikov* poking his nose in and, on the other, there is this comedy. I couldn't abandon it – the Theatre people were being so nice about it with me. But to try and correct it would mean starting all over again from the beginning. So it seems there's no way round the problem. But some way round it has to be found.

Here's what I wanted to ask you, Vikenty Vikentevich. Is there a possibility of renting a dacha in Zvenigorod,* somewhere near where you live? If it's not too much trouble, please could you write or telephone us and let us know about possible owners, location, swimming possibilities? It's mainly for Seryozhka,* but Yelena Sergeyevna would like it for me as well. I'm personally not very keen on the idea, as I'm not keen on the pleasures of suburban Moscow and therefore I won't feel any better there. But for the sake of the company and so as to give my wife and Sergei the possibility of breathing in fresh air, I'm willing to join them. If not Zvenigorod, then we'll find something else close to Moscow.

But now here's the brilliant part: I've decided to ask for permission to go abroad for two months, in August and September. I've been lying here for several days, thinking, wracking my brains, trying to ask people's advice. "Don't mention the fact that you're ill." All right, I won't. But there's one thing I can mention, I must mention: I must see the world, and I have the right to do so. I go over it all in my mind and ask my wife whether I really have this right. Yes, you do, she replies. So what do you think: should I give this as my reason?

The whole question is made infinitely more complicated by the fact that Yelena Sergeyevna has to accompany me. I don't feel well, and my neurasthenia and fear of loneliness would turn the whole trip into a torment of misery otherwise. I wonder what I can give as my reason for wanting to go? When some of the people I ask for advice hear me say "with my wife" they dismiss the idea, and even start waving their arms about. But there's actually no reason at all to behave in this way. This is the truth, and it's a truth that has to be defended. I don't need a doctor, or a rest home, or a sanatorium, or anything of the sort. I know what I need: another city, another sun, another sea, another hotel for two months, and then I believe that, in the autumn, I will be able to rehearse at the Moscow Arts Theatre and perhaps even to write again.

Somebody said I should ask Nemirovich for help.

No, I won't do that! Neither Nemirovich nor Stanislavsky. They won't budge. Let Anton Chekhov address them instead!

So then, I've decided. I'll ask Yelena Sergeyevna. She brings good luck.

It's time to go off on my travels, Vikenty Vikentevich! However strange it may seem, it's already sunset.

Don't wish me success; as the theatre superstition has it, that's unlucky. [...]

28th April

To Pavel Popov

Dear Pavel!

I imagine that, when you get this letter, you'll still be in Yasnaya Polyana.

You can add one more chapter – the 97th – under the heading: "How nothing came of *Bliss*".*

On the 25th I read my play to the Satire Theatre ensemble. They all liked the beginning and the end very much. They all, without exception, fell in love with and latched on to the figure of Ivan the Terrible. Evidently I must have got something wrong somehow or other. Now I've got a big problem. I was thinking of leaving the play alone and moving straight on to writing a film version of *Dead Souls*. But now things have taken a turn for the worse. I feel physically dreadful. Utterly exhausted. Whatever happens, I shall have to give up all work by 1st August and do nothing until the end of September, otherwise it's absolutely clear that I won't be able to make it through next season.

I have asked for permission to go abroad for August and September. I have even been dreaming about Mediterranean waves, Paris museums, a quiet hotel, free from all acquaintances, Molière's fountain, cafés – in other words, the possibility of seeing all of this. I have been discussing with Lyusya for a long time what kind of travel piece I could write! And I remembered Goncharov's immortal *Voyage of the Frigate Pallada*,* and Grigorovich's trip to Paris some eighty years ago!* Oh, if only it could all come true! In which case you could expect a new chapter, the most interesting.

I saw someone once, a writer, who had been abroad. He was wearing a beret with a short tassel. He'd brought nothing back with him apart from this beret! I had the impression that he had been asleep for a couple of months, then he'd bought the beret and come back.

Not a single line, not a single sentence, not a single thought! Oh, immortal Goncharov! Where are you now?

Please, please don't say a word about this to anyone, anyone at all. It's not a question of secrecy: it's simply that I want to shut myself away from the chatter of Moscow gossips and scandal-mongers. I don't want to hear people bandying my name about or discussing my affairs, which are nothing to do with them at all any more. One woman burst in on us the other day and, as soon as she had gone, Lyusya and I spent the next half-hour fulminating against her. She may well have been hiccupping as far away as Myasnitsky Gate. She had asked how much we earned, and told us how much other people earned. One person, she had informed us, earned five hundred thousand a month. And what do we have to drink and to eat? And so on. What a pest! An absolute disaster! For me there's nothing more unpleasant than these Moscow beauties spouting their damned nonsense! I simply don't want such an important question as this to be bandied about everywhere, something which for me is a question of my entire future, even though it may not last for very long, and even though I am in the twilight of my life!

You're the only person I'm talking to seriously about this at the moment. Please note that I haven't spoken even to Kolya about it, and will not do so in the future.

Oh Pavel, what letters I shall write to you! When I see you in the autumn I shall embrace you, but I won't be buying myself a little tassel. Nor a pair of shorts. Nor long checkered socks.

Well, that's all for the moment. I shall look forward to seeing you in Moscow. I hope that Anna Ilinichna is better. Greetings to her from Lyusya and me.

Yours,
Mikhail

10th June

To Y.V. *Stalin*

To Comrade Stalin

From Mikhail Afanasyevich Bulgakov
Playwright and director
The Gorky Moscow Arts Theatre

Highly esteemed Yosif Vissarionovich!
Please permit me to tell you what has been happening to me.

1.

At the end of April of this year I submitted a request to the
Chairman of the Government Commission with responsibility for the Arts Theatre asking for permission to go abroad
for two months accompanied by my wife Yelena Sergeyevna
Bulgakova.

I included in my submission the reason I wanted to undertake
such a journey: I wanted to write a book about travelling in
Western Europe (and on my return to offer it for publication in
the USSR).

Since I am genuinely suffering from exhaustion of the nervous system, linked with a fear of being alone, I asked for permission for my wife to accompany me, on the understanding
that for this period of two months she would leave behind my
seven-year-old stepson, for whose support and education I am
responsible.

Having sent the request, I expected one of two answers: either
permission to travel or a refusal, without considering that there
could be a third answer.

What actually happened, however, was something that I had not
foreseen: a third answer.

On 17th May I received a telephone call, during which the following conversation ensued:

"You have submitted a request concerning your trip abroad?"

"Yes."

"Go to the Foreign Department of the Moscow District Executive Committee and complete the relevant forms for you and your wife."

"When do I need to do this?"

"As soon as possible, since your request will be considered on the 21st or the 22nd."

I was so overcome by joy at this that I didn't even ask the name of the person I was talking to and went straight to the Foreign Department of the Executive Committee with my wife and gave our names. When the official there heard that I had received a summons by telephone from the Department he asked me to wait a moment, went into the office next door and returned, asking me to fill in some forms.

When we had completed the forms he took them and attached two photographs to each, but took no money, saying that the passports would be free of charge. He didn't take in our Soviet passports, saying they would be exchanged for our foreign passports later, when we were at the border. And then he added the following, word for word:

You will be getting your passports very soon, as there have been special instructions about your case. You could have received them today in fact, but it's too late for that. Telephone me on the morning of the 18th.

"But the 18th is a holiday," I said.

"Well then, the 19th," he replied.

When I rang on the morning of the 19th the reply was as follows:

"The passports aren't ready yet. Ring again towards the end of the afternoon. If your passports are ready they will be issued to you then."

When I rang again later as requested I was told that the passports still weren't ready, and I was asked to ring on the 23rd.

On 23rd May my wife and I personally went to the Foreign Department once again, where we learnt that the passports weren't ready. The official made enquiries on the telephone and then suggested that we should ring on 25th or 27th May.

At that I started getting a little alarmed and asked the official whether there really had been special instructions concerning my case, or perhaps I had got the wrong message on the 17th.

The official's reply was as follows:

"You yourself will understand that I don't know who it is who has given the special instructions, *but there are special instructions relating to you and your wife*, just as there are relating to the writer Pilnyak."*

At this any doubts that I might have had vanished, and my joy knew no bounds.

Soon after this came further confirmation that permission for me to travel had been granted. Someone from the Theatre told me that the word had gone out from the Central Executive Committee that "the Bulgakovs' request was being processed".

All this time people were congratulating me on the fulfilment of my long-held writer's dream of travelling abroad, so essential for any writer.

In the meantime, day after day, the Foreign Department of the Executive Committee continued to delay giving me any answer about our passports – to which I reacted with complete equability, believing that, however long the delay, the passports would arrive.

On 7th June a courier from the Arts Theatre went to the Foreign Department with a list of the performers who were to be issued with foreign passports. The Theatre had kindly included the names of me and my wife, even though I had submitted my request independently of the Theatre.

When the courier returned that same afternoon I could see from the bewildered and confused expression on his face that there was something wrong.

The courier informed us that the list of those performers who had been issued foreign passports was in his pocket, but that, as far as my wife and I were concerned, our request had been REFUSED.

Then, on the very next day, the Foreign Department received official confirmation stating that the issue of permission for citizen M.A. Bulgakov to travel abroad had been refused.

After that, so as to avoid listening to expressions of regret, astonishment and so on, I went home, understanding only one thing: that I been placed in a ridiculous and distressingly painful position, not at all befitting my age.

2.

The insult inflicted on me in the Foreign Department of the Moscow District Executive Committee is all the more painful in that my four years of service to MAT give no basis for it whatsoever, which is why I am asking you to intercede in this matter.

26th June

To Pavel Popov

Hotel Astoria, Leningrad
Room No. 430

Dear Pavel!
First of all, enormous thanks for sending me *Bliss*. I'll return the favour in one way or another. I haven't been able to write to you till now. After everything that's happened, not only I, but my missus too, to my absolute horror, have fallen ill. We've been suffering from devilish migraines, and then pain, insomnia and so on. [...] Every day we've been having electric-shock treatment, and we're gradually beginning to stand on our own feet again.

We've just had the five hundredth performance here, on the 20th. The occasion was marked by the presentation of an address to the Theatre by Vyborg House,* and of a silver cigarette case to Zhenya Kaluzhsky.* This took place on the stage with the curtain down, before the third act. (Kaluzhsky was the only one present to have taken part in all 500 performances without exception.)

I had two congratulatory messages: the first was from Moscow, and the second from Sakhnovsky, as deputy director. Both made me feel very happy, as they were both very warmly and elegantly expressed.

Nemirovich also sent his congratulations to the Theatre. Looking through what he'd written I could see that it made no mention at all of the author. I suppose that it wouldn't have been good form to mention the author's name. I hadn't been aware of the fact before, but I clearly wasn't sufficiently a man of the world.

One thing irritated me: the fact that, without asking me, the Theatre sent him their thanks for the message, including those of the author. I only wish I'd been able to remove the word "author". [...]

I'm writing a film version of *Dead Souls* and will bring the finished piece with me. And then all the business with *Bliss* will begin. I've got so much work to do! But my *Margarita* is wandering around inside my head, together with the cat, and the flights over the city*... But I'm still a broken man, and feeling weak. It's true that, as each day goes by, I feel a little stronger.

I will muster all the strength that I possibly can for the summer.

Lyusya has called me Captain Kopeykin.* A brilliant witticism that should be appreciated. If it's no trouble, drop into the apartment and have a look at what we're up to here. And give our beautiful lady a ring from time to time (58-67).

I kiss Anna Ilinishna's hand. Lyusya sends you both her greetings. It would be lovely to get a letter from you.

10th July

To Pavel Popov

Dear Pavel,

Thank you for your letter of the 8th. First of all, please forgive me for not saying how sorry I was to hear of the death of your father – my exhausted brain is still not operating to full capacity. [...]

Lyusya confirms that the screenplay is a great success. I showed it to them in draft form, and was right not to do any more work on it. [...]

I listened carefully to everything that Vaysfeld* and his director said to me and, to their astonishment, immediately replied that I would redo it as they wanted.

Something totally unreal has happened here with *Bliss*.

My room at the Astoria. I am reading the play to the theatre director, who is also the producer. He listens, professes his absolute – and apparently sincere – admiration for the piece, states that he is prepared to put it on, promises me money and says he'll come and have supper with me in forty minutes' time. In forty minutes' time he comes back, has supper, doesn't say a single word about the play and then disappears through a hole in the ground and is no more to be seen!

There's a rumour going around that he's vanished into the fourth dimension.

So that's the kind of miraculous event taking place nowadays!

Our warmest greetings to Anna Ilinishna. I kiss you.

11th July

To Vikenty Veresayev

Dear Vikenty Vikentevich!

[...] I have been thinking of you especially often while I've been ill, but haven't written, because you can't write just about the weather. And in order to write a proper letter, you need to be feeling better. And now you have doubly come to mind, as I have just bought N. Teleshov's book *Literary Reminiscences*.* He writes about the nicknames which have been given in literary circles and taken exclusively from the names of Moscow streets and squares. "Kuprin, because of his passion for the circus – Horse Square"; "Bunin,* for his lean appearance and his wit – Knackers Yard" and so on. And then, "Veresayev, for the indestructibility of his opinions – Stone Bridge". I liked that very much. Perhaps you may have read it?

I want to tell you about my unusual adventures this spring.

At the beginning of spring I became extremely ill. I felt very weak, began to suffer from insomnia and then, to cap it all – the foulest thing that has ever happened to me in my life – a fear of being alone or, to be more precise, the fear of remaining alone. Such a revolting feeling that I would have preferred it if someone had cut off my leg!

Well, of course, doctors, sodium bromide and the like. I'm afraid of going outside, I can't write – people either exhaust me or frighten me, I can't look at the newspapers, I go around clutching Yelena Sergeyevna's or Seryozhka's hand – to be on my own is death!

Well, anyway, at the end of April I wrote a request asking to be allowed to go abroad for two months, to France and Rome, together with Yelena Sergeyevna (I've already written to you about this). Seryozhka would remain here – so, in other words, everything would be fine. I sent this off and then sent another letter to G.* But I didn't expect to get any reply to this second letter. Something had happened there, leading to all communication between us being broken. But it wasn't difficult to guess what it was: someone had turned up and said something, as a result of which a barrier had been erected. And, indeed, I didn't get a reply!

I began to wait for a reply to my first submission (to A.S. Yenukidze at the Government Commission, responsible for MAT).

"And you were refused, of course," I can hear you saying. "Nothing unusual in that."

No, Vikenty Vikentevich, I was not refused.

The first thing I heard was that the request had been passed on to the Central Committee.

On 17th May I was lying on the sofa when the telephone rang and some unknown person – presumably some official – said: "You have submitted a request? Go to the Foreign Department of the Executive Committee and fill in forms for you and your wife."

By four o'clock that afternoon the forms had been completed. An official said: "You will receive your passports very soon, as there have been special instructions regarding your case. If you'd come earlier you would have received them today. You'll get them on the 19th."

Yelena and I walked in the sunshine along Tsvetnoy Boulevard to the city centre talking about only one thing. Had we heard correctly? Yes, we'd both heard the same thing, neither of us had been hallucinating.

One of the reasons for the request had been that I wanted to write a book about travelling in Western Europe.

At home we were in seventh heaven. Just imagine: Paris! The Molière memorial... Hello M. Molière, I have written a book and a play about you. Rome! Hello, Nikolai Vasilyevich, please don't be angry, I've turned your *Dead Souls* into a play. It's rather different from what they're performing on stage, it's true – in fact it's totally dissimilar – but nonetheless I tried... The Mediterranean! Ye Gods!...

And I sat down to map out the chapters of the book. Can you believe it?!

How many of our writers have travelled to Europe, and how many of them have brought back absolutely nothing with them! Nothing at all! If our Seryozhka were to be sent abroad he would have more interesting stories to tell about Europe, I think. But perhaps I won't manage to do that? Forgive me, but I'll have a very good try!

On the 19th there were no passports. Similarly on the 23rd, 25th and 27th. Alarmed, I asked once more whether there had been special instructions. Yes, there had. Through the Theatre we heard that the Government Commission had confirmed that "the Bulgakovs' request had been processed".

What else did we need to do? Nothing.

Except wait patiently. So we waited patiently.

Then people started dropping round and congratulating us. Slightly envious. "You lucky people!"

"Wait a moment," I would say, "we haven't got the passports yet."

"Don't worry!" they'd all reply.

We weren't worried, but dreamt about Rome, a balcony, just as described in Gogol, pine trees, roses... a manuscript... dictating to Yelena Sergeyevna... walks in the evening, absolute peace, fragrant air... Just like a romantic novel, in other words!

By September I'll be starting to feel twinges of conscience: Kamergersky Alley, it'll be drizzling there no doubt, the stage will be in semi-darkness, and who knows? Maybe the studios are getting ready for *Molière*...

And so there I am, in the drizzle, putting in an appearance, with the manuscript in my suitcase. You can't better that, can you!

Our people at MAT are the soberest people in the world. They don't believe in any roses or drizzle. But just imagine: they did believe that Bulgakov was going abroad! It was serious, in other words! They believed this so strongly that, in the list of people from MAT who were to be receiving passports (and this year there happened to be many such people), they included Yelena Sergeyevna and me. They gave the list to the courier: off you go, and get the passports.

The courier went and came back again. The expression on his face struck me so unfavourably that, even before he'd managed to say anything, I clutched at my heart.

In short, he had brought everybody's passports except ours. In his hand there was just a piece of white paper with the words "M.A. Bulgakov, refused".

There was not even a bit of paper about Yelena Sergeyevna. Clearly just some woman or other, Jenny Wren! What was the point of saying anything about her?!

My feelings? They were immense, beyond words, I swear by all of Russian literature! The closest perhaps would be to liken them to the crashing of an express train. An express train ready to go, with everything as it should be, with all the signals on green, setting off on its journey – and then suddenly derailed!

I clambered out of the wreckage looking so terrible that I made an unpleasant sight. But here I am now beginning to recover.

Just before I left for Leningrad I wrote to the General Secretary setting out everything that had happened, saying that I wouldn't remain abroad, but would return within the agreed period, and asking him to review the case. There was no reply. I cannot however guarantee that the letter reached its destination.

On 13th June I abandoned everything and left for Leningrad. We'll be returning to Moscow in two days' time. Maybe I shall go to the country near Zvenigorod for a short while. Seryozhka's there with his female tutor. I shall look for peace and calm there, just as the doctor has ordered.

I would be so pleased to get a letter from you. [...]

Yours,
M. Bulgakov

1935

*To Alexander Gdeshinsky**

Dear Sasha!

Thank you for remembering me, and for your kind invitation.

If you imagine that you're living in Kiev, then you're cruelly mistaken! At least, the Kiev Address Office doesn't recognize you as living there.

I was there last August and a woman's hand passed out a piece of paper through the hatch which clearly stated that the name A.P. Gdeshinsky did not exist. There was no one of that name living in Kiev.

I now see, as I had thought, that those puppets of the Devil in the Address Office were lying. You do "exist", and I am very pleased to get your letter. I had gone to Kiev for one reason only – to walk around my native city and to show my wife places which I have at one time written about. She wanted to see them. Sadly we were able to be there for only five days. I couldn't get a room at the Continental. It was good that someone from the city put us up. […]

6th March

Continuation of the letter to Alexander Gdeshinsky

I couldn't complete the letter in one go, as I was interrupted by theatre business. Anyway, I was up on the hill at Kupechesky looking down at the lights on the river and remembering my life in Kiev.

Walking around the parks in the afternoon I was struck by a strange feeling. This was my land! A sweet sadness, mixed with anxiety!

I would so much like to be there again. This is not possible before the summer, or at best the spring (it's the theatre season). But I think I'll be able to come in the summer.

Write and tell me about yourself. Are you married? Where do you work? And, if you can manage it, something about life in Kiev. The travel question is not that simple. If I do come, it will definitely be with my wife, and then all those anxieties with the Continental and so on will arise. So, please write and tell me about yourself!

Yours,
Mikhail

PS: My wife's name is Yelena Sergeyevna. There are three of us living here: my wife, me and eight-year-old Sergei, my stepson, a highly interesting little boy. A bandit with a tin revolver, learning to play the piano.

I would love to get a letter from you.

22nd April

To K.S. Stanislavsky

Most esteemed Konstantin Sergeyevich!

I received today an extract from the record of the *Molière* rehearsal of 17/04/35 sent to me by the Theatre.

Having read this, I feel compelled to reject categorically the proposed revisions to my play *Molière*, since the suggested changes to the Cabal scene, as well as previously proposed textual changes to other scenes, represent, I am convinced, an absolute breach of my original artistic conception and lead to the composition of a new play, of which I cannot be the author, as I radically disagree with it.

If *Molière* is unacceptable to the Arts Theatre in its present form – even though the Theatre originally accepted it and has been rehearsing it for many years in precisely this form – I would ask you to remove the play from the repertoire and return it to me.

Respectfully yours.

20th May

To Vikenty Veresayev

Dear Vikenty Vikentevich!

I can assure you that I am as astonished as you are disheartened. Above all I am astonished at what you have written about the deadline of 1st October.

At your request, I have undertaken boring and difficult negotiations with the theatres that have taken up a great deal of my time.

I have spent day after day negotiating with Volf* and working on the contract. I accepted the deadline of 1st October suggested by the Theatre, told you about this deadline and then sent the contract to you for your signature. You signed the contract, without expressing any objections to 1st October, but now you tell me that you don't like this deadline. What do you want me to do now, now that the contract has been signed by all sides?

I have dutifully undertaken all this, but I don't want to attempt to carry everything out to the best of my ability, only to find people immediately beginning to reproach me for it. If you find that I am drawing up the contracts incorrectly, I willingly agree to your taking this task upon yourself.

I am saying here and now that there is no link at all between the Leningrad deadline of 1st October and the timescale envisaged for the Moscow readings.

As you so rightly say, the reading to the Vakhtangov Theatre group is very important. I would go further than this: it is of the utmost importance, and it would be out of the question for the authors to go ahead with this reading without first mutually agreeing all the issues in the play.

The reading which has been earmarked for the beginning of June or thereabouts cannot take place, under any circumstances, if an agreed text is not yet ready. We shall find ourselves in an absurd position if we submit a text that leads to disagreements. But after getting your unexpected letter I am beginning to fear that this could happen. In that case we shall have, of course, to postpone the reading.

You write that you don't want simply to play the role of a passive presenter of material. You have told me more than once that you are responsible for collating the material for the play, but that you will leave all the dramatic side of things to me. That's what we've done.

But not only have I always been very careful to make use of the material you have given me as precisely as possible, but each time I have ensured that I have made corrections to the drafts as soon as you have objected to anything, without taking into account whether the matter touches on the historical or the dramatic aspects. I have objected only in those cases when your suggestions were not very convincing from the dramatic point of view. [...]

I would like to say, Vikenty Vikentevich, that you are in no way playing the part of a passive presenter of material.

On the contrary: you have insisted very forcefully and categorically that your views should always and everywhere, down to the slightest detail, be woven into the dramatic cloth.

There are moments, however, when your views are incorrect, and I would like to take this opportunity to say that I would not wish to be a passive (using your word) dramatic functionary, not daring to have an opinion about the accuracy of the material being presented to him. [...]

You call D'Anthès's shot "tasteless".* It's good that you're able to express your literary opinion so sharply and directly; by the same token you will of course grant me the right to do the same. I shall take advantage of this right when talking about D'Anthès.

I think that the shot, deriving as it does from Pushkin's own scene of the Silvio shot,* is the most subtle conclusion possible for this scene, and that any other conclusion would be less convincing. I am willing to acknowledge that I lack taste, but it would be difficult to find anyone who said that I lack experience – just as it would be difficult to find someone to maintain that the shot is unhistorical.

In general, you and I don't see eye to eye with regard to D'Anthès. You write: "I find the image of D'Anthès fundamentally false and, as a Pushkin specialist, I am totally unable to take any responsibility for it."

My reply to you is that I, in my turn, consider your image of D'Anthès to be one that is impossible to stage. He is so thin, shallow and emasculated that he cannot be part of a serious play. You cannot cast the murderer of Pushkin, someone who comes to such a tragic end, as if he were some petty little officer character from a comic opera. [...]

Let's turn now to the conversation between Zhukovsky and Dubelt.*

No, your version isn't better than mine, and the reason is simple: the two versions are the same, but with the single difference that whereas your Dubelt speaks a language that is not suitable for the theatre, mine is. The rejoinders sound different, even though the subject matter of the conversation is the same. In this particular instance, there's nothing for us even to be arguing about, in my opinion.

At the end of your letter you say: "I would like to hope that whatever happens, you will remember that the play's authors will appear as Bulgakov and Veresayev, and that we shall be able to arrive at a happy resolution only by taking each other's position mutually into account." That is what I have done, but it has always seemed to me that I have taken your position into account far more than you have mine.

You are mistaken in what you say concerning the happy resolution. We have already reached a happy resolution, at least in the theatre. The day after the reading I talked to Ruslanov.* He spoke about the sense of joy which both he and the rest of the audience had felt. Having heard the reading of a still unpolished and incomplete work he said how extraordinarily successful the authors had been. As someone who was totally exhausted, I found his words uplifting. And, until your letter arrived, I was in an extremely good frame of mind. But now, I must confess, I feel anxious. Having read through your letter and my reply once again, I am unable to understand what has brought all this on.

In any case, if we destroy this success, we will have destroyed it ourselves, and that will be very sad. We have put too much hard work into this play to allow it to be ruined so easily.*

After reading your letter I find it difficult to raise my pen, but I am making a real effort and am now writing the ball scene.

When the play has been completed I will send a copy to you. And then we shall get together for a critical look at the text, in order to iron out any disagreements, to correct any inaccuracies and to rectify any hackneyed images.

Despite what you have said, I nurture the hope that we shall be able to come to an agreement. With all my heart I would like these letters to sink into oblivion and only the play, which you and I have created with such passion, to live on.

Your devoted M. Bulgakov

27th August

To *Vikenty Veresayev*

Dear Vikenty Vikentevich!

Thank you for your letter of 22nd August saying you would like me to hand over the play to the Theatre in the form that I think is necessary, but that you reserve the right to fight, in so far as you possibly can, for the removal of any distortions of historical truth within the play and for a stronger depiction of the social background.

My view is that you, who were perfectly correct when you wrote that any work of art cannot have two equally powerful masters, that there must be one master and that, in our case, only I, as the person with the greater right, can be that master – and that you, as the person who wrote the following words: "None of this means that I refuse to help you further in any feasible way, on the understanding that it will be interpreted by you as simple advice which does not commit you to anything" – my view is that you are not even in a position to bring up the question of such a fight.

But let's turn now to the business matters which you raise in your letter.

As far as the submission of the play to theatres is concerned I am sending you a copy of the final corrected version, on which I am placing, as before, two names: M. Bulgakov and V. Veresayev. If, having gone through this final version, you should wish to add your signature to mine, I will send it to the theatre with the two signatures appended. But if you should wish to remove your signature, please tell me that this is what you want to do, and I will send off the play under just one name.

In so far as the reading of the play is concerned, you have the right to read the play only to private individuals, whereas I have the right to read it not only to private individuals, but also to all producers, directors and representatives of any theatres to whom I find it necessary to read it. This is in accordance with our agreement, which gives me the right to finalize contracts with theatres, with such readings being not only my right, but also my duty.

But neither of us individually has the right to read the play to the Pushkin Commission or any other such body, as this relates to the very serious question of the agreement not only between the co-authors, but also between the co-authors and the theatres with which there are existing contracts.

In so far as your suggested revisions are concerned, I – for my part – have no objection to you presenting them to theatres. If you decide to do this, you will have to submit these amendments to the Vakhtangov Theatre in Moscow and the Red Theatre in Leningrad, with an explanatory letter, and then inform me that you have done so. For my part, I will then inform the theatres of my absolute refusal to include these amendments in the play, since in my opinion they would be fatal to it.

In so far as the agreement between the co-authors is concerned, this must of course be finalized. In view of the fact that your declaration of war has given rise to a difficult, not to say confused situation, I suggest that you be responsible for working out the clauses of the agreement. We will discuss this and, if there are no disagreements between us, we shall sign it.

There is one clause in this agreement that I see as non-negotiable and incontrovertible: that the co-authors shall divide any royalties from this play into half, with each author receiving 50% of the total.

Yours,

M. Bulgakov

1936

To S.A. Yermolinsky*

I was so pleased, dear Seryozha, to find your letter in the thin bundle waiting for me when I returned home!

Greetings to you and Marika!

Your description of the Sinop* was fantastic; I so want to see the sea.

Kiev is such a dazzling place that I would like to move there from Moscow and live the rest of my life above the River Dnieper.

I suppose that this is simply a temporary flash in the pan, arising from an awareness of the hopelessness of my position, an awareness that is tearing both Lyusya and me to pieces.

There was an extremely interesting reaction when I spoke about my idea to some of the MAT people. They all reacted in the same way: with a bewildered, anxious expression and with total disapproval, as if I had made an indecent remark. I observed them all with great interest!

I don't want to talk about guest performers; I'm tired of the Theatre. They've put on *The Turbins*, but without the Petlyura scene.

Markov has told Lyusya that the press has decided not to write about *The Turbins*.

But I will write about one scene with a guest performer.

I was at the Directorate of Authors' Rights in Kiev settling the advance royalties to be paid to me. Everything was agreed in an atmosphere of astonishing goodwill. I was to come on such and such a date and, moreover, such and such a person would be letting me know exactly when. All very nice.

Such and such a person, however, didn't tell me exactly which date I should come. And when we went again the next day, what do you think? It wasn't the same people. Or rather, it was the same people, but with different faces. But where was this person?

He was ill.

I was very sorry to hear that, but please could I have the money you promised me. Blank expressions!

Finally, they managed to force themselves to ask: "Is it true that *The Turbins* is being taken off?"

I shuddered. What could I say in reply? What? What nonsense was this? And what about *Molière*?

I said that this was the first I had heard of it, but I didn't think it could be true.

As you yourself will understand, I didn't get my money on that day.

They asked me to come again the next day.

And so we go again the next day. Again, what a transformation! Everybody was there. Bright faces, welcoming eyes. "Please come to the cash desk, sign a receipt" and so on. The man who was ill had fully recovered.

I asked who had started that nonsensical rumour.

Awkward pause. I said that I would like to feast my eyes on whoever it was.

Smiles.

"But you have just feasted your eyes on him! You have just been talking to him! Tee-hee!"

And then I remembered. Just before I had been given the money some ghastly-looking chap had fawned up to me.

"Permit me to introduce myself to you, Comrade Bulgakov. I was so enraptured by your *Turbins* that I wanted to come up to you during the performance, but I didn't seize the opportunity. Oh, what a wonderful play! What a…"

Compliments, handshakes and all that dreadful nonsense. I asked him who I had the pleasure of talking to. He turned out to be a writer – couldn't make out the name, the author of *Ukraziya* or something.

I told him how much I regretted that I didn't know this piece.

Then this awful man showered me with more compliments, said goodbye and disappeared. It turned out that he had been the person who had showed up at the Directorate and falsely stated that *The Turbins* was being taken off. It was because of him that the whispering had started, that people had started running about and going off to find out whether the rumour was true.

When we left, Lyusya said: "We can't go on living like this."

When the train left and I was looking, perhaps for the last time, at the Dnieper, someone peddling books came into the compartment and sold Lyusya a copy of *Theatre and Plays* No. 4.

I saw her turn pale as she read it. My name was everywhere. But what stuff it was they were writing about me!

Meyerhold had written some particularly vile things about me. This man is so lacking in principles that you imagine he doesn't wear trousers, but walks about the place just in his underpants.

Yes, she was right. It is impossible to go on living like this, and I won't go on doing it. I keep on thinking what I should do, and will arrive at an answer, whatever it might cost me.

Kisses and friendly greetings to you and to Marika from Lyusya. Also from me.

When are you coming?

Yours,
Mikhail

17th August

*To Ya.L. Leontiev**

Sukhumi, Hotel Sinop

Dear Yakov Leontievich!
My poor head feels as if it's had a rest. I'm beginning to talk to friends that I remember with great fondness.

The Sinop is a wonderful hotel: it's such a relaxing place. It has a park and billiards. There are balconies. It's close to the sea, spacious and clean. There's just one drawback – the food. Boring and monotonous. You'll agree yourself that the use of arcane words on the menu is not any consolation: *Zwiebel klops*, *bœuf Stroganoff*, stuffed something or other... *languette piquante* and so on. Hidden under each of these words lies one and the same thing: a dog's dinner. Many of us, including me, take our foreign medicines and feed on rice and bilberry-milk jelly.

But everything else is fine. There aren't many people I don't like, but I have to say my sister-in-law, Olga, is one of them. She arrived here with such a clatter that even I, with all my imaginative understanding, was astonished. And now, from morning to night, she brings down curses on the entire coastline: the mountains, the air, the magnolias, the cypresses, Zhenya for bringing her here and the balcony for the fact that it has a palm tree next to it. She says that everyone has to be kicked out of here and replaced by citrus plants. In short, she doesn't like anyone, apart from Nemirovich. She started off by nearly succeeding in drowning herself. And if Yershov hadn't dashed into the water as he was, with all his clothes on, and dragged her out, there would have been a major disaster. Lyusya is well, which makes me very happy. Life is difficult for us, and I will be happy if she's able to recoup her energy here.

I didn't read at all at first, trying not to think about anything and to forget it all. But now I have begun to translate *The Merry Wives of Windsor* for MAT. And while we're on the subject, there has been some amazing news from MAT. The sponsors and benefactors are showing such class that one can only gasp open-mouthed. But I'll leave more about that until we meet. Lyusya tells me that I am a prophet!

Oh, my dear Yakov Leontievich, what's going to happen to me in the autumn? What should I do? Go to a fortune-teller?...

We're planning to leave here on 27th–28th August, travelling via Tiflis and Vladikavkaz (Ordzhonokidze).

I would be very pleased if you were able to write to me here. Lyusya sends her warmest friendly greetings. Don't forget!

Yours,

M. Bulgakov

1937

9th February

To Nikolai Bulgakov

Dear Kolya!

[...] Fischer Verlag* have written to say they've broken with Kagansky, and that the Ladyzhnikov Publishing House is planning to start legal proceedings against Kagansky because of *Zoyka's Apartment*. However, he is still behaving as if he is a representative of Fischer-Ladyzhnikov.

I'm hurrying to finish this letter so I can send it off. I'm continuing to look in the archives and will send the next letter to you very soon.

I think the most important point is that, as a result of an oversight in my letter to Ladyzhnikov of 8th October 1928, there's no mention of any termination date. It seems absolutely clear to me that it's null and void. (Otherwise what would we be left with? A never-ending binding obligation?) But if this fact is not acknowledged in Paris and if the battle for my full rights does not meet with success, we must at the very least make sure that that part of my royalties which is recognized as being irrefutably mine should not be sent to Berlin (to Fischer). Please tell the Société that I cannot do business with the people in Berlin, as they are not sending me any money. In other words, my royalties will disappear altogether. The fight with Kagansky must be to the death: it's monstrous to think that a notorious scoundrel like this can get hold of literary royalties. If the worst comes to the worst and he nonetheless succeeds in passing himself off as a "representative", we need to do everything possible to ensure he doesn't get his hands on at least that part of the royalties which is clearly mine.

I understand how difficult and how confusing everything is! But it's all so difficult for me too! Kisses.

11th February

To Nikolai Bulgakov

Dear Kolya!

I don't possess, and have never possessed, any contract in French between M.P. Reinhardt and myself. On 5th July 1933 she sent me a letter in French, which I am enclosing with this letter, and to which I replied with two letters of my own, copies of which I am also enclosing. In addition I am enclosing Fischer's letter to me of 20th October 1933, in which they say the following: "*Ferner haben wir zur Kenntnis genommen, dass Ihr Herr Bruder für Ihr Stück* Zoykas Wohnung *Vollmacht besitzt*", meaning: "In addition, we have been made aware that your brother possesses the rights to your play *Zoyka's Apartment*." It's clear from this that I had told Fischer I had given you the rights relating to the play. And this is what I had said:

"I am writing to inform you that all rights relating to the staging and protection of my play *Zoyka's Apartment* outside the borders of the USSR, together with the receipt of all royalties for this play, have been granted in full under power of attorney to my brother Nikolai Afanasyevich Bulgakov, residing at 11 Rue Jobbé Duval, Paris, XVe, a member of the French Society of Playwrights and Composers. M. Docteur M. Boulgakow. You will need to address all questions relating to the staging of *Zoyka's Apartment* abroad to N.A. Bulgakov." (My letter of 6th October 1933, paragraph 2.)

I ought to add that, in a later letter to me of 21st February 1934, the Fischer company told me that they had understood my declaration as meaning you had been granted the rights to a share of the proceeds deriving from the performances. As far as I can remember, I didn't reply to this.

That's all I can say for the moment.

Yours,

M. Bulgakov

13th February

To B.V. Asafyev*

Dear Boris Vladimirovich!

A young composer called Petunin* has approached me saying he would like to compose an opera about Peter the Great,* for which he would like me to write the libretto.

I replied that I had had such an idea in my head for a long time, and that I intended to write one. But at the same time I said that this theme had been one of your ideas as well, and that if you wanted to compose an opera about Peter I would write the libretto for you.

And so would you like to do Peter, or do you want to focus on something else, something which you and I can think about doing?

If you don't want to do Peter I shall tell Petunin that he will be free to write the opera if he wishes, and since I will, I imagine, be writing the libretto in any case (if the Bolshoi accept the subject), he should start negotiating with the Bolshoi and see how it goes, particularly since he's pinning all his hopes on this opera.

Please write and let me know as soon as possible.

Greetings to your wife and yourself.

M. Bulgakov

22nd March

To P.M. Kerzhentsev*

To the Chairman of the All-Union Committee on Cultural Matters of the USSR Council of Peoples' Commissars Platon Mikhailovich Kerzhentsev.

From Mikhail Afanasyevich Bulgakov, playwright and consultant librettist, Bolshoi Theatre.

I am writing to you to complain about certain actions that the Kharkov Theatre of Russian Drama (director: Ya. Teatralov) have taken concerning me.

On 18th November 1936 I concluded an agreement with said Theatre for the staging of the play *Alexander Pushkin* written by me* in conjunction with V.V. Veresayev.

Today I received a summons from the Theatre to appear at the Moscow City Court with the aim of recovering the sum of 3,038 roubles from V.V. Veresayev and myself, which had been paid to the authors according to the agreement.

According to the Theatre's written statement, the basis for the action was that "M.A. Bulgakov offered his play *Alexander Pushkin* to the Theatre without first obtaining permission to stage the play from the State Repertory Committee, and that he thereby misled the Theatre of Russian Drama, causing the theatre a loss of 3,038 roubles".

I wish to let it be known that, as is evident from the agreement, I never undertook to offer the Theatre a play for which permission had already been granted, and that I, in accordance with the law, have the right to recover money from the Theatre for not staging the play, rather than the Theatre seeking to recover any sum from me. I strongly refute therefore the defamatory claim that I "misled the Theatre", for I have never misled any theatre in my life.

More generally, from my perspective, my position is becoming more and more difficult. I am not referring to the fact that I am not able to put onto the Russian stage a single one of the plays that I have written over the last few years; I have become totally reconciled to that. But now, as if to reward me in some way for my labours as a playwright, including my play about Pushkin, I have not only been forced to defend myself against baseless attempts to demand money from me (the case I have described here is not the first), but have also been subjected to defamation of my literary name.

This is the basis of the complaint I am addressing to you.

M. Bulgakov
22nd March 1937

24th March

To Pavel Popov

I haven't written to you before this because we are so frantically busy the whole time, rushing about in the most trying and unpleasant circumstances. Many people told me that the signs were that 1936 was not good for me, as it was a leap year. But the signs were wrong: I can now see that, in so far as I am concerned, 1937 is no better than its predecessor.

Amongst other things, I have to go to court on 2nd April – smart operators from the Kharkov Theatre are attempting to force some money out of me, taking advantage of the unhappy fate of *Pushkin*. I can't hear the name Pushkin now without shuddering, and I constantly curse myself for conceiving the ill-fated idea of writing a play about him.

Some well-meaning people have chosen a rather strange means of attempting to console me. More than once I've heard suspiciously unctuous voices saying, "Don't worry – everything will be published after your death!" I am of course very grateful to them!

I would like there to be an entr'acte. Yelena Sergeyevna and I invite Anna Ilinichna and you to come and have tea with us on the 28th at ten o'clock in the evening. Drop me a line or give me a ring and let us know whether you can come.

Greetings, kisses!
                         Yours,
                              M. Bulgakov

18th June

To S.A. Yermolinsky

Dear Seryozha!

[...] This is how things are with us: Sergei is at his music teacher's dacha in Lionozovo* with Yekaterina Ivanovna. He's already gashed his leg on a nail, hurt his eye fencing and cut his hand with a penknife. To my great joy, he lost his knife after that happened, and I hope he won't be allowed to slink off to the pond again any more.

We're sitting here in Moscow, settled once and for all like flies in jam, and without hope. I no longer have any hope of travelling anywhere, unless there is some sort of miracle. But, as every grown-up person will understand, there won't be a miracle.

So I take advantage of every opportunity to get to the River Moscow, where I can do some rowing and swimming... Otherwise, everything will come to a sticky end: life is impossible without being able to rest.

I have a pile of material relating to Peter the Great on my desk – I'm beginning work on the libretto. I know for certain that, in any event, nothing will come of it, and that it won't survive, just as *Minin* and *The Black Sea* have not survived,* but I cannot refrain from writing. In any case, I will always be aware that I have always done my duty with regard to the Bolshoi Theatre to the very best of my ability, and it's up to them to decide what to do when I stop being interested not only in the libretto, but in anything else.

What else is there to report? Well, all kinds of life's boring and stupid problems of course.

Kuza came round with an absurd proposal to adapt *Nana* or *Bel-Ami* for the stage.*

I was tempted at first, but came to my senses after I'd reread the novels. Really! Just to be able to go to the seaside somewhere for two weeks and burden oneself with a mass of difficult backbreaking work which will come to nothing in the end! No, that is too high a price to pay!

Lyusya and I sit up until daybreak, always talking about the same topic: the end of my literary life. We've considered every possible way out, and there are no means of salvation left.

It's impossible to undertake anything – it's all totally hopeless.

So there's a cheerful letter for you!

I wish you success in your work, and I hope Marika will fully recover very soon.

Come and see us, and don't forget that there are people in Nashchokinsky who love you.

I embrace you in friendship – twice, once from me and once from Lyusya. Please kiss Marika twice for me and write, if you are able to find the time.

> Yours,
> Mikhail

17th July

To Ya.L. Leontiev

Zhitomir, Bogunya, Tarasevich's dacha*

Dear friends,
It's so lovely here! Here I am, enjoying the sun, the little river, the acacias, the lime trees, the sweet-smelling air, and basking in the hope that I can recover from my exhaustion. Lyusya and I send you tender kisses, and we'll write a detailed letter too.

Yours,

M. Bulgakov

16th August

To *the Board of the Playwrights' Section of the Union of Soviet Writers*

Dear comrades!

I returned to Moscow to find a letter of 29/7/37 from the Board of the Playwrights' Section waiting for me. In this letter the Board asks me how my work on a play to commemorate the twentieth anniversary of the October Revolution is progressing.

To my great regret I have to inform the Board that I have not been writing plays for the theatre for more than a year now.

The reason for this is as follows: at the beginning of 1936 all the theatres suddenly withdrew all the plays that I had written during the last few years. After a number of performances the Moscow Arts Theatre took off my *Molière*; the Moscow Theatre of Satire withdrew my comedy *Ivan Vasilyevich** after the first dress rehearsal; and the Vakhtangov Theatre stopped the work that was just beginning on my play *Alexander Pushkin*.

The removal of these plays of different genres from the repertoire was accompanied by the appearance of articles in the press, the character of which indicated to me with absolute clarity that any further attempt on my part to write plays or to offer them to theatres would be totally pointless.

I have been forced to switch to other work and to become an opera librettist. At present I am completing a libretto for the opera *Peter the Great*.

The Bureau asks me whether I need any help from them. In reply I will tell them that I do need it. The Board would help me in my literary work if they

(1) (immediately) supported me in my hitherto unsuccessful and repeated requests to be offered an apartment on Lavrushinsky Alley, an apartment that is more spacious than my present one at No. 3 Furmanov Street, for in the latter I am quite unable to

engage in literary work because of the cramped circumstances, and

(2) supported me as a matter of urgency in my request to the Directorate of Authors' Rights to release an advance of three thousand roubles on my author's royalties. The fact that my plays have been taken off the stage as described above has made my material circumstances extraordinarily more complicated and has therefore proved to be a hindrance to my work.

With comradely greetings
M. Bulgakov

2nd October

To B.V. Asafyev

Please forgive this typed letter, dear Boris Viktorovich. I have a cold, and I'm just lying here, dictating.

I haven't written to you before now because, until very recently, I didn't actually know what would happen to my *Peter*. And then, suddenly, I've been overwhelmed by a whole mass of urgent work which has taken up all my time recently.

I'll begin with the end: my *Peter* is now no more – that is to say, it's lying here in front of me revised and rewritten, but there's hardly any sense left in it, as they say.

And now, in the right order: when I had completed the libretto I submitted one copy to the Bolshoi and, to speed matters up, I sent another copy to Kerzhentsev. Kerzhentsev then sent me a critical ten-point analysis of my work. The main thing to say about these ten points is that they would be extraordinarily difficult to carry out, and that, in any case, they would mean I would have to start the whole thing from the beginning again, burying my head in the historical material.

Without any further ado, Kerzhentsev says in his letter that much more work needs to be done and that what I had done so far was simply a "first approximation to the topic".

So now I find myself at a crossroads. Should I redo it, not redo it, start on something else or abandon it altogether? I will probably be forced to redo it out of necessity, but I cannot guarantee at all whether I will be successful.

Pashayev* has read through the libretto, and I agree with much of what he says: there are faults of a purely operatic nature. But, I would suggest, they can be corrected. So we are left only with the points in Kerzhentsev's letter.

Now with regard to the composer. The Theatre has told me that I must submit the libretto, and that the question of the choice of a composer is a matter for the Committee and the Theatre. I said as forcefully as I could just how desirable it would be if you could be the composer. I couldn't do any more. But this of course will be a matter that will be decided by the Committee.

It seems to me that, once the libretto has been completed and accepted, you should approach the Committee yourself. And I would of course be genuinely happy if this were to result in success!

I'm now sitting here looking for a solution to this, and I don't seem to have one. It's not simply a question of trying to decide about *Peter*. In the course of the last seven years I have produced sixteen pieces in various different genres and they have all bitten the dust. Such a situation is impossible, and our household is sunk in gloom and despair.

Irrespective of *Peter*, I would be very pleased to get a letter from you. Yelena Sergeyevna and I send our greetings to Irina Stepanovna.*

Yours,
M. Bulgakov

18th December

To B. V. Asafyev

Dear Boris Vladimirovich!
I have received your letter of the 15th; I found it astonishing.
Your idea that people have suggested to me that I should not
have any dealings with you has no foundation whatever. Nobody
has made any such suggestion to me, and if anyone were to
take it into their head to do so, then I'm hardly the sort of
person who would obey! But, in any case, I was convinced
you knew me well enough to know I'm not like other people.
Shame on you!

Now I have some important news for you concerning *Minin*.
On 14th December I was invited to a meeting with Kerzhentsev,
who told me that he had given his progress report on *Minin*, and
there and then asked me, as a matter of urgency, to start work
on amendments to the libretto, which he insisted needed to be
done. [...]

So what do I do about it? I immediately start work on the amendments and, at the same time, try to get Kerzhentsev to listen to the
latest version on the piano. [...]

I don't know what the future has in store for *Minin*, but at this
moment I have the clear impression that it has been restored to
life. In the light of past events, I suppose I can understand the
reaction of the All-Union Committee towards the staging. Of
course I know you didn't write *Minin* when you were asleep,
any more than I wrote the libretto when I was asleep, but for
its part the Committee considers that work on the opera is
proceeding. The opera is being put on as a major work; and
since, in the Committee's opinion, it can proceed, not in its
original form, but with the necessary amendments which I have
referred to above, then it's quite natural that they aren't giving
the go-ahead for the staging and that they're replying that it's

"not yet confirmed" and is "in the process of being written" and so on.

So that's the main thing I wanted to say, and I'm now in a hurry to send the letter off (the haste explains why I'm dictating it – my apologies). Have you got my telegram, which I sent yesterday?

I will of course keep you informed about any future events, but I would ask you please to write to me immediately should you have any questions about what I have written here. Greetings to your wife.

    Yours,
        M. Bulgakov

1938

To Y.V. Stalin

From the playwright Mikhail Afanasyevich Bulgakov

Highly esteemed Yosif Vissarionovich!

Permit me to turn to you with a request concerning the playwright Nikolai Erdman,* who has served out his three-year term of exile in the cities of Yeniseysk and Tomsk, and who is now living in the city of Kalinin.*

Convinced, as I am, of the extraordinary level of literary talent in our country, and aware at the same time that the writer N. Erdman is now deprived of the possibility of applying his particular gifts as a result of the sharply negative attitude towards him in the press, I would respectfully ask that you pay special attention to his fate.

In the hope that N. Erdman's lot will be eased if you are able to view this request in a positive light, I would fervently ask that he be allowed to return to Moscow and to continue with his literary career without any hindrance, so that he may put behind him his state of isolation and spiritual depression.

M. Bulgakov

*Letters to Yelena Bulgakova in Lebedyan**

27th May

To Yelena Bulgakova

My darling Lyusenka,
I send you many loving kisses!

One thing concerns me: how did it all go, getting off the train with all those people accompanying you? I hope you're alive and well after that train journey. I thought there would be a telegram today, but Nastya* said: "What do you mean, telegram? They're all at the market."

When your train left the station it was accompanied by jazz being played over the loudspeaker. The now remunerated Yevgeny* sat on our sofa, thoughtfully counting his money, had lunch with me and wrote letters for Nastya.

That evening there was the scene with Susanin* in the forest at the Bolshoi, then I was at Yakov Leontievich's.* Later – Pilate.* Oh, what difficult, confusing stuff! That was yesterday. But today, I'm afraid, will determine the shape of my entire summer.

At eleven a.m. I was with Solovyov and the librettist (the director is Ivanov)*. Two hours of the most exhausting conversation, with all kinds of problems to solve. And then the telephone rang: Mordvinov on Pototsky, the composer Yurovsky on his *Opanas*,* Olga on the typing of the novel,* and then Yevgeny* inviting himself here for lunch tomorrow, and finally Gorodetsky* also on *Opanas*.

In the middle of all this, Seryozha Yermolinsky. Went for a walk together, then lunch here. He took some old journals and invited me to his dacha, and we talked about you.

This evening Pilate. Not very fruitful. Distracted by Solovyov. There's a gap in the material. It's good that it's not in the second chapter. I hope I'll be able to fill it in while typing.

There's an interesting letter from the Gorky archive (addressed, of course, to Pirogovskaya Street, 35a, Apartment 6!).

"According to our information (?!) you have in your possession some original manuscripts of Alexei Maximovich's…" so please, they ask, would you hand them in to the archive. I will write to them tomorrow and tell them that their information is wrong and that I have no such documents of Gorky's in my possession.

Well, it's night-time already. I'm tired, the bath water's running, and it's time to go to bed.

I kiss you once more, my darling. Please, I beg you, don't forget to rest. Don't give a moment's thought to theatres, or to Nemirovich, or to playwrights, and don't read anything other than grimy and dog-eared foreign novels (or perhaps they don't have such things in Lebedyan?).

May the Lebedyan sun shine on you like a sunflower, and the sunflower (if there are sunflowers in Lebedyan) on you like the sun.

Yours always,

M.

Kiss Sergei, and tell him that I am counting on him to look after you!

Night of 1st–2nd June

To Yelena Bulgakova

Your long letter of the 31st came today, darling Lyu. After I had finished dictating the novel I wanted to start writing a long letter to you, but I don't have the energy. Even Olga, with all her unparalleled typist's stamina, fled from the typewriter today. I'll write to you tomorrow, but for now a bath, a bath! There are 132 pages of typescript. Roughly speaking, that's about one third of the novel (if you include the cutting-down of long-winded passages). <...>*

I shall try to dream about the (Lebedyan) sun and sunflowers. Loving kisses.

      Yours, M.

2nd June

To Yelena Bulgakova

My dear Lyu!
First of all, you'll see glued on the corner a picture of a lady, or to be more precise fragments of this lady, who has been rescued by me from destruction. I'm constantly thinking of this lady, and to help me think I keep fragments like this in front of me.

I shall divide this letter up into small chunks like this: otherwise I won't be able to cope – there's so much that's come up.

To begin with, the novel. As I said in my postcard, almost a third has now been completed in typescript. I have to give Olga her due: she works well. We write for several hours at a time, quietly groaning from tiredness, but it's the right kind of tiredness, not a torment.

And so everything, apparently, is fine, when suddenly an evil genius comes out onto the stage from the wings…With your usual quick-wittedness you will immediately exclaim:
"Nemirovich!"
And you're quite right; that's exactly who it is.
It turns out, as I already knew and have already said, that all those stories your sister tells about him being so thin, with the doctors concealing… and so on, and so on, are just nonsense and lies of the Karlsbad-Marienbad variety. He's as fit as Gogol's coach driver, idling about in Barvikha,* and pestering Olga with all kinds of nonsense.
Disenchanted finally with Barvikha, where there's no Astoria, no actors or actresses and so on, he's begun to threaten us with his presence in Moscow on the 7th. And your sister has already triumphantly announced that there'll now be some interruptions to the work. And that's not all: glowing from happiness, she added that perhaps he'll be "taking her off to Leningrad" on the 15th!

Wouldn't it be good if Woland* were to fly to Barvikha! Alas, such things only happen in novels! Any interruption in the typing would mean the end! I lose the connecting ideas, the thread of the corrections and the harmony of the whole. The typing has to be finished, whatever the cost.

I'm already feverishly beginning to wrack my brains as to where I can find someone to do the typing. It seems an impossible task, of course. He's already taken your sister off to Barvikha today, which means I'm losing a whole day.

I think I'll find out today whether he's taking her off to Leningrad or not.

I must finish the novel! Now! Now!

Please, please, I ask you in all seriousness not to write *a single word* to Olga about the typing and the interruption to my work. Otherwise she'll poison my life once and for all with her rude comments, with her "worm in the apple", with her questions asking whether I think that "I'm the only one", with her howls of "Vladimir Ivanovich!!",* her "poof-poofs" and other shots from her arsenal which are so familiar to you.

I've already had my fill of it all these last few days. So, if you don't want her to ride roughshod over my soul, then *not a word about the typing.* I need to focus all of my mind on the novel.

When she's in an especially good mood she refers to Nemirovich as "that old cynic", erupting in peals of happy laughter.

That's the sort of thing I find nauseating! Oh, goodness, I've written to you asking you not to think about the theatre or Nemirovich, and here I am doing it myself. But could one ever have thought that he could somehow represent a threat even to the novel? But no, no, don't worry: I shall finish it.

In haste to give Nastya the letter. I'll be writing again immediately.

Yours,

M

3rd June
Afternoon

To Yelena Bulgakova

[...] Yes, the novel... I have an unbearable itch in my fingers to convey its spirit as it emerges onto the typed pages, but regretfully I have to forgo this! Otherwise I would have been able to entertain you a little! [...]

You ask me sorrowfully whether I really have so many unnecessary and distracting telephone calls in the course of a single day. What are you saying, Dundik? That I really don't have these calls? But it is as I have described: I really do have them.

The next day I could have added to this list a certain Mokrousov* (perhaps you don't know him – the composer?) talking about some libretto at Stanislavsky's place, and various other things.

I have got used to sharing my burden with you, so that's why I write and tell you about it! When it all mounts up I write and tell you in the order that it happens. But you'll know how to sort it all out.

I like your phrase "you should show your novel to Vladimir Ivanovich". (I read this at a moment when I was feeling especially bewildered and lost in thought.)

Yes, of course, of course! I'm simply dying with impatience to show my novel to such a philistine.

Kukva! I was particularly struck by one point in your letter of the 31st. About the Gorky manuscripts. Cross yourself, Klyunik! You so disturbed my peace of mind that, even though I knew perfectly well that I didn't have a single line – or even a single letter from the alphabet – of Gorky's in my possession, I started totally fruitless

searches, digging around in Zamyatin's and Veresayev's letters, to
see if they contained anything connected with Gorky's, but there
was no trace of him!

I repeat, I don't have any Gorky material! But if I did, what
would be the point of saying I didn't? I would willingly give it to
the museum! I'm not a collector of such material. Your memory is
letting you down, Kukochka, and it's all become a little awkward:
I write and tell you that I don't have any, and then you tell me that
I do!

That must be Korovyov* or the cat playing a joke on you. It's the
work of some magical choirmaster!

Let's stay away from this topic in future! There's quite enough
to write about as it is!

Forgive me! Here's Olga, back from Barvikha. Loving kisses.

Yours,

M.

14th June
Evening

To Yelena Bulgakova

Darling Lyusi!
Your letter (of the 12th), postcard (of the 13th) and telegram (sent today) all arrived today. Fondest love and kisses to you! Lyu! You shouldn't go swimming three times like that! Stay in the shade and don't exhaust yourself going round the market. Let the others get the eggs!... Look around you at the beautiful countryside and remember me. Don't do too much walking. What I mean is: are you keeping well? Please reply!

I wonder why Sergei hasn't replied to my letter marked "Secret. For Sergei's eyes only", in which I charged him to let me know how you were? Surely he must have got it?

Here are some scenes from everyday life, for your entertainment:

1.

Peasant woman. Invites Nastasya to... go on a trip with her.

2.

Old Praskovya, who used to work for us. Claimed some frying pans or other which she had "left with us so that they could be greased". She talked to Nastasya, as I was on the telephone at the time.

3.

A.P.* (*doing her nails*): Is Yelena Sergeyevna missing home yet?
   I (*smoking, lost in thought*): But she's only been away for a few days. Let her relax and have a good time.

197

A.P. (*mistrustfully*): Yes... of course... (*Pause.*) L.K. sends her regards and asked me to say that one of these days she'll come and spend the night here.

I: That's very kind of her. (*I pause for a moment and picture to myself the following scene: I'm talking to Dmitriev,* Nastasya is sleeping at Sergei's and the old woman is asleep on the grand piano.*) My regards to her! (*To myself.*) I've got to put a stop to this!...

4.

Frantic yells from L.K. over the telephone. "Congratulations! Congratulations! Congratulations! Was there a telegram?"

My heart misses a beat. A miracle? *Escape*? "What's going on, L.K.?"

The yelling increases in intensity. "For Konstantin! For Konstantin! Konstantin and Yelena! A telegram!"

"Oh, I see: you're talking about the name day? But that was a few days ago now. I sent my congratulations."

Howls. "No! A telegram! No! There wasn't a telegram! For Konstantin! There wasn't a telegram! For Konstantin! A telegram! From me as well! For Konstantin!"

"L.K.! A.P. has told me that you wanted to come and spend the night here. What's the point of going to so much trouble?" Sudden silence of the grave at the other end of the line. Then an extremely embarrassed and irritated voice: "That would be A.P. lying again. She goes around to other people's apartments and lies about me... Now if you were to invite me, that would be a different matter!"

5.

Sist.* (*joyously, triumphantly*): I have written to Vladimir Ivanovich to say that you were extremely flattered that Vladimir Ivanovich had sent you his respects.

I erupt. How dare she write in my name and say things that I didn't say. I tell her I'm not at all flattered. I remind her that the message sent in response to Nemirovich from Leningrad on the occasion of the *Turbins* celebration included my name without my agreement.

S. greatly bewildered that, for the first time in her life, she was the object rather than the initiator of a row. Mutters that I "can't have understood" and that she can "show me the copy".

6.

Sist. (*in a businesslike voice*): I've written to Zhenya* to say that I still can't see the main point of your novel.

I (*dully*): What did you do that for?

Sist. (*not noticing the look I'm giving her*): Well, I'm not saying that there won't be one at all. After all, I haven't got to the end yet. But I can't see it at the moment.

I (*to myself*): ......!

15th June
a.m.

To Yelena Bulgakova

<...> I've heard that you're still in the habit of burning letters. If you've stopped doing that now, I hope at any rate that my letters aren't lying on the sideboard together with the eggs? My wish is to talk to you and to you alone. Incidentally, Sergei's puzzling silence makes me wonder whether all my letters have arrived. The letter with the brief extract from the dictionary about the helianthus, for example. Please let me know.

About 327 pages of typescript are lying in front of me (about 22 chapters). If I stay fit and healthy the typing will soon be finished. Then the most important thing will remain: the author's correction of the manuscript – important, complicated and painstaking work, including possibly retyping some pages.

"What's going to happen to it?" you ask. I don't know. You'll probably put it away in your desk or in the cupboard, together with all the rejected plays, and you'll think about it from time to time. However, we don't know the future.

I've already formed a judgement about the work and, if I can succeed in developing the conclusion a little more, then I will consider that the whole work is worth correcting, and that it will be worth putting it away into a dark drawer.

I'm now interested in knowing what you think of it, but whether I will ever know what readers think of it is known to no one.

My esteemed typist has been a great help to me in ensuring that my own assessment of the work has been an extremely rigorous one. She smiled just once, on page 245 (the sentence beginning

"The glorious sea…"), out of a total of 327 pages. Why she should find that passage so amusing, I don't know. I'm not sure whether she'll be able to unravel the novel's central thread, but I am sure that it will meet with her total disapproval. This was reflected in the following enigmatic comment: "This novel is your own private thing" (?!). By that she probably meant that it wasn't her fault!

I can just imagine what she'll be saying in Lebedyan, but I can't imagine what she's already been saying in her letters!

Ku! I kiss you tenderly for your invitation and for your care for me. My only happy dream is the thought of seeing you, and I shall try to do everything to see that this is realized. But I cannot guarantee I'll be successful. The fact is, Ku, that I've started to feel unwell and, if it's anything like today and this evening for example, then it will be very unlikely that I will be able to come. I didn't want to write and tell you this, but I can't help it. But I hope I will get better all the same, and then I will try to come.

Don't talk about Zhenya accompanying me. That will make me even more exhausted, and you clearly can't imagine what effect the dazzling combination of Seryozhka, Sashka and Zhenka – who no doubt will get stuck in Lebedyan – will have on you. No, you are not to interrupt your rest!

What you say in the rest of your letter is a sensible idea. No, no and no to the thought of having dinner with the whole group! And as far as S.* is concerned – don't even talk of it. Let Azazello* have dinner with her!

Damn this boiler! Of course, I won't begin to talk about the number of times I've asked Gorshkov* to come, or how much I've had to bustle about dealing with this or that everyday problem. I can't talk to anyone.

Oh, Kuka, from where you are, so far away, you can't see what effect writing this last sunset novel has had on your husband at the end of his appalling literary career. Loving kisses!

Yours, M.

22nd June

To Yelena Bulgakova

Darling Lyusi!
Your letters and postcards have arrived.

My darling Kupik! Before you do anything else make sure you curse my boiler! Nastasya will be of no help to me whatsoever if she brings Gorshkov down on my head! I can bring him down on my head myself, but I can't hold a conversation with him (evidently, we need to install a new boiler).

But in general, my darling, please don't think that you can sort things out from a distance in your letters. You can't do anything, so please don't worry about trifling matters. Just spend time on Zhemchuzhnikov!*

I've written about my poor health only so as to explain why I possibly won't be able to travel to Lebedyan. But please, I beg you in the name of all that's holy, don't think up people who might accompany me! Have pity on me! First it was Yevgeny! And now it's Loli!* They won't be able to help me at all, but will just get in the way!

   Mark Leopoldovich* is going to examine me this evening; everything will become clearer then.

Stenographic record:
   S (*anxiously*): Now, now, now! Why are you so strained?
   I: It's nothing… just a little painful.
   S (*threateningly*): Well, just don't think of writing and telling Lyusya about it.
   I: What are you on about? "Don't think of…"?
   S: Well, I mean that if you do write and tell Lyusya, she'll instantly fly to Moscow, and then what will we do in Lebedyan! No, come on, please, just suffer in silence!

I have this constant pain, low down in my chest. Perhaps it's nothing very serious.

You seem to be puzzled – when does S. ever speak the truth? I can help you with this: she never speaks the truth.

In this particular case, it's her letters that are full of lies. Her lies are like Behemoth's story* about the tiger that's been eaten – that is to say, *a lie from the first word to the last.*

The reason? Knowing what you feel about the novel, she has no intention of ruining her time of relaxation in the garden, under the apple tree. As for me, I'm not a threat to her, and so the bitter truth will emerge of its own accord in Moscow.

But it is the truth!! I regret that I am deprived of the opportunity of producing the kind of pearls that are worth any money (and, I'm sorry to say, a great deal of money!).

But enough of that! Just one piece of friendly advice: if you're interested in this work which people are talking about (I'm already looking on it myself with a sense of quiet sadness), then stop talking about it. Let them do what they like! And instead just let S. roar with laughter in her falsely jocular manner, rave about nature and spout all her usual theatrical rubbish. *That's serious advice.*

All in all, I've had my fill of looking at and listening to people.

Ku! What are you talking about – revising the novel in Lebedyan? And as for *Don Quixote,** hardly! I can't even bear to think about a typewriter!

If I do succeed in coming, it will only be for a short period. Besides, I'm not capable of reading, let alone writing, anything. I need "absolute peace and rest" (your expression, which I liked very much). Yes, and I mean absolute! I can't even look at any *Don Quixote* just now.

I kiss my beautiful, enchanting Yelena!

Yours,

M.

* * *

PS: You see what the novel's done to me?! I'm already beginning
to tear up pieces of paper I don't need any longer, and look:
I've torn up your letter! Gluing it together again affectionately.
Kisses.

22nd July
Evening

To Yelena Bulgakova

[...] Well, we got back to Moscow today at 8 a.m. Airless. We took taxis – Yevgeny to Rzhevsky, and I home. I wanted to have some tea and then go straight to the Sandunovsky baths, and from there to Lavrushinsky, but after the tea I collapsed and went straight to sleep. After a sleep I felt a bit stronger and went to the baths. Really enjoyed my hot bath and getting my hair cut. But the insect bites are tormenting me! The swelling from my Lebedyan bite hasn't gone down at all, and some flying beast bit me so badly on the bottom of my foot in the train that I'm now limping and the foot has swollen up. What a devil!

I have only just realized what rubbish I've been writing! Of course it's so interesting to read about my foot! I'm sorry.

I looked at Moscow with interest. Everything was as it should be. Many people have gone away, it seems. The clothes that people are wearing show just how exhausting the heat has been. No ties, white trousers everywhere, glistening faces.

My telephone calls indicated that many people I wanted to see were away. The Vilyams* are somewhere in the vicinity of Elbrus, and Yakov Leontievich is in Barvikha. I'm sad about that, as I wanted to talk to him.

I didn't get to Lavrushinsky today; Yevgeny had dinner with me.

Nastya greeted him very affectionately. She had rung him to tell him to be careful with the gas, at which he took offence!

She fed me marvellously, and told me that someone had died in our apartment block and that the woman opposite had gassed herself.

So, that's it.

Fondest love and kisses! As I immerse myself in the everyday cares of Moscow existence I remember the moon near the church. Please don't be angry that I joked about your library. I beg you – keep an eye on Sergei when he's in the river. Tell him that on no account is he allowed to do somersaults in the water. According to Nastasya, poor Yura drowned at a shallow spot. I mention this sad event only so that you don't take your eyes off Sergei! Kiss him from me and don't allow him to prattle on.

Kisses from Yevgeny.
                        Yours,
                            M.

Your telegram came as it started to rain!

This letter is so incoherent because I'm exhausted. Now I shall have supper and go to bed.

Greetings, of course, to everyone!

23rd July
a.m.

To Yelena Bulgakova

My darling Lyu!

This is the second day now that I've been rummaging around in the chaotic jumble of papers in your Psyche,* trying to find the documents needed to get the money which I've paid in for the apartment. In particular I need the document indicating the *total number of shares*. Is there such a document? Where is it? I'm just off to Lavrushinsky to get the money, and then to the payments office (Bolshaya Polyanka 28).

It's very airless here. I'm digging about, throwing hundreds of pieces of paper everywhere, in the slight hope of finding what I need.

Fondest kisses.

M.

24th July

To Yelena Bulgakova

My darling Ku!

I'm writing to you in Spanish, firstly to convince you how diligently I'm studying the prince of Spanish writers and secondly to test you to see how much you've forgotten in Lebedyan of the magnificent language in which Miguel Cervantes spoke and wrote. Do you remember the incident with Louis XIV and the courtier? So I put the following question to you: *Sabe, Ud, el castellano?**

I can just imagine how Cervantes would have laughed if he had read my Spanish letter to you! Well, it can't be helped. I confess that writing in Spanish is not easy.

Goodness, how stuffy it is in Moscow, Ku! It's sometimes difficult for Nastya to get hold of any ice. But the working conditions are exceptionally pleasant. Absolute silence. The telephone hardly ever rings, and even the courtyard outside isn't as noisy as usual for some reason. Perhaps the heat has worn everybody out.

The only thing is a radio outside that sometimes poisons life, and then there is some idiot winding up his gramophone from time to time. Let's just hope he manages to break it very soon!

Anna P. was here this morning, telling me about one lady with a "smarmy mug", another who had pinched a nail file and a third with something really nasty on her leg. Very entertaining, as usual. Looking at *Don Quixote* with one eye and at A.P. with the other I listened to her telling me about S. sobbing bitterly on the day of her departure.

"I felt so sorry for her, so very sorry!" she said, and then added, most unexpectedly:

"She was such a nasty woman!"

Please, Ku, I ask you in all seriousness not to say *anything* about A.P. to our fat friend. All right? You yourself will understand why.

I write and tell you about such trivia just so that I can chat to you, *alma mia*.*

Shortly after A.P. had gone, Maria Isakovna* telephoned (there's a direct connection between the two of them). She wanted to ask how much better you were and so on. I said that you looked wonderful and brown as chocolate.

Please don't be angry with me, Lyu, for worrying you with the question of the apartment documents. I'm glad that I was able to cope with it all and will not have to mention the topic again before your return.

Maybe you'll be amused by the following:

Dripping with sweat, I go along to the apartment office. Some unknown official glances at my piece of paper and suddenly asks in an alarmed tone:

"Excuse me... Aren't you the author of *The Days of the Turbins*?"

"Yes, I am," I reply.

His eyes bulge and he drops the document.

"Really?! My God!" he exclaims.

I am so put out by this that I say:

"Word of honour!"

At this he puts his papers down.

"I went to see *Zoyka's Apartment* and also *The Crimson Island*. Oh, I loved *The Crimson Island*!"

So I say:

"Yes, the Chamber Theatre has put on goodness knows what instead of the play."

"No, no, no! It's very good!"

And finally:

"Tell me, how much did you get for writing *The Turbins*?"

And I see that there are occasions when such questions are not asked with any malicious intent, but are just inescapably boorish.

It's not a question of disgusting envy, with which you and I are so familiar, but just curiosity.

Yesterday I had supper with Boris Robertovich* and his wife. Today I meant to ride out to see Sergei Petrovich at his dacha, but I didn't get there. *Hasta la vista!*
  Fondest love!
            Yours,
              M.

26th July
Afternoon

To Yelena Bulgakova

Two postcards, dated 23rd and 24th, came from you today, darling
Ku and Lyu. Aha! You see: they've closed the dam and it's raining!
Now I know when and where it would be a good place to go. But it
would be lovely if they could arrange it so that the rain came here
and you could have the Moscow weather. It would be easier for you
to bear it there, in the parks and gardens. Here the stuffiness hangs
in the air, the sky is overcast and muddy-looking in parts (having
just written that I can now see blue sky again and it's become so
hot!), but there's not a drop of rain. It's so airless you could weep.
You couldn't put on a collar – it would instantly turn into a limp
kind of tourniquet. I'm dying of thirst, but there isn't any Narzan.*
I've been drinking Beryozovsky and Mirgorod mineral waters, but
they're also difficult to get hold of. Yet my work's going quite well,
and my thoughts are fairly sharp. I'll only say something about that,
however, in my longer letters. I'm so glad that Sergei's with you!
That's so good! But please, I beg you, don't give him too much to
eat. It's not good for him. Don't forget that, Ku! Kisses!

Yours,

M.

29th July

To Yelena Bulgakova

Darling Lyu! Your telegram promising to telegraph me about your health has come. The heat is oppressive, it's difficult to do any work. Ku! A couple of important matters: don't go out into the sun too much! I mean it, seriously. I'm afraid you'll pay for it later. Stay in the shade! And secondly: don't let Sergei eat too much! He can see for himself how much it harms him. That's enough of that!

I'll get down to writing you a long letter now. Fondest love and kisses.

Yours, M.

My dearest love!
I get all your letters and read them with great affection. Don't worry too much about these letters in Spanish, my dear Champollion the Younger!*

Make sure you rest, and stay in the shade as much as possible. And remember my instructions to keep out of the sun altogether, my love!

Have pity on me: it's a blazing inferno here. Not only is there no end in sight to the heat, but it becomes worse with each day that passes.

In the evenings the moths fly in the windows and drown themselves in the jam. They're followed by some sort of green flies who come to die on the pages of books. Nastasya spends her time snivelling, with a damp cloth on her head. She tells me that a couple of people collapsed while standing in a queue for ice. It has become difficult to work. If it were possible to hope for such a thing, I would go off somewhere out of Moscow for three or four days and find a room in a hotel, so that I could at least have a view of the sea. But that is quite out of the question.

Dmitriev keeps on asking me to go to Leningrad. And for a moment I was tempted to go. Judging by what he tells me on the telephone, things have turned out badly for him. He himself is unable to come to Moscow. But I can see now it's written in the stars that such a trip would be impossible. Above all I feel rotten and would be physically unable to do anything like that. And besides, I could be faced with a whole heap of things to do precisely during this period. So I will sound the retreat and carry on storming the citadel of Quixote.

Things are not good in Moscow (yesterday I went to the Hermitage and left within ten minutes). Interestingly I didn't come across a single familiar face! Then I went to the Zhurgaz Restaurant, which I also regretted doing. It's true, there were familiar faces everywhere, but I could do without any of them. And just outside the city is even worse in my opinion. I went to the Fyodorovs' dacha, where I was given my usual magnificent welcome, but the countryside around Moscow!... For many kilometres around the dacha area is obscured in haze and covered in litter and dust. And as for the swimming... I thought of the Don and its sandy bottom!

Oh, those dachas – just like little hen coops! As I was on my way home, after sunset, I looked in the windows and felt so sad. I thought of you with especial clarity. I'd so love to be talking to you now!

I don't have the strength to write any more – I'm worn out. I'll write about S., the theatre, the novel and so on in my next letter. Keep happy, stay well (I'm puzzled that there's no promised telegram from you) and fondest love! Stroke Sergei's head for me.

Yours,
M.

I don't feel too well – perhaps it's the heat?

7th August
Late evening

To *Yelena Bulgakova*

As I was writing to you this afternoon, my love, I heard that Stanislavsky had died. The whole time I have been certain that the theatre would let Kaluzhsky know, but I've suddenly been struck by doubt: what if they haven't let him know? I'll go to the telegraph office and send a telegram at once.

Love and kisses!

Yours, M

8th August

To *Yelena Bulgakova*

My darling Lyusenka!

[...] Dmitriev's presence has turned my life into absolute chaos. *Quixote* has stopped, as has any significant train of thought, I can't gather my thoughts to write any letters, the telephone is constantly ringing in my head – the same questions and the same answers twenty times over. I feel sorry for him, as he's absolutely shattered, but he has driven me to such a state that I've started to feel physically ill!

He's going to Leningrad this evening, having managed, thanks to MAT, to delay his case here, which will mean, I hope, that he will no longer be required to settle in Tajikistan. He should have gone yesterday, but he was asked to go to MAT to set up the hall for the funeral.*

I've done everything I can to help him in terms of sympathetic advice – and now, I must confess, I just want to be able to do one thing: to light the lamp, immerse myself in silence and wait for you to arrive.

It's been a nightmare, an absolute nightmare!

I'm finishing the letter quickly so that I can give it to Nastasya to post.

And so, you're leaving on the 14th? That's wonderful. There's no point in you waiting there any longer. Ku, if it's not too much trouble, please could you ask for some headache pills and bring them with you. I'm worried that you might have difficulties on the train. Leave as much as you can in the luggage van.

Everything's swirling around in my head! Fondest love and kisses! Waiting for you!

                    Yours,
                        M.

9th August

To *Yelena Bulgakova*

Darling Lyusi!

This has been the first morning without Dmitriev. You can't imagine what bliss that is, not having lived through the nightmare – which I'll tell you about in detail when I see you. Suffice it to say that I'd started to suffer from total insomnia. As he was leaving, he told me that he'd be back again one of these days, and now I'm seriously wondering how I'll be able to protect my work and preserve my peace and calm. There's a limit to everything!

Having slept well for the first time for days, I was woken by my *cuñada*,* who turned up early in the morning with two boxes. She quickly disappeared, leaving me with two boxes and a headache. I had to telephone her later to find out the date you'll be travelling. After I'd spoken to Kaluzhsky, I was about to put the receiver down when he gave the telephone to my *cuñada*, who proceeded to start talking, incoherently and at great speed, about some jam and some Russian butter or other, and to tell me what I needed to do with them, something which I won't do of course, since I moved the receiver a little away from my ear and stopped listening to all that rubbish.

So, you're travelling on the 14th. Are you all right for money? (Olga says you are). I'm so happy I'll be seeing you soon. I remember with such loving feelings how concerned you were about my peace and calm in Lebedyan.

It's now coming up to midday and Nastasya has made off somewhere, which is something she never does. I hope nothing's happened to her. It's all right – I can take today off again, but tomorrow I'll be able, I'm sure, to get back to *Quixote*. I'll start revising it.

Here's Nastya! So everything's all right.

As you can understand, I'm still reacting to the news of Konstantin's death and am constantly thinking about it. Since my thoughts

about the fate of writers and about the way I have been treated
by MAT have become burdensome and persistent, and in order
to switch them onto a different set of rails, I will present to you
a number of scenes relating to the *death*.

On the afternoon of the 7th, when somebody happened to telephone
the Theatre about a matter that concerned him, one MAT lady (pos-
sibly Ripsi's sister, is there such a person?) replied, falteringly, as follows:
   "You know that... um... something's happened here..."
   "What is it?"
   "What's happened is that... Konstantin Sergeyevich... has died...
But please, I beg you, *not a word to anybody!...*"

I: Nastya, do you know who Stanislavsky is?
   Nastasya: Stanislavsky? No, no! I don't know him! Never heard
of him!
   I: I see... not to worry.
   (*A few hours later.*)
   Nastasya (*embarrassed*): You asked if I knew Stanislavsky? I was
busy with my own thoughts at the time... Of course, how could I not
know him!... Polya has just rung me... I'm so fond of the theatre!...
And my mum loved him so much... Every evening we used to sit
together talking about him... She used to say: "Oh, Nastya, Nastya!
Wouldn't it be wonderful to be given a bouquet of flowers or some
perfume by him!" And I used to reply: "Yes, mum, wouldn't it!"
   And now Olya's been told that they're making Nikolai Vasilyevich*
the new director! (Recorded verbatim.)

There's two scenes for you. That's all for the time being, as Seryozha
Yermolinsky has just arrived. I enclose a note from him.
   Fondest love and kisses.
                           Yours,
                              M.

PS: Yevgeny has arrived from Archangel and will be coming to have
a meal.

1939

To V.V. Veresayev

Dear Vikenty Vikentevich!

I've been meaning to write to you for ages, but work keeps on getting in the way. In addition, I've wanted to put together our agreement on *Pushkin*.

I'm enclosing two copies of the contract with this letter. If you have no objections, could you please sign both copies and return one to me.

I often find myself wanting to talk to you, but I am embarrassed to do so since, as with all shattered and persecuted writers, my thoughts are constantly harping on the gloomy topic of my situation, and this is tiring for those around me.

Having become convinced over recent years that not a single line I've written will appear either in print or on the stage, I try to cultivate an attitude of indifference towards it all. And I may well have had significant success in this.

One of my most recent efforts has been the play *Don Quixote* from the novel by Cervantes, written under contract with the Vakhtangov Theatre. It's now stuck with them, and will remain stuck until it rots, despite the fact that they met it with acclaim and that it came with the approbatory stamp of the Repertory Committee.

They have placed the play in such a remote part of their plan that it will never be performed there. And it won't be performed anywhere else of course. This doesn't sadden me at all, since I have already become accustomed to seeing everything I've written from one particular angle: how much unpleasantness will it cause me? And if it doesn't look as if it's going to be very much, I'm sincerely grateful even for that.

At the moment I'm preoccupied with something that is completely pointless from a practical point of view – making the final corrections to my novel.

And yet, however hard you try to suppress the impulse in yourself, it's difficult not to pick up your pen. I'm tormented by the vague idea that I must bring my literary career to a conclusion.

What are you working on? Have you finished your translation?*

I would like to see you. Are you free in the evenings? I'll give you a ring and drop round.

Keep well. All good wishes for future success in your work.

Yours,

M. Bulgakov

Barvikha
3rd December

*To Ye.A. Svetlayeva**

Dear Lyolya!
Here is some news about me. There has been a significant improvement in my left eye. The right eye is lagging behind somewhat, but it's also trying to behave itself. The doctors say that any improvement in the eyes is marked by a corresponding improvement in the kidneys.

And if that is so, then there is hope that I shall escape the old man with the scythe for the time being, and that I shall be able to finish one or two things that I've wanted to finish.

I've been held back a little by being in bed with the flu – but I had already started going out and had been for walks in the forest. And I am significantly stronger.

So, let me tell you about Barvikha. It is a magnificently equipped and comfortable clinic. But what I want more than anything of course is to be able to go home! It's fine to be away, but there's nothing like one's own home!

I am receiving meticulous treatment, mostly with a special, blended diet. Mainly all sorts of vegetables and fruit. I'm bored to death with both, but I'm told that that's how it has to be, and that such a diet is necessary for my recovery. And anyway, reading and writing are so important to me that I'm prepared to chew rubbish like carrots.

I don't know how much longer we shall have to be here. If, as I very much hope, you write to me, please use our Moscow address. Greetings to Varya and Nadya. Lyusya sends her kisses, and her greetings to you and to them.

Yours,
Mikhail

Barvikha
6th December

To Pavel Popov

Yes, dear Pavel, you're right: never try to guess in advance what's going to happen. We've both been laid low by flu, and everything seems to be crumbling to dust – by everything I mean fresh air and further progress. I don't feel at all well; I lie here the whole time and dream only about returning to Moscow and about a respite from all the difficult treatment and every kind of procedure which, after three months, have finally worn me out.

I've had enough of it all!

I'm strictly forbidden to read and write – nothing new in that, and I am told that this situation will last "for a long time".

Now there's a phrase that is full of uncertainty! Perhaps you could tell me what "for a long time" means?

Whatever happens, I shall do my best to be back in Moscow by 20th December.

Greetings to Anna Ilinichna!

Yours,

M.

28th December

To Alexander Gdeshinsky

Moscow

I haven't been able to answer your letter for some time, my dear friend, or to thank you for your delightful news. So, here I am back in Moscow, home from the sanatorium. How do I feel? To tell you frankly and in confidence, I'm haunted by the thought that I have come back to die.

I find this a disturbing thought for one reason and one reason only: it's all so painful, boring and banal. As is well known, there is only one decent way to die, and that is by a gun, but, regretfully, I do not have one available.

To be a little more detailed about my illness: I can distinctly sense a struggle between life and death going on inside me. In particular, on the positive side, there is a marked improvement in my eyesight.

But that's enough about my illness!

There's just one more thing to add: approaching the end of my life I have come to experience yet one more disillusionment: in therapists and doctors.

It would be wrong to call them murderers – that would be too harsh – but I'm not at all averse to calling them incompetent posturers and charlatans.

There are exceptions, of course, but they are extremely rare!

And anyway, how can these exceptions be of any use if traditional medics, let's say, not only do not possess any means to fight illnesses such as mine, but are sometimes unable even to diagnose what illness it is.

Time will pass, and people will laugh at our doctors, just as they did in Molière's time. But this does not apply to surgeons, oculists or dentists. Or to the best doctor treating Yelena

Sergeyevna. But she can't do everything on her own, and I've therefore adopted a new faith and changed to a homoeopath. But the person who can help us sick people more than anyone else is God!

Please do write to me. Regards to L.N.!*

With all my heart I wish you the best of health – to see the sun, to hear the sea and to listen to music.

Yours,
M.

1940

To his nieces

Thank you, my dear Olya and Lena,* for your letter. I wish you every happiness in life.

M. Bulgakov

[*A little over a month later, on 10th March 1940, Mikhail Bulgakov died.*]

Notes

p. 3, *Varvara Mikhailovna Voskresenskaya*: Mikhail Bulgakov's mother (1869–1922); married a second time to Ivan Pavlovich Voskresensky, a family friend.

p. 3, *Taska*: Tatyana Nikolayevna Lappa (1892–1982), Bulgakov's first wife, from 1913 to 1924.

p. 4, *Andrei's room is a life-saver*: Andrei Mikhailovich Zemsky (1892–1946), Mikhail's brother-in-law.

p. 4, *When Nadya comes*: Nadezhda Afanasyevna Zemskaya (1893–1971), Bulgakov's sister, married to Andrei.

p. 5, *A Country Doctor's Notebook*: A collection, also known as *A Young Doctor's Notebook*, of autobiographical stories relating to Bulgakov's experiences as a country doctor. It was published in medical journals from 1925 to 1927.

p. 5, *The Ailment*: A discarded version of the early autobiographical story *Morphine*.

p. 6, *an article by Boris*: Boris Mikhailovich Zemsky (1891–1941), brother of Andrei.

p. 6, *Eugene Onegin*: Novel in verse (1833) by Alexander Pushkin (1799–1837).

p. 6, *Nekrasov*: Nikolai Alexeyevich Nekrasov (1821–78), poet and journalist.

p. 7, *some "basement" satirical article on Moscow*: The "basement" was the section towards the bottom of the page in many newspapers reserved for satirical articles.

p. 8, *Korolenko's death*: Vladimir Galaktionovich Korolenko (1853–1921), prose writer.

p. 8, *K.G.'s*: The reference is to Nikolai Leonidovich Gladyrevsky (1896–1973), a friend of the Bulgakov family.

p. 9, *Meyerhold's son*: Vsevolod Emilevich Meyerhold (1874–1940), distinguished theatre director and producer.

p. 9, *A Doctor's Notebook*: A devastatingly honest autobiographical account (1902) of the trials and tribulations of a young provincial doctor by Vikenty Vikentevich Veresayev (1867–1945).

p. 11, *Vera Bulgakova*: Vera Afanasyevna Bulgakova (1892–1973), Bulgakov's sister.

p. 12, *Lyolya*: Yelena Afanasyevna Bulgakova (1902–54), Bulgakov's sister.

p. 12, *Ivan Pavlovich*: Ivan Pavlovich Voskresensky, the Bulgakovs' stepfather.

p. 12, *Kolya and Vanya*: Nikolai Afanasyevich Bulgakov (1898–1966) and Ivan Afanasyevich Bulgakov (1900–68), brothers of Mikhail. Both had emigrated.

p. 13, *Varvara*: Varvara Afanasyevna Bulgakova (1895–1956), Bulgakov's sister.

p. 13, *Bucha*: A town some fifteen miles to the south-west of Kiev, where the Bulgakovs' dacha was situated.

p. 14, *The Soviet representative Vatslav Vatslavovich Vorovsky was murdered in Lausanne by Conradi*: Vatslav Vatslavovich Vorovsky (1871–1923), Soviet diplomat and representative in Italy, assassinated by Conradi, an unknown White Russian.

p. 14, *Curzon's ultimatum to Russia*: Lord George Curzon (1859–1925), British Foreign Secretary from 1919 to 1924. The ultimatum to the Soviet government was delivered on 8th May 1923.

p. 14, *Weinstein's impudent diplomatic messages*: Aron Isaakovich Veinstein (Weinstein, 1877–1938), head of the Soviet Finance Control Committee.

p. 14, *Marshall Foch has visited Poland*: Marshall Ferdinand Foch (1851–1929), French general and military strategist, awarded the title of Marshall of Poland in 1923.

p. 14, *Krasin*: Leonid Borisovich Krasin (1870–1926), from 1920 the Soviet People's Commissar for External Trade and Trade Attaché in Great Britain.

p. 15, *Count Alexei Tolstoy has arrived from Berlin*: Alexei Nikolayevich Tolstoy (1883–1945), novelist. Author, among other works, of *Road to Calvary* (1943) and *Peter the First* (1945).

p. 15, *Patriarch Tikhon*: Patriarch Tikhon (1865–1925), Orthodox Patriarch of Moscow and All Russia.

p. 15, *the chervonets*: A currency introduced by the Soviet government in 1922, parallel to the rouble. The chervonets was fully convertible and backed by the gold standard.

p. 16, *the Hooter*: Official organ of the Railway Workers' Union – the vehicle for satirical articles by many writers.

p. 16, *On the Eve*: Berlin-based newspaper, with an affiliated branch in Moscow, set up in 1922 to bridge the divide between the émigré community and the Soviet Union.

p. 16, *The Berlin book*: The reference is to 'Notes on a Cuff', an autobiographical work by Bulgakov recording his experiences in Vladikavkaz and his early months in Moscow. It was to be published later that year.

p. 16, *Change of Landmarks group*: A group of former émigrés who believed in the need for reconciliation and cooperation with Soviet Russia. The name derives from a collection of articles entitled *Change of Landmarks*, published in 1921.

p. 16, *Professor Klyuchnikov...Vasilyevsky-Ne-Bukva*: Yuri Veniaminovich Klyuchnikov (1886–1938), lawyer, foreign minister in the administration of Admiral Kolchak during the civil war; Alexander Vladimirovich Bobrishchev-Pushkin (1875–1937), writer; Ilya Markovich Vasilyevsky (Ne-Bukva), writer, formerly married to Bulgakov's second wife Lyubov Belozerskaya.

p. 17, *Katayev*: Valentin Petrovich Katayev (1897–1986), author, amongst other works, of *Time, Forward!* (1932) and *The Holy Well* (1966).

p. 17, *Sofochka arrived yesterday, with her mother, husband and child*: The reference is to the Davidoviches, relatives of Bulgakov's first wife.

p. 18, *Kalmens*: Semyon Nikolayevich Kalmens, head of the finance department at the Moscow office of the newspaper *On the Eve*.

p. 19, *Diaboliad*: The story was first published in *Nedra* in 1924.

p. 19, *Zvezda*: Monthly literary journal, founded in Petrograd in 1923.

p. 19, *a certain Stresemann... the German Kerensky*: Gustav Stresemann (1878–1929), Chancellor of the Weimar Republic for a brief period in 1923. Alexander Fyodorovich Kerensky (1881–1970), prime minister in the Russian Provisional Government between the February and October revolutions of 1917.

p. 19, *Radek*: Karl Radek (1885–1939), Comintern secretary in the early 1920s.

p. 20, *A. Erlich... Komorsky and Davy*: Aron Isayevich Erlich (1896–1963), journalist and author of memoirs of Bulgakov; Vladimir Yevgenevich Komorsky, lawyer, friend of Bulgakov in the early 1920s; David Alexandrovich Kiselgof (Davy), friend of Bulgakov in the early 1920s, later married Bulgakov's first wife, Tatyana Lappa.

p. 20, *Bogdanov... Krasnoshchekov*: Pyotr Alexeyevich Bogdanov (1882–1939); Alexander Mikhailovich Krasnoshchekov (1880–1937).

p. 20, *NEP*: The New Economic Policy, initiated by Lenin in 1921, and resulting in a partial return to market forces after the exigencies of revolution and civil war.

p. 20, *Qui vivra – verra*: "We'll have to wait and see" (French).

p. 21, *Wrangel's troops are joining in*: Pyotr Nikolayevich Wrangel (Vrangel) (1858–1928), commander of the anti-Bolshevik forces in southern Russia during the civil war.

p. 22, *Kolarov and Dimitrov*: Vasil Petrov Kolarov (1877–1950), Bulgarian communist leader; Georgi Mikhailovich Dimitrov (1882–1949), Bulgarian communist leader, arrested in Berlin in 1933 for setting fire to the Reichstag.

p. 22, *Tsankov*: Alexander Tsolov Tsankov (1879–1959), Bulgarian fascist politician.

p. 22, *Kahr*: Gustav Ritter von Kahr (1862–1934), right-wing politician and prime minister of Bavaria from 1920 to 1921.

p. 22, *Izvestiya*: *Izvestiya* (*News*), official national publication of the Soviet government, founded in 1917.

p. 22, *Vilensky-Sibiryakov*: Vladimir Dmitrievich Vilensky-Sibiryakov (1888–1942), writer and specialist on Siberia and the Far East.

p. 23, *Konstantin arrived from St Petersburg today*: Konstantin Petrovich Bulgakov, first cousin of Mikhail.

p. 23, *the journal Krokodil*: *Krokodil*, a satirical journal, founded in 1922.

p. 23, *Brandler, Heckert and Böttcher*: Heinrich Brandler (1881–1967), together with Fritz Heckert and Paul Böttcher, leading members of the German Communist Party (KPD) in the early 1920s.

p. 24, *Workers' Copeck*: Daily popular Moscow newspaper, founded in 1924 and later renamed *Evening Moscow*.

p. 24, *Koltsov*: Mikhail Yefimovich Koltsov (1898–1940), leading Soviet journalist and founder of the *Workers' Copeck*.

p. 25, *my uncles*: The reference is to Nikolai Mikhailovich and Mikhail
Mikhailovich Pokrovsky ("Uncle Misha" below).

p. 25, *a speech by Trotsky*: Leon Trotsky (1879–1940), born Lev Davidovich
Bronstein, from 1919 to 1925 People's Commissar for Military and Naval
Affairs.

p. 27, *P.N. Zaytsev*: Pyotr Nikanorovich Zaytsev (1889–1970), secretary of the
Nedra publishing house and journal.

p. 27, *Veresayev... likes it a lot*: Vikenty Vikentevich Veresayev, born Smidovich.
Prose writer and editor (see second note to p. 9).

p. 27, *The Last of the Mohicans*: Novel (1826) by the American writer James
Fenimore Cooper (1789–1851)

p. 28, *Sokolov-Mikitov*: Ivan Sergeyevich Sokolov-Mikitov (1892–1975), writer.

p. 28, *Lidin*: Vladimir Germanovich Lidin (1894–1979), writer.

p. 28, *Alexander Drozdov*: Alexander Mikhailovich Drozdov (1885–1963),
writer working for émigré publications.

p. 28, *Markov the second*: The reference is to Pavel Alexandrovich Markov
(1897–1980), theatre critic and director.

p. 30, *Mozalevsky*: Viktor Ivanovich Mozalevsky (1889–1970), writer.

p. 30, *Mitya Stonov and Gaidovsky*: Dmitry Mironovich Stonov (1892–1963)
and Georgy Nikolayevich Gaidovsky (1902–62), writers.

p. 30, *Andrei*: Andrei Mikhailovich Zemsky. See first note to p. 4.

p. 30, *Mikhail Chekhov's... book on his great brother*: Bulgakov was presumably referring to *Anton Chekhov as Storyteller* (1923), by Mikhail Pavlovich
Chekhov (1865–1936).

p. 30, *Kolya Gladyrevsky*: See second note to p. 8.

p. 30, *My Universities*: The final part, published in 1923, of an autobiographical
trilogy by Maxim Gorky (1868–1936), born Alexei Maximovich Peshkov, dramatist
and prose writer, one of the founding members of the Soviet Writers' Union.

p. 30, *Lezhnev's*: Isay Grigorovich Lezhnev (1891–1955), journalist and editor.

p. 32, *Boris's*: See first note to p. 6.

p. 33, *Poincaré*: Raymond Poincaré (1860–1934), French prime minister.

p. 33, *death sentences*: The Kiev court had sentenced a number of eminent
scientists to death for conspiring to bring down the state. In the event, although
one or two of the sentences were commuted, most were carried out.

p. 33, *Nikolai Nikolayevich*: Grand Prince Nikolai Nikolayevich (1856–1929),
grandson of Tsar Nicholas I. After the death of Nicholas II one of the main
claimants to the throne.

p. 34, *Kalinin*: Mikhail Ivanovich Kalinin (1875–1946), nominal head of state
of the Soviet Union from 1919 to 1946.

p. 34, *Mordkin and the ballerina Kriger*: Mikhail Mikhailovich Mordkin
(1881–1944), ballet-master with the Bolshoi ballet; Viktorina Vladimirovna
Kriger (1896–1978), principal ballerina at the Bolshoi.

p. 34, *Viktorov*: Viktor Yaklovlevich Viktorov (1882–1965), soloist with the Bolshoi Theatre.

p. 34, *Golovin*: Dmitry Danilovich Golovin (1894–1966), soloist with the Bolshoi theatre.

p. 34, *the Demon*: Main character in *The Demon*, opera (1871) by Anton Rubinstein (1829–94), based on the poem by Mikhail Lermontov (1814–41).

p. 34, *Zinoviev*: Grigory Yevseyevich Zinoviev (1883–1936), born Ovsey-Gershon Aronovich Apfelbaum, leading Bolshevik politician and member of Lenin's politburo. Executed, on Stalin's orders, in 1936.

p. 35, *Ramsay MacDonald*: James Ramsay MacDonald (1866–1937), British Labour prime minister in 1924.

p. 35, *Lyubov Yevgenyevna's*: Lyubov Yevgenyevna Belozerskaya (1895–1987) became Bulgakov's second wife.

p. 35, *Deinka's*: A reference to Yevgeny Nikitovich Tarnovsky, a relative of Lyubov Yevgenyevna Bulgakova's, familiarly known as "Dei" and the prototype for the character of Professor Persikov in Bulgakov's story *The Fatal Eggs*.

p. 35, *Ilf and Yuri Olyesha*: Ilya Ilf, born Ilya Arnoldovich Fainzilberg (1897–1937), together with Yevgeny Petrov, was the author, among other works, of *The Twelve Chairs* (1928); Yuri Karlovich Olyesha (1899–1960), author of *Envy* (1927).

p. 36, *Red Pepper*: Moscow satirical journal, founded in 1923.

p. 36, *Furman*: Georgy Vasilyevich Furman (b.1891), journalist.

p. 36, *Dawn of the East*: Newspaper, based in Georgia, founded in 1922.

p. 36, *Sven*: Ilya Lvovich Sven (Kremlyov) (1897–1971), writer.

p. 36, *Splinter*: Moscow satirical journal.

p. 36, *Kagansky*: Zakhar Leontievich Kagansky, publisher of the journal *Russia*, later to leave the Soviet Union for Berlin, from where he attempted to seize control of Bulgakov's royalties (see letter of 28th November 1927).

p. 36, *The White Guard won't now be published*: *The White Guard*, Bulgakov's first full-length novel, was first published in full in Paris in 1929.

p. 37, *GPU*: Glavnoye Politicheskoye Upravlenie (Chief Political Administration), Soviet secret police, predecessor of OGPU and the NKVD.

p. 37, *Evening Moscow*: See first note to p. 24.

p. 37, *Yeremeyev*: Konstantin Stepanovich Yeremeyev (1874–1931), Party functionary and editor of *The Worker* newspaper.

p. 37, *The Joker*: Weekly satirical journal published in Moscow and Leningrad from 1924 to 1928.

p. 38, *Rakovsky*: Christian Rakovsky (1873–1941), Bulgarian revolutionary and Bolshevik diplomat.

p. 39, *Galya Syngayevskaya*: Wife of a childhood friend of Bulgakov's, Nikolai Nikolayevich Syngyaevsky.

p. 39, *Zina Komorskaya's*: Zinaida Vasilyevna Komorskaya, wife of a friend of Bulgakov's, Vladimir Yevgenyevich Komorsky.

p. 39, *The Contemporary*: *The Russian Contemporary*, literary journal published in Leningrad in 1924.

p. 39, *I.M. Vasilyevsky*: See fifth note to p. 16.

p. 39, *Blyumkin... Mirbach*: In 1918 the left socialist-revolutionary Yakov Grigorevich Blyumkin (1898–1929) assassinated the German ambassador in Moscow, Wilhelm Graf von Mirbach-Harff (1871–1918). The presumed reference is to a biography of Felix Edmundovich Dzerzhinsky (1877–1926), Bolshevik functionary and head of the Soviet secret police (Cheka, later OGPU) from 1917 to 1926.

p. 40, *Lemke's 250 Days at Headquarters*: An account of the activities of the imperial-headquarters staff during the First World War, published in 1920 and written by the historian Mikhail Konstantinovich Lemke (1872–1923)

p. 40, *Kubuv*: Russian acronym for the Committee for the Improvement of Everyday Life for Doctors.

p. 40, *Professor Martynov*: Alexei Vasilyevich Martynov (1868–1934), leading Russian surgeon.

p. 40, *Boris Savinkov*: Boris Viktorovich Savinkov (1879–1925), leading socialist revolutionary. Arrived from abroad illegally in 1924 and arrested for anti-Soviet activities. He was sentenced to death, but the sentence was commuted to ten years in jail. He is thought to have committed suicide in 1925.

p. 40, *Chepedaleva*: Unidentified.

p. 40, *Sun Yat-sen's*: Sun Yat-sen (1866–1925), Chinese revolutionary and first president of the Republic of China.

p. 41, *Yevgeny Nikitich*: Yevgeny Nikitovich Tarnovsky, see third note to p. 35.

p. 42, *Bryusov*: Valery Yakovlevich Bryusov (1873–1924), Symbolist poet and literary critic.

p. 42, *The Fatal Eggs*: The story was first published in 1925.

p. 42, *Angarsky*: Nikolai Semyonovich Angarsky (1873–1941), editor of the journal *Nedra*.

p. 42, *The Lessons of October*: The preface to a volume of Trotsky's writings published in 1924.

p. 43, *Chamberlain*: Arthur Neville Chamberlain (1869–1940), British politician and statesman.

p. 43, *Zinoviev's famous letter*: Controversial document, published by the British government in 1924, purporting to be a directive from Moscow calling for increased communist agitation in Great Britain. For Zinoviev, see sixth note to p. 34.

p. 43, *the French premier Herriot*: Édouard Herriot (1872–1957), politician and statesman, three times premier of France.

p. 44, *this Dickson woman*: Real identity uncertain. She went under the name of Mariya Dickson-Yevgenyeva.

p. 44, *Lunacharsky*: Anatoly Vasilyevich Lunacharsky (1875–1933), Soviet People's Commissar of Enlightenment from 1917 to 1929.

p. 44, *Rykov's tipple*: Alexei Ivanovich Rykov (1881–1938), leading Bolshevik politician, Soviet premier from 1924 to 1930.

p. 44, *Schmidt*: Otto Yulevich Schmidt (1891–1956), head of the State Publishing House from 1921 to 1924.

p. 44, *Ivanov or Rabinovich*: In *The Lessons of October* Trotsky accuses Stalin's Politburo of anti-Semitism, quoting the following anecdote: "If they imprison Ivanov [i.e. a typical Russian name] for theft, that's simply because he's a thief. But if they imprison Rabinovich [i.e. a typical Jewish name] for theft, then that's anti-Semitism." Rabinovich was also Trotsky's real name.

p. 45, *new calendar*: The Soviet government moved from the Julian (Old Style) Calendar to the Gregorian (New Style) Calendar on 1st February 1918.

p. 45, *my wife*: Bulgakov was now divorced and living with Lyubov Yevgenyevna Belozerskaya (1895–1987). They were to be married on 30th April 1925.

p. 46, *R.O.L.*: Unidentified.

p. 46, *Aron*: Aron Isayevich Erlich, (see first note to p. 20).

p. 46, *Pototsky*: Avgust Vladislavovich Pototsky, journalist with the *Hooter*.

p. 46, *Immortality… till the end*: From the poem 'A Bard in the Camp of Russian Warriors' by Vasily Andreyevich Zhukovsky (1783–1852), commemorating the victory over Napoleon in 1812.

p. 46, *the Shali-Aul campaign*: Shali-Aul, a settlement in Chechnya, was the scene of fierce fighting in the Russian civil war in 1919. Bulgakov's experiences are recorded in his autobiographical story 'The Unusual Adventures of a Doctor' (1922).

p. 47, *Blest he whom battle's overwhelmed*: This is the next line of the Zhukovsky poem quoted above.

p. 47, *the dog with the owl*: The reference is to an incident in Bulgakov's novella *A Dog's Heart*, written in 1925 but unpublished during Bulgakov's lifetime.

p. 48, *Mitya Stonov*: Dmitry Mironovich Stonov (see second note to p. 20).

p. 48, *Bobrishchev-Pushkin (Volodarsky)*: For Bobrishchev-Pushkin see fifth note to p. 16. V. Volodarsky (1891–1918), real name Moisey Markovich Goldshtein, revolutionary activist.

p. 48, *old man Arsenyev*: Probably a reference to Konstantin Konstantinovich Arsenyev (1837–1919), academic and lexicographer.

p. 48, *all these Pavel Nikolayeviches and Pasmaniks ensconced in Paris*: The reference is to Pavel Nikolayevich Milyukov and D.S. Pasmanik, leading Russian émigrés.

p. 48, *The Wanderer Playing on Muted Strings*: Novel (1909) by the Norwegian writer Knut Hamsun (1859–1952).

p. 48, *Demyan Bedny*: Demyan Bedny (1883–1945), Soviet poet.

p. 49, *Sigayev*: On 20th December 1924 the newspaper *Soviet Siberia* carried a brief report of a meeting in a village near Rostov-on-Don, during which a rural correspondent, Nikolai Sigayev, a former Red Army soldier, had been murdered.

p. 50, *Veresayev… Lvov-Rogachevsky*: Mikhail Yakovlevich Kozyrev (1892–1941), poet and prose writer; Nikolai Nikandrovich Nikandrov (1878–1964), writer; Vladimir Timofeyevich Kirillov (1889–1943), poet; Nikolai Nikolayevich Lyashko

(1884–1953), writer; Vasily Lvov-Rogachevsky (1873–1930), literary critic. For Veresayev see second note to p. 9 and for Zaytsev see first note to p. 27.

p. 51, *the sensational letter/pamphlet of Bernard Shaw... in yesterday's Izvestiya*: Shaw's letter took the Soviet government to task for its negative attitude towards European socialism.

p. 52, *Russia*: Literary journal, also known as New Russia, published 1922–26, edited by Isay Grigorovich Lezhnev (see seventh note to p. 30).

p. 52, *Nikitina's*: Yevdokia Fyodorovna Nikitina (1893–1973), literary historian.

p. 53, *"places that are not so far away"*: Ironic reference to a legal term used by the Tsarist government. Prisoners exiled to Siberia were sent either to "places that are far away" or "places that are not so far away".

p. 53, *Lydia Vasilyevna's*: Lydia Vasilyevna Kiryakova, journalist.

p. 53, *Sabashnikov*: Mikhail Vasilyevich Sabashnikov (1871–1943), publisher.

p. 54, *the Central Committee has dropped out of his name*: "TsK" is the Russian acronym for "Central Committee".

p. 54, *Ehrenburg*: Ilya Grigorevich Ehrenburg (1891–1967), novelist and journalist.

p. 55, *Yuri Potekhin*: Yuri Nikolayevich Potekhin (1888–c.1927), a member of the Change of Landmarks group. See fourth note to p. 16.

p. 55, *Chekhov's notebook*: The reference is unclear, but Chekhov's notebooks were first published in full in Russian in vol. 23 of the *Complete Works of Anton Chekhov* in 1916.

p. 55, *Sadyker/Change of Landmarks persuasion*: The reference is to Pavel Abramovich Sadyker, the managing director of *On the Eve*.

p. 55, *Auslender*: Sergei Abramovich Auslender (1886–1943), writer.

p. 56, *Krasnaya Niva*: Literally 'Red Cornfield', literary journal.

p. 56, *Nadya's*: See second note to p. 4.

p. 56, *the lovely Lyamins*: Nikolai Nikolayevich Lyamin (1892–1941), philologist and close friend of Bulgakov, and his wife, Natalya Abramovna Ushakova (1899–1993), artist.

p. 57, *the Atheist*: Monthly journal, published in Moscow from 1923 to 1941.

p. 57, *M.S. was with me*: The presumed reference is to Mitya Stonov (see second note to p. 30).

p. 58, *L.L.*: Unidentified.

p. 59, *"But I will explain that owl"*: The reference is to an incident in Bulgakov's story *A Dog's Heart*. See second note to p. 47.

p. 59, *Andrei Bely*: Andrei Bely (1880–1934), born Boris Nikolayevich Bugayev, Symbolist poet and novelist.

p. 59, *S.Z. Fedorchenko*: Sofya Zakharovna Fedorchenko (1880–1959), writer.

p. 60, *M.A. Voloshin*: Maximilian Alexandrovich Voloshin (1877–1932), poet and artist. Over a period of many years he invited writers and artists to spend part of the summer at his dacha in the resort of Koktebel on the Crimean peninsula.

p. 61, *Vasily Luzhsky*: Vasily Vasilyevich Luzhsky (1869–1931), director at the Moscow Arts Theatre.

p. 61, *some difficulties associated with my play*: The reference is to the Moscow Arts Theatre's proposal that Bulgakov adapt his novel *The White Guard* for the stage. The play was first performed by the Arts Theatre in 1926 under the title *The Days of the Turbins*.

p. 63, *Budyonny's wife had died*: Semyon Mikhailovich Budyonny (1883–1973), commander of the First Cavalry Army during the civil war.

p. 64, *OGPU*: The acronym for the All-Union State Political Directorate, the Soviet secret police, formed under this name in 1923 and dissolved in 1934. Forerunner of the NKVD and the KGB.

p. 65, *the Petlyura scene*: Symon Vasylyovych Petlyura (1879–1926) was the Ukrainian nationalist leader in 1918–19, portrayed in both the novel *The White Guard* and the play *The Days of the Turbins*.

p. 66, *Alexei Popov*: Alexei Dmitrievich Popov (1892–1961), leading theatre director.

p. 66, *Zoyka's Apartment*: The play was first produced, by Studio No. 3 of the Moscow Arts Theatre (later the Vakhtangov Theatre), in 1926.

p. 66, *the Vakhtangov Theatre*: Theatre in Moscow dating back to 1913. Named after the actor and theatre director Yevgeny Bagrationovich Vakhtangov (1883–1922).

p. 68, *the Moscow Arts Theatre Studio*: The Moscow Arts Theatre (MAT), founded in 1898 by Konstantin Sergeyevich Stanislavsky (1863–1938) and Vladimir Ivanovich Nemirovich-Danchenko (1858–1943).

p. 69, *Vladikavkaz*: Capital city of the Republic of North Ossetia-Alania in the Caucasus. Renamed Ordzhonikidze during the Soviet period.

p. 69, <...>: The top of the page is torn off.

p. 72, *Revel*: Old name for Tallinn, the capital of Estonia (German Reval).

p. 72, *a Mr Kagansky*: See fifth note to p. 36.

p. 74, *Escape*: The play, also known as *Flight*, was written between 1926 and 1928 and completely rewritten in 1932, but it was not performed in Soviet Russia until 1957.

p. 76, *Yevgeny Zamyatin*: Yevgeny Ivanovich Zamyatin (1884–1937), prose writer and author, among many other works, of *We* (1924). Left the Soviet Union in 1931 and settled in Paris.

p. 76, *The Première*: An unpublished article on the theatre which Bulgakov had promised to produce for Zamyatin.

p. 76, *The Crimson Island*: The play received its première in Moscow in 1928.

p. 77, *Lyudmila Nikolayevna*: Lyudmila Nikolayevna Zamyatina (1887–1965, née Usova), wife of Yevgeny Zamyatin.

p. 77, *The old boy*: Humorous reference to Marika (Mariya Artemyevna) Chimishkian (1904–97), friend of Bulgakov and his second wife Lyubov Belozerskaya.

p. 79, *A.I. Svidersky*: Alexei Ivanovich Svidersky (1878–1933), Soviet functionary and diplomat.

p. 79, *A.M. Gorky*: See sixth note to p. 30.

p. 80, *Adventures of Chichikov*: Satirical tale by Bulgakov, written in 1922 and included in *Diaboliad*.

p. 80, *my wife Lyubov Yevgenyevna Bulgakova*: See second note to p. 35.

p. 85, *A.S. Yenukidze*: Avel Safronovich Yenukidze (1877–1937).

p. 88, *play about Molière*: Bulgakov completed the play by the end of 1929, with the original title *The Cabal of Hypocrites*. It was later performed as *Molière*.

p. 90, *Vladimir Lvovich*: Unidentified.

p. 90, *Vanya*: See third note to p. 12.

p. 95, *Mikhail Saltykov-Shchedrin*: Mikhail Yevgrafovich Saltykov-Shchedrin (1826–89), author, amongst other works, of the novel *The Golovlyov Family* (1880).

p. 95, *V. Blyum*: Vladimir Ivanovich Blyum (pseudonym Sadko) (1877–1941), theatre critic.

p. 96, *R. Pikel*: Richard Vitoldovich Pikel (1896–1936), literary and theatre critic.

p. 96, *a novel about the Devil*: A reference to Bulgakov's novel *The Master and Margarita*, written during the period 1928–1940, but not published until 1966–67.

p. 97, *a second novel, The Theatre*: An earlier version of what would later become his *Theatrical Novel*, published posthumously in 1965.

p. 97, *L. Averbakh*: Leopold Leonidovich Averbakh (1903–1937), literary critic and militant leader of the Association of Proletarian Writers.

p. 99, *Nikolai Gogol*: Nikolai Vasilyevich Gogol (1809–1852), prose writer and dramatist, author of *The Government Inspector* (1836) and *Dead Souls* (1842). The quotation comes from *An Author's Confession* (1847).

p. 100, *TRAM*: Young Workers' Theatre, operating in Moscow and Leningrad during the 1920s and '30s.

p. 104, *lasciate ogni speranza*: "Abandon all hope" (Italian), from Dante, *Inferno* III, 9.

p. 105, *"existence determines consciousness"*: a saying from Karl Marx.

p. 107, *Mariya Germogenovna*: Veresayev's wife.

p. 108, *Adam and Eve*: The play was not to be published or performed during Bulgakov's lifetime. It was first published in Paris in 1971 and in the Soviet Union in 1987.

p. 110, *Dead Souls*: Stage adaptation of the novel by Nikolai Gogol (1809–52). First produced in Moscow in 1932.

p. 110, *Manilov*: A landowner in Gogol's *Dead Souls*, whom Chichikov visits in an attempt to extract from him a list of serfs that have died since the last census.

p. 111, *Pavel Popov*: Pavel Sergeyevich Popov (1892–1956). Bulgakov's first biographer.

p. 114, *a very familiar figure... expression in his eyes*: The reference is to Nikolai Gogol (see note to p. 99).

p. 114, *Shalyapin is coming, and Kachalov has had his leg amputated*: Fyodor Ivanovich Shalyapin (1873–1938), renowned Russian bass. Vasily Ivanovich Kachalov, actor with the Moscow Arts Theatre.

p. 115, *the Fontanka*: The Fontanka is one of the tributaries of the River Neva flowing through St Petersburg.

p. 116, *... the commander of our Russian order of writers was shot*: The reference is to Alexander Pushkin, killed in a duel in 1837.

p. 117, *Faust*: Opera (1859) by Charles Gounod (1818–93).

p. 117, *The play was staged on 18th February*: The reference is to *The Days of the Turbins*.

p. 118, *Toporkov*: Vasily Vladimirovich Toporkov (1889–1970), actor and theatre director.

p. 118, *K.S.*: Konstantin Sergeyevich Stanislavsky (see note to p. 68).

p. 120, *Citizen Vishnevsky's*: Vsevolod Vitalevich Vishnevsky (1900–51), journalist.

p. 120, *the Ramzin affair*: Leonid Konstantinovich Ramzin (1887–1948), engineer, implicated as a "saboteur" in the so-called "Industrial Party" trial in 1930.

p. 122, *Turgenev, Leskov, Brockhaus-Efron? Ostrovsky?*: Ivan Sergeyevich Turgenev (1818–83), prose writer and dramatist; Nikolai Semyonovich Leskov (1831–95), prose writer; *Brockhaus-Efron*, an encyclopedic dictionary in thirty-five volumes, published in St Petersburg and Leipzig (1890–1906); Alexander Nikolayevich Ostrovsky (1823–86), dramatist.

p. 122, *Sakhnovsky, Telesheva*: Vasily Grigorevich Sakhnovsky (1886–1945), Moscow Arts Theatre director; Yelizaveta Sergeyevna Telesheva (1892–1943), actress and director at MAT.

p. 123, *Gogol's poem*: The novel *Dead Souls* is subtitled 'A Poem'.

p. 123, *Captain Kopeykin*: The story of Captain Kopeykin, a seriously wounded army officer, is told in Chapter 10 of Gogol's *Dead Souls*.

p. 123, *Nemirovich's*: Vladimir Ivanovich Nemirovich-Danchenko (see note to p. 68).

p. 124, *K.S.*: Konstantin Stanislavsky (see note to p. 68).

p. 125, *V.G. Sakhnovsky*: See second note to p. 122.

p. 125, *I am getting married in the Registry Office*: Bulgakov's third marriage was to Yelena Sergeyevna Shilovskaya (1892–1970, née Nyurenberg). She is later referred to by various endearing nicknames, such as "Dundik", "Klyunik", "Ku", "Kuka", "Kukva", "Lyu", "Lyusenka", "Lyusi" and "Lyusya".

p. 127, *Sergei*: Sergei Yevgenyevich Shilovsky (1926–77).

p. 129, *I have completed a volume of... Molière*: The Life of Monsieur de Molière, first published in 1962.

p. 129, *Tikhonov*: Alexander Nikolayevich Tikhonov (1880–1950), born Seryebrov, writer and editor.

p. 130, *N.A. Ekke*: Secretary of the series *The Lives of Remarkable People*, originally published from 1890 to 1924, and then renewed in 1933 on the initiative of Maxim Gorky.

p. 131, *Ye.S. and K.*: The first is Yelena Sergeyevna Bulgakova. "K." has not been identified.

p. 131, *sent the book to Sorrento*: The addressee was Maxim Gorky, who lived in Sorrento before returning finally to Moscow.

p. 133, *What will you be doing after your Sisters*: Veresayev's novel *Sisters* was published in 1933.

p. 134, *your Gogol*: Veresayev's biography of Gogol, *Gogol in Life* (1933).

p. 141, *Fischer*: Fischer Verlag, Berlin publishing house, founded by Samuel Fischer in 1886.

p. 142, *Professor d'Hérelle*: Felix d'Hérelle (1873–1949), renowned French-Canadian microbiologist, Nikolai Bulgakov's boss in Paris.

p. 144, *The Pickwick Club*: A stage adaptation by N.A. Venkstern, of the novel by Charles Dickens.

p. 144, *The Storm*: Play (1859) by Alexander Ostrovsky (1823–86).

p. 144, *After Sudakov... Kirshon*: Ilya Yakovlevich Sudakov (1890–1969), actor and director; Boris Arkadevich Mordvinov (1899–1953), theatre director; Vladimir Mikhailovich Kirshon (1902–38), playwright.

p. 144, *Yasnaya*: The presumed reference is to Yasnaya Polyana, the estate of Leo Tolstoy, near Tula.

p. 144, *Anna Ilinichna's*: Anna Ilinichna Popova (1888-1954), the wife of Pavel Popov and the granddaughter of Leo Tolstoy.

p. 145, *Chichikov*: Chichikov, the hero of Gogol's *Dead Souls*.

p. 145, *Zvenigorod*: A town on the River Moscow.

p. 145, *Seryozhka*: Sergei Shilovsky (see note to p. 127).

p. 147, *How nothing came of Bliss*: The play, with the full title *Bliss (The Dream of Engineer Rein in Four Acts)* was first published in 1966.

p. 147, *Goncharov's immortal Voyage of the Frigate Pallada*: An account of a journey undertaken by the writer Ivan Alexandrovich Goncharov (1812–91) to England, Japan and Africa, published in two volumes in 1858.

p. 147, *Grigorovich's visit to Paris some eighty years ago*: Dmitry Vasilyevich Grigorovich (1822–1900), prose writer. He recorded the details of his trip to Europe in 1858 in his book *The Retzivan* (1859–63).

p. 151, *Pilnyak*: Boris Andreyevich Pilnyak (1894–1938), born Vogau, prose writer.

p. 153, *Vyborg House*: Vyborg House (Palace of Culture), cultural centre in St Petersburg/Leningrad.

p. 153, *Zhenya Kaluzhsky*: Yevgeny Vasilyevich Kaluzhsky (1896–1966), actor with the Moscow Arts Theatre. He was Yelena Bulgakova's brother-in-law.

p. 154, *But my Margarita... the flights over the city*: A reference to *The Master and Margarita* (see second note to p. 96).

p. 154, *Captain Kopeykin*: See second note to p. 123.

p. 155, *Vaysfeld*: Ilya Veniaminovich Vaysfeld (1909-2003), critic and writer on the cinema.

p. 156, *N. Teleshov's Literary Reminiscences*: Nikolai Dmitrievich Teleshov (1867–1957), prose writer. His *Literary Reminiscences* were published in 1931.

p. 156, *Kuprin... Bunin*: Alexander Ivanovich Kuprin (1870–1938), prose writer. Ivan Alexeyevich Bunin (1870–1953), prose writer, winner of the Nobel Prize for Literature.

p. 156, *G*: Maxim Gorky.

p. 160, *Alexander Gdeshinsky*: Alexander Petrovich Gdeshinsky (1893–1951), a close friend of Bulgakov's since childhood.

p. 163, *Volf*: Veniamin Yevgenyevich Volf (1898–1959), theatre director and administrator.

p. 164, *You call D'Anthès's shot "tasteless"*: Georges D'Anthès (1812–95), the adopted son of the Dutch ambassador to the Russian court, fatally wounded the writer Alexander Pushkin in a duel.

p. 164, *Pushkin's own scene of the Silvio shot*: A reference to Pushkin's short story 'The Shot' (1831).

p. 165, *Zhukovsky… Dubelt*: Leonty Vasilyevich Dubelt (1792–1862) was the police chief who removed the seals from Pushkin's study after the poet's death in 1837. He then helped Zhukovsky (see fourth note to p. 46) read, assess and organize Pushkin's papers.

p. 165, *Ruslanov*: Lev Petrovich Ruslanov (1894–1937), writer on the theatre.

p. 166, *We have put too much… ruined so easily*: The play under discussion is *The Final Days (Pushkin)*, first performed in 1943. The final version was Bulgakov's alone, achieved without the collaboration of Veresayev.

p. 169, *S.A. Yermolinsky*: Sergei Alexandrovich Yermolinsky (1900–1984), journalist.

p. 169, *the Sinop*: A hotel in Sukhumi on the Black Sea coast.

p. 172, *Ya.L. Leontiev*: Yakov Leontievich Leontiev (1890–1948), theatre director.

p. 174, *Fischer Verlag*: See note to p. 141.

p. 176, *B.V. Asafyev*: Boris Vladimirovich Asafyev (1884–1949), composer and music critic (literary pseudonym: Igor Glebov).

p. 176, *Petunin*: Yevgeny V. Petunin, opera composer.

p. 176, *an opera about Peter the Great*: Bulgakov completed the libretto, but the work was rejected on political grounds.

p. 177, *P.M. Kerzhentsev*: Platon Mikhailovich Kerzhentsev (1881–1940), born Lebedev. Communist Party functionary and diplomat.

p. 177, *the play Alexander Pushkin written by me*: See note to p. 166.

p. 180, *Lionozovo*: District of Moscow on the north-eastern edge of the city.

p. 180, *just as Minin and the Black Sea have not survived*: Operas for which Bulgakov wrote the librettos, but which were not performed in Bulgakov's lifetime. *Minin and Pozharsky*, opera by Asafyev.

p. 180, *Kuza came round… to adapt Nana or Bel-Ami for the stage*: Vasily Vasilyevich Kuza (1902–1941), actor and theatre director. *Nana* (1880), novel by Émile Zola (1840–1902); *Bel-Ami* (1885), novel by Guy de Maupassant (1850–93).

p. 182, *Tarasevich's dacha*: The dacha belonged to Yulia Lvovna Tarasevich, the wife of the theatre director Vladimir Avgustovich Stepun (1898–1974).

p. 183, *my comedy Ivan Vasilyevich*: *Ivan Vasilyevich* was not performed in Bulgakov's lifetime. It was first published in Moscow in 1965.

p. 185, *Pashayev*: Alexander Shamilovich Melik-Pashayev (1905–64), composer and conductor.

p. 186, *Irina Stepanovna*: Presumably Asafyev's wife.

p. 189, *the playwright Nikolai Erdman*: Nikolai Robertovich Erdman (1900–1970), author, amongst other works, of *The Mandate* (1925) and *The Suicide* (1931).

p. 189, *Kalinin*: A city to the north-west of Moscow, named after the Soviet head of state M.I. Kalinin (see first note to p. 34). Upon the collapse of the Soviet Union in 1991 the city reverted to its pre-revolutionary name of Tver.

p. 190, *to Yelena Bulgakova*: Bulgakov's wife spent the summer of 1938 in Lebedyan, a town south of Moscow on the river Don.

p. 190, *Nastya*: Short for Nastasya, the Bulgakovs' home help.

p. 190, *Yevgeny*: The reference is to Yevgeny Shilovsky, Yelena Bulgakova's elder son by her previous marriage.

p. 190, *the scene with Susanin*: The reference is to the opera *Ivan Susanin (A Life for the Tsar*, 1836) by Mikhail Ivanovich Glinka (1804–57).

p. 190, *Yakov Leontievich's*: See note to p. 172.

p. 190, *Pilate*: Character in *The Master and Margarita*.

p. 190, *Ivanov*: Unidentified.

p. 190, *Mordvinov on Pototsky, the composer Yurovsky on his Opanas*: For Mordvinov see third note to p. 144; Sergei Ivanovich Pototsky (1883–1958), composer; Vladimir Mikhailovich Yurovsky (1915–72), composer. *Opanas* (1926) is an opera based on the poem 'Duma pro Opanasa' by Eduard Georgievich Bagritsky (1895–1934).

p. 190, *Olga on the typing of the novel*: Olga Sergeyevna Bokshanskaya, Yelena Bulgakova's sister and wife of Yevgeny Kaluzhsky (see second note to p. 153). She was Nemirovich-Danchenko's secretary at the Moscow Arts Theatre, engaged by Bulgakov to type the manuscript of *The Master and Margarita*.

p. 190, *Yevgeny*: Yevgeny Vasilyevich Kaluzhsky (see second note to p. 153).

p. 190, *Gorodetsky*: Sergei Mitrofanovich Gorodetsky (1884–1967), writer and librettist.

p. 192, <...>: Two further lines were crossed out in Indian ink by Yelena Bulgakova.

p. 193, *Barvikha*: Village near Moscow.

p. 194, *Woland*: Professor of black magic and incarnation of the Devil in *The Master and Margarita*.

p. 194, *Vladimir Ivanovich*: Vladimir Ivanovich Nemirovich-Danchenko (see note to p. 68).

p. 195, *Mokrousov*: Boris Andreyevich Mokrousov (1909–68). Composer.

p. 196, *Korovyov*: Korovyov, one of Woland's attendants in *The Master and Margarita*.

p. 197, *A.P.*: Anna, wife of Pavel Popov. See note to p. 111.

p. 198, *Dmitriev*: V.V. Dmitriev, stage designer.

p. 198, *Sist.*: written by Bulgakov in English; short for "sister-in-law" i.e. Olga Bokshanskaya.

p. 199, *Zhenya*: Yevgeny Kaluzhsky, Yelena Bulgakova's brother-in-law (see second note to p. 153).

p. 201, *S.*: Here and elsewhere in these letters to his wife Bulgakov writes "S." in Roman script to refer to his sister-in-law Olga.

p. 201, *Azazello*: Azazello, one of Woland's attendants in *The Master and Margarita*.

p. 201, *Gorshkov*: A plumber who had been asked by Bulgakov to repair a faulty boiler.

p. 202, *Zhemchuzhnikov*: The presumed reference is to one of the Zhemchuzhnikov brothers, Alexei Mikhailovich (1821–1908), Alexander Mikhailovich (1826–96), or Vladimir Mikhailovich (1830–84). All three, together with the poet Alexei Konstantinovich Tolstoy (1817–75), were the creators of one of Russia's best-known satirical figures, the fictional Kozma Prutkov, who appeared in journals published during the 1850s and '60s.

p. 202, *And now it's Loli!*: The family's nickname for Yekaterina Ivanovna Bush, tutor to Yelena Bulgakova's son Sergei.

p. 202, *Mark Leopoldovich*: Unidentified.

p. 203, *Behemoth's story*: Behemoth is the name of the walking, talking cat in Bulgakov's *The Master and Margarita*.

p. 203, *And as for Don Quixote*: Bulgakov's play *Don Quixote*, from the novel by Cervantes, was first performed in Leningrad in 1941.

p. 205, *The Vilyams*: The presumed reference is to Pyotr Vladimirovich Vilyams (1902–47), artist and theatre designer, and his wife.

p. 207, *your Psyche*: The familiar term used to refer to Yelena Sergeyevna's desk.

p. 208, *Sabe, Ud, el castellano?*: "Do you know Spanish?"

p. 209, *alma mia*: "My soul" (Spanish).

p. 209, *Maria Isakovna*: Possibly Maria Isaakovna Brian (real name Shmargoner) (1886–1965), lyrical soprano.

p. 210, *Boris Robertovich*: The presumed reference is to Boris Robertovich Erdman (1899–1960), theatre designer, a close friend of Bulgakov and the brother of the playwright Nikolai Erdman (see first note to p. 189).

p. 211, *Narzan*: A brand of Russian mineral water.

p. 212, *my dear Champollion the Younger!*: Jean-François Champollion (1790–1832), orientalist and decipherer of Egyptian hieroglyphs.

p. 215, *set up the hall for the funeral*: The reference is to the funeral service for Konstantin Stanislavsky.

p. 216, *cuñada*: "Sister-in-law" (Spanish).

p. 217, *Nikolai Vasilyevich*: Nikolai Vasilyevich Yerokhov, deputy director of the Moscow Arts Theatre.

p. 219, *your translation*: At this time Veresayev was working on a translation of Homer's *Iliad*.

p. 220, *Ye.A. Svetlayeva*: Yelena Afanasyevna Svetlayeva (Lyolya), Bulgakov's sister. See first note to p. 12.

p. 223, *L.N.*: The presumed reference is to Gdeshinsky's wife.

p. 224, *Olya and Lena*: This note was Bulgakov's penultimate autograph, written on a photograph of himself that he presented to his Zemsky nieces.

Index

Extra Material

on

Mikhail Bulgakov's

Diaries and Selected Letters

Mikhail Bulgakov's Life

Mikhail Afanasyevich Bulgakov was born in Kiev – then in the Russian Empire, now the capital of independent Ukraine – on 15th May 1891. He was the eldest of seven children – four sisters and three brothers – and, although born in Ukraine, his family were Russians, and were all members of the educated classes – mainly from the medical, teaching and ecclesiastical professions. His grandfathers were both Russian Orthodox priests, while his father lectured at Kiev Theological Academy. Although a believer, he was never fanatical, and he encouraged his children to read as widely as they wished, and to make up their own minds on everything. His mother was a teacher and several of his uncles were doctors.

In 1906 his father became ill with sclerosis of the kidneys. The Theological Academy immediately awarded him a full pension, even though he had not completed the full term of service, and allowed him to retire on health grounds. However, he died almost immediately afterwards.

Every member of the Bulgakov family played a musical instrument, and Mikhail became a competent pianist. There was an excellent repertory company and opera house in Kiev, which he visited regularly. He was already starting to write plays which were performed by the family in their drawing room. He was a conservative and a monarchist in his school days, but never belonged to any of the extreme right-wing organizations of the time. Like many of his contemporaries, he favoured the idea of a constitutional monarchy as against Russian Tsarist autocracy.

A few years after her first husband's death, Mikhail's mother married an uncompromising atheist. She gave the children supplementary lessons in her spare time from her own teaching job and, as soon as they reached adolescence, she encouraged them to take on younger pupils to increase the family's meagre income. Mikhail's first job, undertaken when he was still at school, was as a part-time guard and ticket inspector on the local railway, and he continued such part-time employment when he entered medical school in Kiev in 1911.

Birth, Family Background and Education

He failed the exams at the end of his first year, but passed the resits a few months later. However, he then had to repeat his entire second year; this lack of dedication to his studies was possibly due to the fact that he was already beginning to write articles for various student journals and to direct student theatricals. Furthermore, he was at this time courting Tatyana Lappa, whom he married in 1913. She came from the distant Saratov region, but had relatives in Kiev, through whom she became acquainted with Bulgakov. He had already begun by this time to write short stories and plays. Because of these distractions, Bulgakov took seven years to complete what was normally a five-year course, but he finally graduated as a doctor in 1916 with distinction.

War   In 1914 the First World War had broken out, and Bulgakov enlisted immediately after graduation as a Red Cross volunteer, working in military hospitals at the front, which involved carrying out operations. In March 1916 he was called up to the army, but was in the end sent to work in a major Kiev hospital to replace experienced doctors who had been mobilized earlier. His wife, having done a basic nursing course by this time, frequently worked alongside her husband.

In March 1917 the Tsar abdicated, and the Russian monarchy collapsed. Two forces then began to contend for power – the Bolsheviks and the Ukrainian Nationalists. Although not completely in control of Ukraine, the latter declared independence from the former Tsarist Empire in February 1918, and concluded a separate peace deal with Germany. The Germans engineered a coup, placed their own supporters at the helm in Ukraine and supported this puppet regime against the Bolsheviks, the now deposed Nationalists and various other splinter groups fighting for their own causes. The Government set up its own German-supported army, the White Guard, which provided the background for Bulgakov's novel of the same name. The Bolsheviks ("The Reds"), the White Guard ("The Whites") and the Ukrainian Nationalists regularly took and retook the country and Kiev from each other: there were eighteen changes of government between the beginning of 1918 and late 1919.

Early in this period Bulgakov had been transferred to medical service in the countryside around the remote town of Vyazma, which provided him with material for his series of short stories *A Young Doctor's Notebook*. Possibly to blunt the distress caused to him by the suffering he witnessed there, and to cure fevers he caught from the peasants he was tending, he dosed himself heavily on his own drugs, and rapidly became addicted to morphine. When his own supplies had run out, he sent his wife to numerous pharmacies to pick up new stocks for imaginary patients. When she finally refused to acquiesce in this any further, he became abusive and violent, and even threatened her with a gun. No more mention is made at any later date of his addiction, so it is uncertain whether he obtained professional help for the problem or weaned himself off his drug habit by his own will-power.

He returned to Kiev in February 1918 and set up in private practice. Some of the early stories written in this period show that he was wrestling with problems of direction and conscience: a doctor could be pressed into service by whichever faction was in power at that moment; after witnessing murders, torture and pogroms, Bulgakov was overwhelmed with horror at the contemporary situation. He was press-ganged mainly by the right-wing Whites, who were notoriously anti-Semitic and carried out most of the pogroms.

Perhaps as a result of the suffering he had seen during his enforced military service, he suffered a "spiritual crisis" – as an acquaintance of his termed it – in February 1920, when he gave up medicine at the age of twenty-nine to devote himself to literature. But things were changing in the literary world: Bulgakov's style and motifs were not in tune with the new proletarian values which the Communists, in the areas where they had been victorious, were already beginning to inculcate. The poet Anna Akhmatova talked of his "magnificent contempt" for their ethos, in which everything had to be subordinated to the creation of a new, optimistic mentality which believed that science, medicine and Communism would lead to a paradise on earth for all, with humanity reaching its utmost point of development. *Turning to Literature*

He continued to be pressed into service against his will. Although not an ardent right-winger, he had more sympathy for the Whites than for the Reds, and when the former, who had forced him into service at the time, suffered a huge defeat at the hands of the Communists, evidence suggests that Bulgakov would rather have retreated with the right-wing faction, and maybe even gone into emigration, than have to work for the victorious Communists. However, he was prevented from doing this as just at this time he became seriously ill with typhus, and so remained behind when the Whites fled. Incidentally, both his brothers had fled abroad, and were by this time living in Paris.

From 1920 to 1921 Bulgakov briefly worked in a hospital in the Caucasus, where he had been deployed by the Whites, who finally retreated from there in 1922. Bulgakov, living in the town of Vladikavkaz, produced a series of journalistic sketches, later collected and published as *Notes on a Cuff*, detailing his own experiences at the time, and later in Moscow. He avowedly took as his model classic writers such as Molière, Gogol and particularly Pushkin, and his writings at this time attracted criticism from anti-White critics, because of what was seen as his old-fashioned style and material, which was still that of the cultured European intellectuals of an earlier age, rather than being in keeping with the fresh aspirations of the new progressive proletarian era inaugurated by the Communists. The authorities championed literature and works of art which depicted the life of the masses and assisted in the development of the new Communist ethos. At the time, this tendency was still only on the level of advice and encouragement from the Government, rather than being a categorical demand. It only began to crystallize around the mid-1920s into an obligatory uncompromising line, ultimately leading to the repression, under Stalin, of any kind of even mildly dissident work, and to an increasingly oppressive state surveillance.

In fact, although never a supporter of Bolshevism as such, Bulgakov's articles of the early 1920s display not approval of the Red rule, but simply relief that at last there seemed to be stable government in Russia, which had re-established law and order and was gradually rebuilding the country's infrastructure. However, this relief at the new stability did not prevent him producing stories satirizing the new social order; for instance, around this time he published an experimental satirical novella entitled *Crimson Island*, purporting to be a novella by "Comrade Jules Verne" translated from the French. It portrayed the Whites as stereotypical monsters and was written in the coarse, cliché-ridden agitprop style of the time – a blatant lampoon of the genre.

But by 1921, when he was approaching the age of thirty, Bulgakov was becoming worried that he still had no solid body of work behind him. Life had always been a struggle for him and his wife Tatyana, but he had now begun to receive some money from his writing and to mix in Russian artistic circles. After his medical service in Vladikavkaz he moved to Moscow, where he earned a precarious living over the next few years, contributing sketches to newspapers and magazines, and lecturing on literature. In January 1924 he met the sophisticated, multilingual Lyubov Belozerskaya, who was the wife of a journalist. In comparison with her, Tatyana seemed provincial and uncultured. They started a relationship, divorced their respective partners, and were entered in the local registers as married in late spring 1924, though the exact date of their marriage is unclear.

Between 1925 and 1926 Bulgakov produced three anthologies of his stories, the major one of which received the overall title *Diaboliad*. This collection received reasonably favourable reviews. One compared his stories in *Diaboliad* to those of Gogol, and this was in fact the only major volume of his fiction to be published in the USSR during his lifetime. According to a typist he employed at this time, he would dictate to her for two or three hours every day, from notebooks and loose sheets of paper, though not apparently from any completely composed manuscript.

But in a review in the newspaper *Izvestiya* of *Diaboliad* and some of Bulgakov's other writings in September 1925, the Marxist writer and critic Lev Averbakh, who was to become head of RAPP (the Russian Association of Proletarian Writers) had already declared that the stories contained only one theme: the uselessness and chaos arising from the Communists' attempts to create a new society. The critic then warned that, although Soviet satire was permissible and indeed requisite for the purposes of stimulating the restructuring of society, totally destructive lampoons such as Bulgakov's were irrelevant, and even inimical to the new ethos.

The Government's newly established body for overseeing literature subsequently ordered *Diaboliad* to be withdrawn, although it allowed a reissue in early 1926. By April 1925, Bulgakov was reading his long story *A Dog's Heart* at literary gatherings, but finding it very difficult to get this work, or anything else, published. In May 1926, Bulgakov's flat was searched by agents of OGPU, the precursor of the KGB. The typescript of *A Dog's Heart* and Bulgakov's most recent diaries were confiscated; the story was only published in full in Russian in 1968 (in Germany), and in the USSR only in 1987, in a literary journal. In 1926 Bulgakov had written a stage adaptation of the story, but again it was only produced for the first time in June 1987, after which it became extremely popular throughout the USSR.

Between 1922 and 1924 Bulgakov was engaged in writing his first novel, ultimately to be known as *The White Guard*. The publishing history of this volume – which was originally planned to be the first part of a trilogy portraying the whole sweep of the Russian Revolution and Civil War – is extremely complex, and there were several different redactions. The whole project was very important to him, and was written at a period of great material hardship. By 1925 he was reading large sections at literary gatherings. Most of the chapters were published as they were produced, in literary magazines, with the exception of the ending, which was banned by the censors; pirated editions, with concocted endings, were published abroad. The novel appeared finally, substantially rewritten and complete, in 1929 in Paris, in a version approved by the author. Contrary to all other Soviet publications of this period, which saw the events of these years from the point of view of the victorious Bolsheviks, Bulgakov described that time from the perspective of one of the enemy factions, portraying them not as vile and sadistic monsters, as

The White Guard

was now the custom, but as ordinary human beings with their own problems, fears and ideals.

It had a mixed reception; one review found it inferior to his short stories, while another compared it to the novelistic debut of Dostoevsky. It made almost no stir, and it's interesting to note that, in spite of the fact that the atmosphere was becoming more and more repressive as to the kind of artistic works which would be permitted, the party newspaper *Pravda* in 1927 could write neutrally of its "interesting point of view from a White-Guard perspective".

First Plays   Representatives of the Moscow Arts Theatre (MAT) had heard Bulgakov reading extracts from his novel-in-progress at literary events, realized its dramatic potential, and asked him to adapt the novel for the stage. The possibility had dawned on him even before this, and it seems he was making drafts for such a play from early 1925. This play – now known as *The Days of the Turbins* – had an extremely complicated history. At rehearsals, Bulgakov was interrogated by OGPU. MAT forwarded the original final version to Anatoly Lunacharsky, the People's Commissar for Education, to verify whether it was sufficiently innocuous politically for them to be able to stage it. He wrote back declaring it was rubbish from an artistic point of view, but as far as subject matter went there was no problem. The theatre seems to have agreed with him as to the literary merit of the piece, since they encouraged the author to embark on an extensive revision, which would ultimately produce a radically different version.

During rehearsals as late as August 1926, representatives of OGPU and the censors were coming to the theatre to hold lengthy negotiations with the author and director, and to suggest alterations. The play was finally passed for performance, but only at MAT – no productions were to be permitted anywhere else. It was only allowed to be staged elsewhere, oddly enough, from 1933 onwards, when the party line was being enforced more and more rigorously and Stalin's reign was becoming increasingly repressive. Rumour had it that Stalin himself had quite enjoyed the play when he saw it at MAT in 1929, regarded its contents as innocuous, and had himself authorized its wider performances.

It was ultimately premiered on 26th October 1926, and achieved great acclaim, becoming known as "the second *Seagull*", as the first performance of Chekhov's *Seagull* at MAT in 1898 had inaugurated the theatre's financial and artistic success after a long period of mediocrity and falling popularity. This was a turning point in the fortunes of MAT, which had been coming under fire for only performing the classics and not adopting styles of acting and subject matter more in keeping with modern times and themes. The play was directed by one of the original founders of MAT, Konstantin Stanislavsky, and he authorized a thousand-rouble advance for the playwright, which alleviated somewhat the severe financial constraints he had been living under.

The play received mixed reviews, depending almost entirely on the journal or reviewer's political views. One critic objected to its "idealization of the Bolsheviks' enemies", while another vilified its "petit-bourgeois vulgarity". Others accused it of using means of expression dating from the era of classic theatre which had now been replaced in contemporary plays by styles – often crudely propagandistic – which were more in tune with the Soviet proletarian ethos. The piece was extremely popular, however, and in spite of the fact that it was only on in one theatre, Bulgakov could live reasonably well on his share of the royalties.

At this time another Moscow theatre, the Vakhtangov, also requested a play from the author, so Bulgakov gave them *Zoyka's Apartment*, which had probably been written in late 1925. It was premiered on 28th October, just two days after *The Days of the Turbins*. The theatre's representatives suggested a few textual (not political) changes, and Bulgakov first reacted with some irritation, then acknowledged he had been overworked and under stress, due to the strain of the negotiations with OGPU and the censors over *The Days of the Turbins*.

Various other changes had to be made before the censors were satisfied, but the play was allowed to go on tour throughout the Soviet Union. It is rather surprising that it was permitted, because, in line with party doctrine, social and sexual mores were beginning to become more and more puritanical, and the play brought out into the open the seamier side of life which still existed in the workers' paradise. Zoyka's apartment is in fact a high-class brothel, and the Moscow papers had recently reported the discovery in the city of various such establishments, as well as drug dens. The acting and production received rave reviews, but the subject matter was condemned by some reviewers as philistine and shallow, and the appearance of scantily clad actresses on stage was excoriated as being immoral.

The play was extremely successful, both in Moscow and on tour, and brought the author further substantial royalties. Bulgakov was at this time photographed wearing a monocle and looking extremely dandified; those close to him claimed that the monocle was worn for genuine medical reasons, but this photograph attracted personal criticism in the press: he was accused of living in the past and being reactionary.

Perhaps to counteract this out-of-touch image, Bulgakov published a number of sketches in various journals between 1925 and 1927 giving his reminiscences of medical practice in the remote countryside. When finally collected and published posthumously, they were given the title *A Young Doctor's Notebook*. Although they were written principally to alleviate his financial straits, the writer may also have been trying to demonstrate that, in spite of all the criticism, he was a useful member of society with his medical knowledge.

Censorship   Bulgakov's next major work was the play *Escape* (also translated as *Flight*), which, according to dates on some of the manuscript pages, was written and revised between 1926 and 1928. The script was thoroughly rewritten in 1932 and only performed in the USSR in 1957. The play was banned at the rehearsal stage in 1929 as being not sufficiently "revolutionary", though Bulgakov claimed in bafflement that he had in fact been trying to write a piece that was more akin to agitprop than anything he'd previously written.

Escape is set in the Crimea during the struggle between the Whites and Reds in the Civil War, and portrays the Whites as stereotypical villains involved in prostitution, corruption and terror. At first it seems perplexing that the piece should have been banned, since it seems so in tune with the spirit of the times, but given Bulgakov's well-known old-fashioned and anti-Red stance, the play may well have been viewed as in fact a satire on the crude agitprop pieces of the time.

The year 1929 was cataclysmic both for Bulgakov and for other Soviet writers: by order of RAPP (Russian Association of Proletarian Writers) *Escape*, *The Days of the Turbins* and *Zoyka's Apartment* had their productions suspended. Although, with the exception of *Zoyka*, they were then granted temporary runs, at least until the end of that season, their long-term future remained uncertain.

Bulgakov had apparently started drafting his masterpiece *The Master and Margarita* as early as 1928. The novel had gone through at least six revisions by the time of the writer's death in 1940. With the tightening of the party line, there was an increase in militant, politically approved atheism, and one of the novel's major themes is a retelling of Christ's final days, and his victory in defeat – possibly a response to the atheism of Bulgakov's time. He submitted one chapter, under a pseudonym, to the magazine *Nedra* in May 1929, which described satirically the intrigues among the official literary bodies of the time, such as RAPP and others. This chapter was rejected. Yevgeny Zamyatin, another writer in disfavour at the time, who finally emigrated permanently, stated privately that the Soviet Government was adopting the worst excesses of old Spanish Catholicism, seeing heresies where there were none.

In July of that year Bulgakov wrote a letter to Stalin and other leading politicians and writers in good standing with the authorities, asking to be allowed to leave the USSR with his wife; he stated in this letter that it appeared he would never be allowed to be published or performed again in his own country. His next play, *Molière*, was about problems faced by the French playwright in the period of the autocratic monarch Louis XIV; the parallels between the times of Molière and the Soviet writer are blatant. It was read in January 1930 to the Artistic Board of MAT, who reported that, although it had "no relevance to contemporary questions", they had now admitted a couple of modern propaganda plays to their repertoire, and so they thought the authorities might stretch a point and permit Bulgakov's play. But in March he was told that the Government artistic authorities had not passed the piece. MAT now demanded the return of the thousand-rouble advance they had allowed Bulgakov for *Escape*, also now banned; furthermore the writer was plagued by demands for unpaid income tax relating to the previous year. None of his works were now in production.

On Good Friday Bulgakov received a telephone call from Stalin himself promising a favourable response to his letter to the authorities, either to be allowed to emigrate, or at least to be permitted to take up gainful employment in a theatre if he so wished. Stalin even promised a personal meeting with the writer. Neither meeting nor response ever materialized, but Bulgakov was shortly afterwards appointed Assistant Director at MAT, and Consultant to the Theatre of Working Youth, probably as a result of some strings being pulled in high places. Although unsatisfactory, these officially sanctioned positions provided the writer with some income and measure of protection against the torrent of arbitrary arrests now sweeping through the country. *Help from Stalin*

Although there was now some stability in Bulgakov's professional life, there was to be another major turn in his love life. In February 1929 he had met at a friend's house in Moscow a woman called Yelena Shilovskaya; she was married with two children, highly cultured, and was personal secretary at MAT to the world-famous theatre director Vladimir Nemirovich-Danchenko. They fell in love, but then did not see each other again for around eighteen months. When they did meet again, they found they were still drawn to each other, divorced their partners, and married in October 1932. She remained his wife till his death, and afterwards became the keeper of his archives and worked tirelessly to have his works published. *Yelena Shilovskaya*

Over the next few years Bulgakov wrote at least twice more to Stalin asking to be allowed to emigrate. But permission was not forthcoming, and so Bulgakov would never travel outside the USSR. He always felt deprived because of this and sensed something had been lacking in his education. At this time, because of his experience in writing such letters, and because of his apparent "pull" in high places, other intellectuals such as Stanislavsky and Anna Akhmatova were asking for his help in writing similar letters.

While working at MAT, Bulgakov's enthusiasm quickly waned and he felt creatively stifled as his adaptations for the stage of such classic Russian novels as Gogol's *Dead Souls* were altered extensively either for political or artistic reasons. However, despite these changes, he also provided screenplays for mooted films of both *Dead Souls* and Gogol's play *The Government Inspector*. Once again, neither ever came to fruition. There were further projects at this time for other major theatres, both in Moscow and Leningrad, such as an adaptation of Tolstoy's novel *War and Peace* for the stage. This too never came to anything. In May 1932 he wrote: "In nine days' time I shall be celebrating my forty-first birthday... And so towards the conclusion of my literary career I've been forced to write adaptations. A brilliant finale, don't you think?" He wrote numerous other plays and adaptations between then and the end of his life, but no new works were ever produced on stage.

Things appeared to be looking up at one point, because in October 1931 *Molière* had been passed by the censors for production and was accepted by the Bolshoi Drama Theatre in Leningrad. Moreover, in 1932, MAT had made a routine request to be allowed to restage certain works, and to their surprise were permitted to put *Zoyka's Apartment* and *The Days of the Turbins* back into their schedules. This initially seemed to herald a new thaw, a new liberalism, and these prospects were enhanced by the dissolution of such bodies as RAPP, and the formation of the Soviet Writers' Union. Writers hitherto regarded with suspicion were published.

However, although *Molière* was now in production at the Leningrad theatre, the theatre authorities withdrew it suddenly, terrified by the vituperative attacks of a revolutionary and hard-line Communist playwright, Vsevolod Vishnevsky, whose works celebrated the heroic deeds of the Soviet armed forces and working people and who would place a gun on the table when reading a play aloud.

Bulgakov was then commissioned to write a biography of Molière for the popular market, and the typescript was submitted to the authorities in March 1933. However, it was once again rejected, because Bulgakov, never one to compromise, had adopted an unorthodox means of telling his story, having a flamboyant narrator within the story laying out the known details of Molière's life, but also commenting on them and on the times in which he lived; parallels with modern Soviet times were not hard to find. The censor who rejected Bulgakov's work suggested the project should only be undertaken by a "serious Soviet historian". It was finally published only in 1962, and was one of the writer's first works to be issued posthumously. It is now regarded as a major work, both in content and style.

In December 1934 Bulgakov made his acting debut for MAT as the judge in an adaptation of Dickens's *Pickwick Papers*, and the performance was universally described as hilarious and brilliant. However, though he obviously had great acting ability, he found the stress and the commitment of performing night after night a distraction from his career as a creative writer. He was still attempting to write plays and other works – such as *Ivan Vasilyevich*, set in the time of Ivan the Terrible – which were rejected by the authorities.

Acting

At about this time, Bulgakov proposed a play on the life of Alexander Pushkin, and both Shostakovich and Prokofiev expressed an interest in turning the play into an opera. But then Shostakovich's opera *Lady Macbeth of Mtsensk* was slaughtered in the press for being ideologically and artistically unsound, and Bulgakov's play, which had not even gone into production, was banned in January 1936.

Molière, in a revised form, was passed for performance in late 1935, and premiered by MAT in February 1936. However, it was promptly savaged by the newspaper *Pravda* for its "falsity", and MAT immediately withdrew it from the repertoire. Bulgakov, bitterly resentful at the theatre's abject capitulation, resigned later in the year, and swiftly joined the famous Moscow Bolshoi Opera Theatre as librettist and adviser. In November 1936, in just a few hours he churned out *Black Snow* (later to be called *A Theatrical Novel*), a short satire on the recent events at MAT.

In mid-1937 he began intensive work on yet another redaction of *The Master and Margarita*, which was finally typed out by June 1938. Soon afterwards, he started work on a play about Stalin, *Batum*. The dictator, although in the main disapproving of the tendency of Bulgakov's works, still found them interesting, and had always extended a certain amount of protection to him. Bulgakov had started work in 1936 on a history of the USSR for schools and, although the project remained fragmentary, he had gathered a tremendous amount of material on Stalin for the project, which he proposed to incorporate in his play. It is odd that this ruthless dictator and Bulgakov – who was certainly not a supporter of the regime and whose patrician views seemed to date from a previous era – should have been locked in such a relationship of mutual fascination.

Play on Stalin

Although MAT told him that the play on Stalin would do both him and the theatre good in official eyes, Bulgakov, still contemptuous of the theatre, demanded that they provide him with a new flat where he could work without interruption from noise. MAT complied with this condition. He submitted the manuscript in July 1939, but it was turned down, apparently by the dictator himself.

Illness and Death Bulgakov was devastated by this rejection, and almost immediately began to suffer a massive deterioration in health. His eyesight became worse and worse, he developed appalling headaches, he grew extremely sensitive to light and often could not leave his flat for days on end. All this was the first manifestation of the sclerosis of the kidneys which finally killed him, as it had killed his father. When he could, he continued revising *The Master and Margarita*, but only managed to finish correcting the first part. He became totally bedridden, his weight fell to under fifty kilograms, and he finally died on 10th March 1940. The next morning a call came through from Stalin's office – though not from the leader himself – asking whether it was true the writer was dead. On receiving the answer, the caller hung up with no comment. Bulgakov had had no new work published or performed for some time, yet the Soviet Writers' Union, full of many of the people who had pilloried him so mercilessly over the years, honoured him respectfully. He was buried in the Novodevichy Cemetery, in the section for artistic figures, near Chekhov and Gogol. Ultimately, a large stone which had lain on Gogol's grave, but had been replaced by a memorial bust, was placed on Bulgakov's grave, where it still lies.

Posthumous Publications and Reputation After the Second World War ended in 1945, the country had other priorities than the publication of hitherto banned authors, but Bulgakov's wife campaigned fearlessly for his rehabilitation, and in 1957 *The Days of the Turbins* and his play on the end of Pushkin's life were published, and a larger selection of his plays appeared in 1962. A heavily cut version of *The Master and Margarita* appeared in a specialist literary journal throughout 1966–67, and the full uncensored text in 1973. Subsequently – especially post-Glasnost – more and more works of Bulgakov's were published in uncensored redactions, and at last Western publishers could see the originals of what they had frequently published before in corrupt smuggled variants. Bulgakov's third wife maintained his archive, and both she and his second wife gave public lectures on him, wrote memoirs of him and campaigned for publication of his works. Bulgakov has now achieved cult status in Russia, and almost all of his works have been published in uncensored editions, with unbiased editorial commentary and annotation.

Mikhail Bulgakov's Works

It is difficult to give an overall survey of Bulgakov's works, which, counting short stories and adaptations, approach a total of almost one hundred. Many of these works exist in several versions, as the author revised them constantly to make them more acceptable to the authorities. This meant that published versions – including translations brought out abroad – were frequently not based on what the author might have considered the "definitive" version. In fact to talk of "definitive versions" with reference to Bulgakov's works may be misleading. Furthermore, no new works of his were published after 1927, and they only began to be issued sporadically, frequently in censored versions, from 1962 onwards. Complete and uncut editions of many of the works have begun to appear only from the mid-1990s. Therefore the section below will contain only the most prominent works in all genres.

Despite the wide variety of settings of his novels – Russia, the *Themes* Caucasus, Ukraine, Jerusalem in New Testament times and the Paris of Louis XIV – the underlying themes of Bulgakov's works remain remarkably constant throughout his career. Although these works contain a huge number of characters, most of them conform to certain archetypes and patterns of behaviour.

Stylistically, Bulgakov was influenced by early-nineteenth-century classic Russian writers such as Gogol and Pushkin, and he espoused the values of late-nineteenth-century liberal democracy and culture, underpinned by Christian teachings. Although Bulgakov came from an ecclesiastical background, he was never in fact a conventional believer, but, like many agnostic or atheistic Russian nineteenth-century intellectuals and artists, he respected the role that the basic teachings of religion had played in forming Russian and European culture – although they, and Bulgakov, had no liking for the way religions upheld obscurantism and authority.

Some works portray the struggle of the outsider against society, such as the play and narrative based on the life of Molière, or the novel *The Master and Margarita*, in which the outsider persecuted by society and the state is Yeshua, i.e. Jesus. Other works give prominent roles to doctors and scientists, and demonstrate what happens if science is misused and is subjected to Government interference. Those works portraying historical reality, such as *The White Guard*, show the Whites – who were normally depicted in Communist literature as evil reactionaries – to be ordinary human beings with their own concerns and ideals. Most of all, Bulgakov's work is pervaded by a biting satire on life as he saw it around him in the USSR, especially in the artistic world, and there is frequently a "magical realist" element – as in *The Master and Margarita* – in which contemporary reality and fantasy are intermingled, or which show the influence of Western science fiction (Bulgakov admired the works of H.G. Wells enormously).

The White Guard   Bulgakov's major works are written in a variety of forms, including novels, plays and short stories. His first novel, *The White Guard*, was written between 1922 and 1924, but it received numerous substantial revisions later. It was originally conceived as the first volume of a trilogy portraying the entire sweep of the post-revolutionary Civil War from a number of different points of view. Although this first and only volume was criticized for showing events from the viewpoint of the Whites, the third volume would apparently have given the perspective of the Communists. Many chapters of the novel were published separately in literary journals as they appeared. The ending – the dreams presaging disaster for the country – never appeared, because the journal it was due to be printed in, *Rossiya*, was shut down by official order, precisely because it was publishing such material as Bulgakov's. Different pirate versions, with radically variant texts and concocted endings, appeared abroad. The novel only appeared complete in Russian, having been proofread by the author, in 1929 in Paris, where there was a substantial émigré population from the Tsarist Empire/USSR.

The major part of the story takes place during the forty-seven days in which the Ukrainian Nationalists, under their leader Petlyura, held power in Kiev. The novel ends in February 1919, when Petlyura was overthrown by the Bolsheviks. The major protagonists are the Turbins, a family reminiscent of Bulgakov's own, with a similar address, who also work in the medical profession: many elements of the novel are in fact autobiographical. At the beginning of the novel, we are still in the world of old Russia, with artistic and elegant furniture dating from the Tsarist era, and a piano, books and high-quality pictures on the walls. But the atmosphere is one of fear about the future, and apprehension at the world collapsing. The Turbins' warm flat, in which the closely knit family can take refuge from the events outside, is progressively encroached on by reality. Nikolka Turbin, the younger son, is still at high school and in the cadet corps; he has a vague feeling that he should be fighting on the side of the Whites – that is, the forces who were against both the Nationalists and Communists. However, when a self-sacrificing White soldier dies in the street in Nikolka's arms, he realizes for the first time that war is vile. Near the conclusion of the novel there is a family gathering at the flat, but everything has changed since the beginning of the book: relationships have been severed, and there is no longer any confidence in the future. As the Ukrainian Nationalists flee, they brutally murder a Jew near the Turbins' flat, demonstrating that liberal tolerant values have disintegrated. The novel ends with a series of sinister apocalyptic dreams – indeed the novel contains imagery throughout from the Biblical Apocalypse. These dreams mainly presage catastrophe for the family and society, although the novel ends with the very short dream of a child, which does seem to prefigure some sort of peace in the distant future.

The Life of Monsieur de Molière is sometimes classed not as a novel but as a biography. However, the treatment is distinctive enough to enable the work to be ranked as semi-fictionalized. Bulgakov's interpretative view of the French writer's life, rather than a purely historical perspective, is very similar to that in his play on the same theme. The book was written in 1932, but was banned for the same reasons which were to cause problems later for the play. Molière's life is narrated in the novel by an intermediary, a flamboyant figure who often digresses, and frequently comments on the political intrigues of the French author's time. The censors may have felt that the description of the French writer's relationship to an autocrat might have borne too many similarities to Bulgakov's relationship to Stalin. The book was only finally published in the USSR in 1962, and is now regarded as a major work. *The Life of Monsieur de Molière*

Although he had written fragmentary pieces about the theatre before, Bulgakov only really settled down to produce a longer work on the theme – a short, vicious satire on events in the Soviet theatre – in November 1936, after what he saw as MAT's abject capitulation in the face of attacks by Communists on *Molière*. *A Theatrical Novel* was only published for the first time in the Soviet Union in 1969. There is a short introduction, purporting to be by an author who has found a manuscript written by a theatrical personage who has committed suicide (the reason for Bulgakov's original title, *Notes of the Deceased*; other mooted titles were *Black Snow* and *White Snow*). Not only does Bulgakov take a swipe at censorship and the abject and pusillanimous authorities of the theatre world, but he also deals savagely with the reputations of such people as the theatre director Stanislavsky, who, despite his fame abroad, is depicted – in a thinly veiled portrait – as a tyrannical figure who crushes the individuality and flair of writers and actors in the plays which he is directing. The manuscript ends inconclusively, with the dead writer still proclaiming his wonder at the nature of theatre itself, despite its intrigues and frustrations; the original author who has found the manuscript does not reappear, and it's uncertain whether the point is that the theatrical figure left his memoirs uncompleted, or whether in fact Bulgakov failed to finish his original project. *A Theatrical Novel*

The Master and Margarita is generally regarded as Bulgakov's masterpiece. He worked on it from 1928 to 1940, and it exists in at least six different variants, ranging from the fragmentary to the large-scale narrative which he was working on at the onset of the illness from which he died. Even the first redaction contains many of the final elements, although the Devil is the only narrator of the story of Pilate and Jesus – the insertion of the Master and Margarita came at a later stage. In 1929 the provisional title was *The Engineer's Hoof* (the word "engineer" had become part of the vocabulary of the Soviet demonology of the times, since in May and June 1928 a large group of mining engineers had been tried for anti-revolutionary activities, and they were equated in the press to the Devil who was trying to undermine the new Soviet society). The last variant written before the author's death was completed around mid-1938, and Bulgakov began proofreading and revising it, making numerous corrections and sorting out loose ends. In his sick state, he managed to revise only the first part of the novel, and there are still a certain number of moot points remaining later on. The novel was first published in a severely cut version in 1966–67, in a specialist Russian literary journal, while the complete text was published only in 1973. At one stage, Bulgakov apparently intended to allow Stalin to be the first reader of *The Master and Margarita*, and to present him with a personal copy.

The multi-layered narrative switches backwards and forwards between Jerusalem in the time of Christ and contemporary Moscow. The Devil – who assumes the name Woland – visits Moscow with his entourage, which includes a large talking black cat and a naked witch, and they cause havoc with their displays of magic.

In the scenes set in modern times, the narrative indirectly evokes the atmosphere of a dictatorship. This is paralleled in the Pilate narrative by the figure of Caesar, who, although he is mentioned, never appears.

The atheists of modern Moscow who, following the contemporary party line, snigger at Christ's miracles and deny his existence, are forced to create explanations for what they see the Devil doing in front of them in their own city.

There are numerous references to literature, and also to music – there are three characters with the names of composers, Berlioz, Stravinsky and Rimsky-Korsakov. Berlioz the composer wrote an oratorio on the theme of Faust, who is in love with the self-sacrificing Margarita; immediately we are drawn towards the idea that the persecuted writer known as the Master, who also has a devoted lover called Margarita, is a modern manifestation of Faust. Bulgakov carried out immense research on studies of ancient Jerusalem and theology, particularly Christology. The novel demands several readings, such are the depths of interconnected details and implications.

Apart from novels, another important area for Bulgakov to channel his creative energy into was plays. *The Days of the Turbins* was the first of his works to be staged: it was commissioned by the Moscow Arts Theatre in early 1925, although it seems Bulgakov had already thought of the possibility of a stage adaptation of *The White Guard*, since acquaintances report him making drafts for such a project slightly earlier. It had an extremely complex history, which involved numerous rewritings after constant negotiations between the writer, theatre, secret police and censors. Bulgakov did not want to leave any elements of the novel out, but on his reading the initial manuscript at the Moscow Arts Theatre it was found to be far too long, and so he cut out a few of the minor characters and pruned the dream sequences in the novel. However, the background is still the same – the Civil War in Kiev after the Bolshevik Revolution. The family are broadly moderate Tsarists in their views, and therefore are anti-Communist but, being ethnically Russian, have no sympathy with the Ukrainian Nationalists either, and so end up fighting for the White Guards. Their flat at the beginning is almost Chekhovian in its warmth, cosiness and air of old-world culture, but by the end one brother has been killed in the fighting and, as the sounds of the 'Internationale' offstage announce the victory of the Communists, a feeling of apprehension grips the family as their world seems to be collapsing round them. The final lines of the play communicate these misgivings (Nikolka: "Gentlemen, this evening is a great prologue to a new historical play." / Studzinsky: "For some a prologue – for others an epilogue."). The final sentence may be taken as representing Bulgakov's fear about the effect the Communist takeover might have on the rest of his own career.

The Soviet playwright Viktor Nekrasov, who was in favour of the Revolution, commented that the play was an excellent recreation of that time in Kiev, where he had also been participating in the historic events on the Bolshevik side – the atmosphere was all very familiar, Nekrasov confirmed, and one couldn't help extending sympathy to such characters as the Turbins, even if they were on the other side: they were simply individuals caught up in historical events.

At around the time of the writing of *The Days of the Turbins*, another Moscow theatre, the Vakhtangov, requested a play from Bulgakov, so he provided them with *Zoyka's Apartment*, which had been first drafted in late 1925. Various alterations had to be made before the censors were satisfied. At least four different

The Days of the Turbins

Zoyka's Apartment

texts of *Zoyka* exist, the final revision completed as late as 1935; this last is now regarded as the authoritative text, and is that generally translated for Western editions.

The setting is a Moscow apartment run by Zoyka; it operates as a women's dress shop and haute-couturier during the day, and becomes a brothel after closing time. At the time the play was written, various brothels and drug dens had been unearthed by the police in the capital, some run by Chinese nationals. Bulgakov's play contains therefore not only easily recognizable political and social types who turn up for a session with the scantily clad ladies, but also stereotypical Chinese drug dealers and addicts. Zoyka is however treated with moral neutrality by the author: she operates as the madam of the brothel in order to raise money as fast as possible so that she can emigrate abroad with her husband, an impoverished former aristocrat, who is also a drug addict. In the final act the ladies and clients dance to decadent Western popular music, a fight breaks out and a man is murdered. The play ends with the establishment being raided by "unknown strangers", who are presumably government inspectors and the police. At this point the final curtain comes down, so we never find out the ultimate fate of the characters.

The Crimson Island   In 1924 Bulgakov had written a rather unsubtle short story, *The Crimson Island*, which was a parody of the crude agitprop style of much of the literature of the time, with its stereotypical heroic and noble Communists, and evil reactionaries and foreigners trying to undermine the new Communist state, all written in the language of the person in the street – often as imagined by educated people who had no direct knowledge of this working-class language. In 1927 he adapted this parody for the stage. The play bears the subtitle: *The Dress Rehearsal of a Play by Citizen Jules Verne in Gennady Panfilovich's theatre, with music, a volcanic eruption and English sailors: in four acts, with a prologue and an epilogue.* The play was much more successful than the story. He offered it to the Kamerny ["Chamber"] Theatre, in Moscow, which specialized in mannered and elegant productions, still in the style of the late 1890s; it was passed for performance and premiered in December 1928, and was a success, though some of the more left-wing of the audience and critics found it hard to swallow. However, the critic Novitsky wrote that it was an "interesting and witty parody, satirizing what crushes artistic creativity and cultivates slavish and absurd dramatic characters, removing the individuality from actors and writers and creating idols, lickspittles and panegyrists". The director of the play, Alexander Tairov, claimed that the work was meant to be self-criticism of the falsity and crudeness of some revolutionary work. Most reviews found it amusing and harmless, and it attracted good audiences. However, there were just a few vitriolic reviews; Stalin himself commented that the production of such a play underlined how reactionary the Kamerny Theatre still was. The work was subsequently banned by the censor in March 1929.

The Crimson Island takes the form of a play within a play: the prologue and epilogue take place in the theatre where the play is to be rehearsed and performed; the playwright – who, although Russian, has taken the pen name Jules Verne – is progressive and sensitive, but his original work is increasingly censored and altered out of all recognition. The rest of the acts show the re-written play, which has now become a crude agitprop piece. The play within *Crimson Island* takes place on a sparsely populated desert island run by a white king and ruling class, with black underlings. There is a volcano rumbling in the background, which occasionally erupts. The wicked foreigners are represented by the English Lord and Lady Aberaven, who sail in on a yacht crewed by English sailors who march on singing 'It's a Long Way to Tipperary'. During the play the island's underlings stage a revolution and try unsuccessfully to urge the English sailors to rebel against the evil Lord and Lady. However, they do not succeed, and the wicked aristocrats sail away unharmed, leaving the revolutionaries in control of the island.

Bulgakov's play *Escape* (also translated as *Flight*), drafted *Escape* between 1926 and 1928, and completely rewritten in 1932, is set in the Crimea during the conflicts between the Whites and Reds in the Civil War after the Revolution.

The Whites – who include a general who has murdered people in cold blood – emigrate to Constantinople, but find they are not accepted by the locals, and their living conditions are appalling. One of the women has to support them all by resorting to prostitution. The murderous White general nurses his colleagues during an outbreak of typhus, and feels he has expiated some of his guilt for the crimes he has committed against humanity. He and a few of his colleagues decide to return to the USSR, since even life under Communism cannot be as bad as in Turkey. However, the censors objected that these people were coming back for negative reasons – simply to get away from where they were – and not because they had genuinely come to believe in the Revolution, or had the welfare of the working people at heart.

Molière was one of Bulgakov's favourite writers, and some *Molière* aspects of his writing seemed relevant to Soviet reality – for example the character of the fawning, scheming, hypocritical anti-hero of *Tartuffe*. Bulgakov's next play, *Molière*, was about problems faced by the French playwright during the reign of the autocratic monarch Louis XIV. It was written between October and December 1929 and, as seen above, submitted in January 1930 to the Artistic Board of MAT. Bulgakov told them that he had not written an overtly political piece, but one about a writer hounded by a cabal of critics in connivance with the absolute monarch. Unfortunately, despite MAT's optimism, the authorities did not permit a production. In this piece the French writer at one stage, like Bulgakov, intends to leave the country permanently. Late in the play, the King realizes that Molière's brilliance would be a further ornament to his resplendent court, and extends him his protection; however, then this official attitude changes, Molière is once again an outcast, and he dies on stage, while acting in one of his own plays, a broken man. The play's original title was *The Cabal of Hypocrites*, but it was probably decided that this was too contentious.

Bliss and Ivan Vasilyevich   A version of the play *Bliss* appears to have been drafted in 1929, but was destroyed and thoroughly rewritten between then and 1934. Bulgakov managed to interest both the Leningrad Music Hall Theatre and Moscow Satire Theatre in the idea, but they both said it would be impossible to stage because of the political climate of the time, and told him to rewrite it; accordingly he transferred the original plot to the time of Tsar Ivan the Terrible in the sixteenth century, and the new play, entitled *Ivan Vasilyevich*, was completed by late 1935.

The basic premise behind both plays is the same: an inventor builds a time machine (as mentioned above, Bulgakov was a great admirer of H.G. Wells) and travels to a very different period of history: present-day society is contrasted starkly with the world he has travelled to. However, in *Bliss*, the contrasted world is far in the future, while in *Ivan Vasilyevich* it is almost four hundred years in the past. In *Bliss* the inventor accidentally takes a petty criminal and a typically idiotic building manager from his own time to the Moscow of 2222: it is a utopian society, with no police and no denunciations to the authorities. He finally returns to his own time with the criminal and the building manager, but also with somebody from the future who is fed up with the bland and boring conformity of such a paradise (Bulgakov was always sceptical of the idea of any utopia, not just the Communist one).

Ivan Vasilyevich is set in the Moscow of the tyrannical Tsar, and therefore the contrast between a paradise and present reality is not the major theme. In fact, contemporary Russian society is almost presented favourably in contrast with the distant past. However, when the inventor and his crew – including a character from Ivan's time who has been transported to the present accidentally – arrive back in modern Moscow, they are all promptly arrested and the play finishes, emphasizing that, although modern times are an improvement on the distant past, the problems of that remote period still exist in contemporary reality. For all the differences in period and emphasis, most of the characters of the two plays are the same, and have very similar speeches.

Even this watered-down version of the original theme was rejected by the theatres it was offered to, who thought that it would still be unperformable. It was only premiered in the Soviet Union in 1966. Bulgakov tried neutering the theme even further, most notably by tacking on an ending in which the inventor wakes up in his Moscow flat with the music of Rimsky-Korsakov's popular opera *The Maid of Pskov* (set in Ivan the Terrible's time) wafting in from offstage, presumably meant to be from a radio in another room. The inventor gives the impression that the events of the play in Ivan's time have all been a dream brought on by the music. But all this rewriting was to no avail, and the play was never accepted by any theatre during Bulgakov's lifetime.

In January 1931 Bulgakov signed a contract with the Leningrad Red Theatre to write a play about a "future world"; he also offered it, in case of rejection, to the Vakhtangov Theatre, which had premiered *Zoyka's Apartment*. However, it was banned even before rehearsals by a visiting official from the censor's department, because it showed a cataclysmic world war in which Leningrad was destroyed. Bulgakov had seen the horror of war, including gas attacks, in his medical service, and the underlying idea of *Adam and Eve* appears to be that all war is wrong, even when waged by Communists and patriots. *Adam and Eve*

The play opens just before a world war breaks out; a poison gas is released which kills almost everybody on all sides. A scientist from the Communist camp develops an antidote, and wishes it to be available to everybody, but a patriot and a party official want it only to be distributed to people from their homeland. The Adam of the title is a cardboard caricature of a well-meaning but misguided Communist; his wife, Eve, is much less of a caricature, and is in love with the scientist who has invented the antidote. After the carnage, a world government is set up, which is neither left- nor right-wing. The scientist and Eve try to escape together, apparently to set up civilization again as the new Adam and Eve, but the sinister last line addressed to them both is: "Go, the Secretary General wants to see you." The Secretary General of the Communist Party in Russia at the time was of course Stalin, and the message may well be that even such an apparently apolitical government as that now ruling the world, which is supposed to rebuild the human race almost from nothing, is still being headed by a dictatorial character, and that the proposed regeneration of humanity has gone wrong once again from the outset and will never succeed.

The Final Days   In October 1934 Bulgakov decided to write a play about Pushkin, the great Russian poet, to be ready for the centenary of his
death in 1937. He revised the original manuscript several times,
but submitted it finally to the censors in late 1935. It was passed
for performance, and might have been produced, but just at
this time Bulgakov was in such disfavour that MAT themselves
backtracked on the project.

Bulgakov, as usual, took an unusual slant on the theme: Pushkin was never to appear on stage during the piece, unless one
counts the appearance at the end, in the distance, of his body
being carried across stage after he has been killed in a duel.
Bulgakov believed that even a great actor could not embody the
full magnificence of Pushkin's achievement, the beauty of his
language and his towering presence in Russian literature, let alone
any of the second-rate hams who might vulgarize his image in
provincial theatres. He embarked on the project at first with a
Pushkin scholar, Vikenty Veresayev. However, Veresayev wanted
everything written strictly in accordance with historical fact,
whereas Bulgakov viewed the project dramatically. He introduced
a few fictitious minor characters, and invented speeches between
other characters where there is no record of what was actually
said. Many events in Pushkin's life remain unclear, including who
precisely engineered the duel between the army officer d'Anthès
and the dangerously liberal thinker Pushkin, which resulted in
the writer's death: the army, the Tsar or others? Bulgakov, while
studying all the sources assiduously, put his own gloss and interpretation on these unresolved issues. In the end, Veresayev
withdrew from the project in protest. The play was viewed with
disfavour by critics and censors, because it implied that it may
well have been the autocratic Tsar Nicholas I who was behind
the events leading up to the duel, and comparison with another
autocrat of modern times who also concocted plots against dis-
sidents would inevitably have arisen in people's minds.

The Last Days was first performed in war-torn Moscow in
April 1943, by MAT, since the Government was at the time
striving to build up Russian morale and national consciousness
in the face of enemy attack and invasion, and this play devoted
to a Russian literary giant was ideal, in spite of its unorthodox
perspective on events.

Batum   Commissioned by MAT in 1938, *Batum* was projected as a
play about Joseph Stalin, mainly concerning his early life in the
Caucasus, which was to be ready for his sixtieth birthday on 21st
December 1939. Its first title was *Pastyr* ["The Shepherd"], in reference to Stalin's early training in a seminary for the priesthood,
and to his later role as leader of his national "flock". However,
although most of Bulgakov's acquaintances were full of praise

for the play, and it passed the censors with no objections, it was finally rejected by the dictator himself.

Divided into four acts, the play covers the period 1898–1904, following Stalin's expulsion from the Tiflis (modern Tbilisi) Seminary, where he had been training to be an Orthodox priest, because of his anti-government activity. He is then shown in the Caucasian town of Batum organizing strikes and leading huge marches of workers to demand the release of imprisoned workers, following which he is arrested and exiled to Siberia. Stalin escapes after a month and in the last two scenes resumes the revolutionary activity which finally led to the Bolshevik Revolution under Lenin. Modern scholars have expressed scepticism as to the prominent role that Soviet biographers of Stalin's time ascribed to his period in Batum and later, and Bulgakov's play, although not disapproving of the autocrat, is objective, and far from the tone of the prevailing hagiography.

Varying explanations have been proposed as to why Stalin rejected the play. Although this was probably because it portrayed the dictator as an ordinary human being, the theory has been advanced that one of the reasons Stalin was fascinated by Bulgakov's works was precisely that the writer refused to knuckle under to the prevailing ethos, and Stalin possibly wrongly interpreted the writer's play about him as an attempt to curry favour, in the manner of all the mediocrities around him.

One Western commentator termed the writing of this play a "shameful act" on Bulgakov's part; however, the author was now beginning to show signs of severe ill health, and was perhaps understandably starting to feel worn down both mentally and physically by his lack of success and the constant struggle to try to make any headway in his career, or even to earn a crust of bread. Whatever the reasons behind the final rejection of *Batum*, Bulgakov was profoundly depressed by it, and it may have hastened his death from hereditary sclerosis of the kidneys.

Bulgakov also wrote numerous short stories and novellas, the most significant of which include 'Diaboliad', 'The Fatal Eggs' and *A Dog's Heart*.

'Diaboliad' was first published in the journal *Nedra* in 1924, *Diaboliad* and then reappeared as the lead story of a collection of stories under the same name in July 1925; this was in fact the last major volume brought out by the author during his lifetime in Russia, although he continued to have stories and articles published in journals for some years. In theme and treatment the story has reminiscences of Dostoevsky and Gogol.

The "hero" of the tale, a minor ordering clerk at a match factory in Moscow, misreads his boss's name – Kalsoner – as *kalsony*, i.e. "underwear". In confusion he puts through an order for underwear and is sacked. It should be mentioned here that both he and the boss have doubles, and the clerk spends the rest of the story trying to track down his boss through an increasingly nightmarish bureaucratic labyrinth, continually confusing him with his double; at the same time he is constantly having to account for misdemeanours carried out by his own double, who has a totally different personality from him, and is a raffish philanderer. The clerk is robbed of his documents and identity papers, and can no longer prove who he is – the implication being that his double is now the real him, and that he doesn't exist any longer. Finally, the petty clerk, caught up in a Kafkaesque world of bureaucracy and false appearances, goes mad and throws himself off the roof of a well-known Moscow high-rise block.

The Fatal Eggs   'The Fatal Eggs' was first published in the journal *Nedra* in early 1925, then reissued as the second story in the collection *Diaboliad*, which appeared in July 1925. The title in Russian contains a number of untranslatable puns. The major one is that a main character is named "Rokk", and the word "rok" means "fate" in Russian, so "fatal" could also mean "belonging to Rokk". Also, "eggs" is the Russian equivalent of "balls", i.e. testicles, and there is also an overtone of the "roc", i.e. the giant mythical bird in the *Thousand and One Nights*. The theme of the story is reminiscent of *The Island of Doctor Moreau* by H.G. Wells. However, Bulgakov's tale also satirizes the belief of the time, held by both scientists and journalists, that science would solve all human problems, as society moved towards utopia. Bulgakov was suspicious of such ideals and always doubted the possibility of human perfection.

In the story, a professor of zoology discovers accidentally that a certain ray will increase enormously the size of any organism or egg exposed to it – by accelerating the rate of cell multiplication – although it also increases the aggressive tendencies of any creatures contaminated in this manner. At the time, chicken plague is raging throughout Russia, all of the birds have died, and so there is a shortage of eggs. The political activist Rokk wants to get hold of the ray to irradiate eggs brought from abroad, to replenish rapidly the nation's devastated stock of poultry. The professor is reluctant, but a telephone call is received from "someone in authority" ordering him to surrender the ray. When the foreign eggs arrive at the collective farm, they look unusually large, but they are irradiated just the same. Soon Rokk's wife is devoured by an enormous snake, and the country is plagued by giant reptiles and ostriches which wreak havoc. It turns out that a batch of reptile eggs was accidentally substituted for the hens' eggs. Chaos and destruction ensue, creating a sense of panic, during which the professor is murdered. The army is mobilized unsuccessfully, but – like the providential extermination of the invaders by germs in

Wells's *The War of the Worlds* – the reptiles are all wiped out by an unexpected hard summer frost. The evil ray is destroyed in a fire.

A Dog's Heart was begun in January 1925 and finished the following month. Bulgakov offered it to the journal *Nedra*, who told him it was unpublishable in the prevailing political climate; it was never issued during Bulgakov's lifetime. Its themes are reminiscent of *The Island of Doctor Moreau*, *Dr Jekyll and Mr Hyde* and *Frankenstein*. *A Dog's Heart*

In the tale, a doctor, Preobrazhensky ["Transfigurative", or "Transformational"] by name, transplants the pituitary glands and testicles from the corpse of a moronic petty criminal and thug into a dog (Sharik). The dog gradually takes on human form, and turns out to be a hybrid of a dog's psyche and a criminal human being. The dog's natural affectionate nature has been swamped by the viciousness of the human, who has in his turn acquired the animal appetites and instincts of the dog. The monster chooses the name Polygraf ["printing works"], and this may well have been a contemptuous reference to the numerous printing presses in Moscow churning out idiotic propaganda, appealing to the lowest common denominator in terms of intelligence and gullibility. The new creature gains employment, in keeping with his animal nature, as a cat exterminator. He is indoctrinated with party ideology by a manipulative official, and denounces numerous acquaintances to the authorities as being ideologically unsound, including his creator, the doctor. Although regarded with suspicion and warned as to his future behaviour, the doctor escapes further punishment. The hybrid creature disappears, and the dog Sharik reappears; there is a suggestion that the operation has been reversed by the doctor and his faithful assistant, and the human part of his personality has returned to its original form – a corpse – while the canine characteristics have also reassumed their natural form. Although the doctor is devastated at the evil results of his experiment, and vows to renounce all such researches in future, he appears in the last paragraph already to be delving into body parts again. The implication is that he will never be able to refrain from inventing, and the whole sorry disaster will be repeated ad infinitum. Again, as with 'The Fatal Eggs', the writer was voicing his suspicion of science and medicine's interference with nature, and his scepticism as to the possibility of utopias.

From 1920 to 1921, Bulgakov worked in a hospital in the Caucasus, where he produced a series of sketches detailing his experiences there. The principal theme is the development of a writer amid scenes of chaos and disruption. An offer was made to publish an anthology of the sketches in Paris in 1924, but the project never came to fruition. *Notes on a Cuff*

A Young Doctor's Notebook

A Young Doctor's Notebook was drafted in 1919, then published mainly in medical journals between 1925–27. It is different in nature from Bulgakov's most famous works, being a first-person account of his experiences of treating peasants in his country practice, surrounded by ignorance and poverty, in a style reminiscent of another doctor and writer, Chekhov. Bulgakov learns by experience that often in this milieu what he has learnt in medical books and at medical school can seem useless, as he delivers babies, treats syphilitics and carries out amputations. The work is often published with *Morphine*, which describes the experience of a doctor addicted to morphine. This is autobiographical: it recalls Bulgakov's own period in medical service in Vyazma, in 1918, where, to alleviate his distress at the suffering he was seeing, he dosed himself heavily on his own drugs and temporarily became addicted to morphine.

Select Bibliography

Standard Edition of Bulgakov's Works:
Bulgakov, Mikhail, *Sobranie sochinenii v vos'mi tomakh*, 8 vols. (St Petersburg: Azbuka, 2002)

Biographies:
Drawicz, Andrzey, *The Master and the Devil*, tr. Kevin Windle (New York, NY: Edwin Mellen Press, 2001)
Haber, Edythe C., *Mikhail Bulgakov: The Early Years* (Cambridge, MS: Harvard University Press, 1998)
Milne, Lesley, *Mikhail Bulgakov: A Critical Biography* (Cambridge: Cambridge University Press, 1990)
Proffer, Ellendea, *Bulgakov: Life and Work* (Ann Arbor, MI: Ardis, 1984)
Proffer, Ellendea, *A Pictorial Biography of Mikhail Bulgakov* (Ann Arbor, MI: Ardis, 1984)
Wright, A. Colin, *Mikhail Bulgakov: Life and Interpretation* (Toronto, ON: University of Toronto Press, 1978)

Letters, Memoirs:
Belozerskaya-Bulgakova, Lyubov, *My Life with Mikhail Bulgakov*, tr. Margareta Thompson (Ann Arbor, MI: Ardis, 1983)
Curtis, J.A.E., *Manuscripts Don't Burn: Mikhail Bulgakov: A Life in Letters and Diaries* (London: Bloomsbury, 1991)
Vozdvizhensky, Vyacheslav, ed., *Mikhail Bulgakov and his Times – Memoirs, Letters*, tr. Liv Tudge (Moscow: Progress Publishers, 1990)

Other books by MIKHAIL BULGAKOV
published by Alma Classics

Diaboliad and Other Stories

A Dog's Heart

The Fatal Eggs

The Life of Monsieur de Molière

The Master and Margarita

A Young Doctor's Notebook

The White Guard